GOD, GOODNESS AND PHILOSOPHY

God, Goodness and Philosophy *is an extraordinary collection of new, first-rate work on religion and values by the best philosophers of religion working today. The writing, throughout, is clear, engaging, and accessible to both students and scholars in philosophy, theology, and religious studies.*

Charles Taliaferro, St. Olaf College, USA

Does belief in God yield the best understanding of value? Can we provide transcendental support for key moral concepts? Does evolutionary theory undermine or support religious moralities? Is divine forgiveness unjust? Can a wholly good God understand evil? Should philosophy of religion proceed in a faith-neutral way?

Public and academic concerns regarding religion and morality are proliferating as people wonder about the possibility of moral reassurance, and the ability of religion to provide it, and about the future of religion and the relation between religious faiths. This book addresses current thinking on such matters, with particular focus on the relationship between moral values and doctrines of the divine. Leading scholars in the field test the scope of philosophy of religion, and engage with the possibilities and difficulties of attempting trans-faith philosophy. Chapters also relate to a number of cross-disciplinary contemporary debates: on evolution and ethics; politics, justice and forgiveness; and the relation between reason and emotions. Another set of chapters tests the coherence of Anselmian theism and concepts of an Omni-God in relation to divine knowledge and goodness.

This book will be of interest to scholars and undergraduates in philosophy of religion, as well as moral philosophers, philosophers of science, theologians, and those working in theology and science.

The British Society for the Philosophy of Religion Series

Philosophy of religion is undergoing a fascinating period of development and transformation. Public interest is growing as the power of religion for both good and ill is becoming ever more apparent, as energetic forms of atheism open up the public imagination to many philosophical questions about God, and as fresh perspectives and questions arise due to the unprecedented level of interaction between different religious faiths. The British Society for the Philosophy of Religion harnesses, reflects and further promotes these interests, within the UK and internationally. The BSPR is the UK's main forum for the interchange of ideas in the philosophy of religion. This series, in association with the BSPR, presents books devoted to themes of major concern within the field of philosophy of religion – books which will significantly shape contemporary debate around key themes both nationally and internationally.

God, Goodness and Philosophy

Edited by

HARRIET A. HARRIS
University of Edinburgh, UK

ASHGATE

Published by
Ashgate Publishing Limited
Wey Court East
Union Road
Farnham
Surrey, GU9 7PT
England

Ashgate Publishing Company
Suite 420
101 Cherry Street
Burlington
VT 05401-4405
USA

www.ashgate.com

British Library Cataloguing in Publication Data
God, goodness and philosophy – (The British Society for the Philosophy of Religion series)
  1. Religion and ethics. 2. Religious ethics. 3. God—Goodness.
  4. Religion—Philosophy.
  I. Series II. Harris, Harriet A.
  210–dc22

Library of Congress Cataloging-in-Publication Data
God, goodness, and philosophy / [edited by] Harriet A. Harris.
     p. cm. — (The British Society for the Philosophy of Religion series)
  Includes bibliographical references and index.
  ISBN 978-1-4094-2851-0 (hardcover : alk. paper) — ISBN 978-1-4094-2852-7
(pbk. : alk. paper) — ISBN 978-1-4094-2853-4 (ebook) 1. Religious ethics.
2. Ethics. 3. Religion—Philosophy. 4. God—Goodness. I. Harris, Harriet A.

  BJ1188.G63 2011
  205—dc23
                                                                        2011021377

ISBN 9781409428510 (hbk)
ISBN 9781409428527 (pbk)
ISBN 9781409428534 (ebk)

Printed and bound in Great Britain by the
MPG Books Group, UK.

Contents

List of Figures

List of Contributors

Robin Attfield is a Professorial Research Fellow at Cardiff University, where he has taught and held a Chair in Philosophy. His latest monograph is *Creation, Evolution and Meaning* (Ashgate, 2006). He is also the editor of *The Ethics of the Environment* (Ashgate, 2008).

Timothy Chappell is Professor of Philosophy at the Open University, Director of the Open University Ethics Centre and Honorary Research Fellow at the Department of Philosophy, University of St Andrews. His most recent book is *Ethics and Experience: Life Beyond Moral Theory* (Acumen, 2009).

John Cottingham is Professor Emeritus of Philosophy at Reading University, Professorial Research Fellow at Heythrop College, University of London, and an Honorary Fellow of St John's College, University of Oxford. He is the author of numerous books, including *On the Meaning of Life* (Routledge, 2003), *The Spiritual Dimension: Religion, Philosophy and Human Value* (Cambridge University Press, 2005) and *Why Believe?* (Continuum, 2009).

Jaco Gericke is Senior Lecturer in Biblical Studies at the North West University in South Africa and specializes in interdisciplinary research involving a philosophical clarification of the Hebrew Bible with the aid of descriptive currents in the philosophy of religion.

Alicja A. Gescinska is a researcher at Ghent University in Belgium, offered a grant from the Research Foundation Flanders (FWO). She is currently finishing her doctoral thesis on the meaning of the human person, freedom and intersubjectivity in the thought of Max Scheler and Karol Wojtyla. She previously published articles on Scheler's ethics, the idea of freedom as praxis in Nikolaj Berdjaev's and August Cieszkowski's writings and on Catholic sexual ethics. She is author of *De verovering van de vrijheid* (*The Conquest of Liberty*) (Lemniscaat Publishers, 2011), in which she combines a philosophical analysis of boredom with a plea for the renewal of positive liberty.

Vasil Gluchman is Director of the Institute of Philosophy and Ethics, and Professor of Philosophy and Ethics at the Institute of Philosophy and Ethics, Faculty of Arts, University of Presov (Slovakia), as well as holding the Chair of the Slovak Unit of the International Network of the UNESCO Chairs in Bioethics at the University of Presov. His many books include *Slovak Lutheran Social Ethics* (Edwin Mellen, 1997), *Human Being and Morality in Ethics of Social Consequences* (Edwin

Mellen, 2003) and *Morality of the Past from the Present Perspective* (Cambridge Scholars Publishing, 2007).

Harriet A. Harris is Chaplain to the University of Edinburgh, where she also teaches philosophy in the School of Divinity. Her books include *Fundamentalism and Evangelicals* (Oxford University Press, 1998/2008) and *Faith and Philosophical Analysis: The Impact of Analytical Philosophy upon Philosophy of Religion* (Ashgate, 2005, ed. with Christopher J. Insole).

Victoria S. Harrison is Reader and Director of the Centre for Philosophy and Religion in the Department of Philosophy at the University of Glasgow. Her publications include *The Apologetic Value of Human Holiness* (Kluwer, 2000) and *Religion and Modern Thought* (SCM, 2007). Her current work is concerned with theories of religious and ethical pluralism.

Anders Kraal holds a PhD in the Philosophy of Religion and an MA in Logic and Metaphysics from Uppsala University. His specialism is the relation between formal logic and theism, and his publications include 'The Status of Logic in Christian-Zen Buddhist Dialogue', *Studies in Interreligious Dialogue* 18(2) (2008), 169–83, 'The Use of Logic in Lutheran Theology', *LOGIA* 17(4) (2008), 25–9, and 'Logic and Divine Simplicity', *Philosophy Compass* 6(4) (2011), 282–94.

Dan O'Brien is a Senior Lecturer in Philosophy at Oxford Brookes University, an Honorary Research Fellow at the University of Birmingham and Associate Lecturer with the Open University. His books include *An Introduction to the Theory of Knowledge* (Polity, 2006) and *Hume's* Enquiry Concerning Human Understanding: *Reader's Guide* (Continuum, 2006, with Alan Bailey).

Ioanna-Maria Patsalidou will be awarded her PhD in Philosophy of Religion in November 2011 from the University of Glasgow, where she is also Assistant to the Director of the Centre for Philosophy and Religion. She received a Masters degree in Philosophy from the University of Reading, UK and a BA (Hons) in Philosophy and Social Studies at the University of Rethymnon, Crete. Her main research interests are in Philosophy of Religion and Metaphysics; in particular on the problem of evil, the problem of hell, moral responsibility and free will.

Herman Philipse holds a University Professorship in philosophy at the University of Utrecht. He has written widely on Heidegger, Husserl and the philosophy of science. His books include *Heidegger's Philosophy of Being: A Critical Interpretation* (Princeton University Press, 1998), *Filosofische polemieken* (Prometheus-Bert Bakker, 2009) and the forthcoming *God in the Age of Science? A Critique of Religious Reason* (Oxford University Press).

Roger Scruton in a resident scholar at AEI and a visiting professor at the University of Oxford. He is a well-known writer and philosopher, specializing in questions concerning art, culture, religion and society. His recent publications include *Beauty* (Oxford University Press, 2009), *Understanding Music* (Continuum, 2009) and *I Drink Therefore I Am: a Philosopher's Guide to Wine* (Continuum, 2010).

Nicholas Wolterstorff is Noah Porter Professor Emeritus of Philosophical Theology at Yale University and Senior Fellow at the Institute for Advanced Studies in Culture, University of Virginia. He is author of many books, including *Justice: Rights and Wrongs* (Princeton University Press, 2008), *John Locke and the Ethics of Belief* (Cambridge University Press, 1996) and the landmark *Faith and Rationality: Reason and Belief in God* (University of Notre Dame Press, 1983), which he co-edited with Alvin Plantinga.

Foreword

The British Society for the Philosophy of Religion was founded in 1994, its aim being 'to advance the education of the public in the Philosophy of Religion, with special reference to the Christian religion'. Its membership is not limited to academic philosophers, but includes all those with an interest in the philosophy of religion, from whatever perspective. As a UK charity with limited funds, its direct support for activities has perforce to be limited in both a financial and geographical sense, but through its publications it aims to reach a wide audience, and this volume represents a milestone in this respect.

The Society's main activity is the biennial conference, the theme of which varies from occasion to occasion but is always broadly defined so as to reflect the variety of interests and perspectives of the Society's members. The present volume is the first of a planned series of volumes which will contain a selection of the papers presented at each conference. Whereas, before, some conference papers might have appeared in various scattered locations, there is now the opportunity of collecting them together, with an introduction which sets the scene and draws out some common threads between them. And it is entirely appropriate that this first volume should begin by a discussion of the purpose and usefulness of philosophy of religion.

I am very grateful to Ashgate, which has long had a distinctive commitment to the philosophy of religion, for launching the series, and to Harriet Harris, who is both series editor and editor of this volume, for bringing a much-cherished idea to fruition.

Robin Le Poidevin

Acknowledgements

I am grateful to Robin Baird Smith at Continuum for his kind permission to reprint parts of Chapter 2 of John Cottingham's book *Why Believe?* (London: Continuum, 2009) in the chapter by John Cottingham, 'The Source of Goodness'. I would also like to thank Janusz Salaman for allowing us to reprint Timothy Chappell's work, 'Euthyphro's "Dilemma", Socrates' Daimonion, and Plato's God', which first appeared in the *European Journal for Philosophy of Religion* 2(1) (2010); and Andries G. van Aarde for granting us permission to reprint Jaco Gericke's piece, 'Beyond Divine Command Theory: Moral Realism in the Hebrew Bible', which first appeared in *Reformed Theological Studies* 65(1) (2009). A version of Nicholas Wolsterstorff's 'What Makes Generosity Sometimes Unjust?' appears in his new book, *Justice in Love* (Grand Rapids, MI: Eerdmans, 2011) and I thank the author and William B. Eerdman's Publishing Co. for enabling parallel publication.

I greatly appreciate the support that Robin Le Poidevin has given me throughout the preparation of this volume and the launching of a BSPR Series, during his Presidency of the BSPR. The BSPR Committee and I are grateful for the work of John Cottingham and Tim Mawson, as former President and Secretary of the Society, in putting together the 2009 Conference on 'God and Morality', from which this volume proceeds.

We most especially thank Sarah Lloyd at Ashgate for backing this volume and the ensuing series with sound advice and enthusiasm, and for her support of the BSPR over many years. I also thank Beatrice Beaup at Ashgate for her ever-helpful guidance and Lesley McCorkindale in Edinburgh for invaluable assistance in preparing the manuscript for publication.

Harriet A. Harris, Edinburgh, 2011

List of Abbreviations

Primary Sources from Aquinas

SCG	*Summa Contra Gentiles*
ST Ia	*Summa Theologica*, Part I
ST I-II	*Summa Theologica*, First part of the Second Part
ST II-II	*Summa Theologica*, Second part of the Second Part
ST IaIIae	*Summa Theologiae*

Introduction
Philosophizing about God, Goodness and Morality

Harriet A. Harris

When the British Society for the Philosophy of Religion turned its attention to 'God and Morality', central questions were raised:

- Can we find an ultimate explanation for goodness?
- Does belief in God yield the best understanding of why we have moral values?
- Do we need transcendental support for key moral concepts?
- If God is understood to be the source of goodness, does this imply any particular theory about how goodness is conveyed, communicated or transmitted?
- Can evolutionary theory provide moral reassurance?
- Does evolution undermine or support religious moralities?
- Is divine forgiveness unjust?
- Can a doctrine of hell be compatible with the goodness of God?
- Can a wholly good God understand evil?
- What is 'sin' and does it yield any benefits?
- Can such questions be addressed only within particular religious traditions or can and should philosophy of religion proceed in a trans-faith or faith-neutral way?

We will map below how these questions affect key debates within philosophy of religion. But it is to the final question that we first turn, for it calls our attention to the very task of the discipline.

Prolegomena

The Task of Philosophy of Religion

We are used to philosophy of religion focusing on questions about God, but challenges are afoot that it should focus on 'religion' instead. For example, John Schellenberg proposes for philosophers such questions as 'what *is* this form of life

– or these forms of life – we call religious?' and 'what attitudes should we take to the conceptions and claims at the heart of religious forms of life?'.[1]

What would happen to philosophy of religion if the questions Schellenberg identifies took centre stage? It is not all that straightforward to predict, not least because the concept 'religion' has evolved to cover so many disparate entities.[2] We could perhaps foresee that the discipline would increase its contact with religious studies and with the sociology and psychology of religion. At present it is most strongly aligned with theology, which is part of Schellenberg's complaint. Enhanced contact with other disciplines would be helpful in widening our scope for understanding, but it would also raise questions about the interface between philosophical and social-scientific investigation. Some would ask whether we were still doing philosophy and others would ask 'does that matter?'. What is philosophy and who decides? These are the questions let out of the box by the challenges posed by Schellenberg and by Nick Trakakis, which form the starting point for Victoria Harrison's opening chapter in this volume.

Before looking further at these challenges, it is as well to clarify that philosophy of religion in this volume falls within well-established expectations of the discipline. For most of its history, philosophy of religion has attended to one particular dimension of religion, *viz*, the content of beliefs, and has tested its rationality or otherwise. The contributors to this volume are engaged in precisely this exercise. Like the majority of philosophers of religion, they speak to a tradition of 'theism' in a variety of consenting and dissenting ways, and are in varying degrees of contact with theology.

It is also worth saying at this point that the relationship of philosophy of religion to theology is not at all straightforward and raises its own questions about the nature of the discipline. So, alongside the challenges of new questions from Schellenberg et al., are a set of longer running challenges from theological quarters.

Theism and Theology

Philosophy of religion has been practised overwhelmingly within a theistic framework and, moreover, in one which broadly presupposes that its subject is the God of the Abrahamic religions, and most usually of Christianity. The reasons for this are largely historical. The discipline emerged within the same broadly Christian culture as the European Enlightenment, and is a product partly of that Enlightenment. However, the reasons are also to some extent religion-specific: Christianity by nature is more discursive on the nature of God than are its sibling faiths Judaism and Islam. Their discourse focuses more, though not exclusively, on

---

[1]   John L. Schellenberg, 'Imagining the Future: How Scepticism can Renew Philosophy of Religion', in David Cheetham and Rolfe King (eds), *Contemporary Practice and Method in the Philosophy of Religion: New Essays* (London: Continuum, 2008), p. 21.

[2]   A point well illustrated by Peter Harrison in his Gifford Lectures, 'Science, Religion and Modernity', Edinburgh, 2011.

the will of God. This difference between the Abrahamic religions is due to the need for early Christian theologians to clarify both the humanity and divinity of Jesus Christ, and therefore also to consider the nature of the Godhead, to which Christ came to be seen to belong. Discourse about the nature of God has been central to Christian identity from the beginnings of Christianity; therefore, Christianity is a natural host religion for the discipline of thinking philosophically about God.

However, it does not follow that within philosophy of religion God is understood in terms of the most distinctive Christian doctrines: the Trinity and the Incarnation. Rather, philosophy of religion has followed the trajectory of natural rather than revealed theology. As such, it has focused on beliefs (such as that God exists) that are judged to be accessible to reason without the assistance of special revelation, and not on beliefs (such as that God is Three) that are said to depend on special revelation. The distinction between natural and revealed theology is a contested one, but the history of that distinction helps to explain why it is only in the last three decades that some philosophers of religion have turned their attention to Scripture, the Trinity, the Resurrection or other doctrines more typically associated with revealed theology.[3]

Once philosophers of religion take on board such distinctive beliefs within a religious tradition, how, if at all, are they distinguishable from theologians? Well, there are differences of focus, skills, training and approach, which make themselves felt when philosophers are judged to have strayed into the territory of theology without understanding theological tools. Writing in this volume, Jaco Gericke, who is both a philosopher and biblical scholar, detects what he calls a 'fundamentalist' bent amongst some mainstream philosophers of religion – those who take the Bible factually if they can and argue their philosophy from a sometimes unfeasibly factual interpretation of biblical texts. His judgment is reminiscent of the criticism made by Maurice Wiles of Richard Swinburne in the 1980s: 'I do not see how any theologian who has given serious attention to the work done by biblical scholars could begin to pursue the work of Christian theology in the way that Swinburne proposes.'[4]

---

[3]   Richard Swinburne has made the most forays into these areas: for example, *Responsibility and Atonement*, (Oxford: Clarendon, 1989); *Revelation: From Metaphor to Analogy* (Oxford: Clarendon, 1991, 2007); *The Christian God* (Oxford: Oxford University Press, 1994); *The Resurrection of God Incarnate* (Oxford: Oxford University Press, 2003); and *Was Jesus God?* (Oxford: Oxford University Press, 2010). For examples of philosophers of religion engaging with theologians and biblical scholars on Christian doctrine, see the Oxford University Press Interdisciplinary Symposium series edited by Stephen T. Davis, Daniel Kendall and Gerald O'Collins: *The Resurrection* (1997), *The Trinity* (2003); *The Incarnation* (2004); and *The Redemption* (2006).

[4]   Maurice Wiles, 'The Reasonableness of Christianity', in William J. Abraham and Steven W. Holtzer (eds), *The Rationality of Religious Belief: Essays in Honour of Basil Mitchell* (Oxford: Clarendon, 1987), p. 48.

At the baseline, perhaps we can say that the theologian is ultimately beholden to scripture (and to some extent tradition), and the philosopher to logic, and that differences in focus, skills, training and approach reflect this fundamental difference in loyalty. If this assessment bears any truth, it helps to explain why philosophers of religion who engage theologically are accused by other philosophers of reneging on their proper philosophical duties. Hence, Nicholas Wolterstorff finds himself fielding an almost opposite accusation to that made by Gericke, *viz*, that those practising 'philosophical theology within the analytic tradition' are 'religious fundamentalists, employing the techniques of philosophy for apologetic purposes without displaying anything of the critical spirit of the true philosopher'.[5]

Notwithstanding the hazards of theological engagement, many philosophers of religion are moving closer to theology. Some now call their discipline 'philosophical theology'[6] and they have much in common with the newly emerging school of 'analytical theologians'.

Oliver Crisp, the leading advocate of analytical theology, sets out a theological method that uses critical analysis in much the same way as it is used within analytical philosophy of religion, and which tests the coherence of beliefs about, for example, the threeness of God, or God's relationship to time.[7] This new discipline seems very close to the kind of philosophy of religion rejected by John Schellenberg because it is a vehicle for apologetics.[8] Both analytical theologians and a large number of philosophers of religion are engaged in a 'faith-seeking-understanding project' in which, as Crisp puts it, '"metaphysical" analysis is the means by which theologians make sense of what they already believe'.[9]

Thus, it seems that there is very little distance, if any, between analytical theology and theologically engaged philosophy of religion – within a Christian milieu, it is important to add. Nicholas Wolterstorff writes as though there is an easy flow and perhaps even an identity between the two.[10] Moreover, he argues that analytical philosophy is more friendly to theological concerns than is Continental philosophy. This is the opposite of what many theologians and Continental thinkers have assumed, but Wolterstorff believes that Continental philosophers are still preoccupied by a theme that has dominated modern philosophy, from John Locke onwards: that there are limits to what can be thought and asserted. This

---

[5]   Wolterstorff, 'How Philosophical Theology Became Possible within the Analytic Tradition of Philosophy', in Oliver D. Crisp and Michael C. Rea (eds), *Analytical Theology: New Essays in the Philosophy of Theology* (Oxford: Oxford University Press, 2009), p. 156.

[6]   Consider Charles Taliaferro and Chad Meister (eds), *The Cambridge Companion to Philosophical Theology* (Cambridge: Cambridge University Press, 2010) and Wolterstorff, 'How Philosophical Theology Became Possible'.

[7]   Oliver Crisp, 'On Analytical Theology', in Crisp and Rea (eds), *Analytical Theology*, pp. 33–53.

[8]   Schellenberg, 'Imagining the Future', p. 21.

[9]   Crisp, 'On Analytical Theology', p. 51.

[10]   Wolterstorff, 'How Philosophical Theology Became Possible'.

theme reached its culmination, perhaps, in logical positivism. With the collapse of that movement and the self-defeating nature of the verification principle, the possibilities for practising philosophy in previously closed territory have widened. Nick Trakakis, whom we will consider below, encourages philosophers of religion to break out of the constraints of their analytical discipline and to work in a poetic or visionary way. However, Wolterstorff believes that analytical philosophers have already broken through their constraints and that this is what has made 'the flowering of philosophical theology … possible'.[11]

By now it will be apparent that there are quite different verdicts on the benefits of philosophical analysis, the directions that philosophy of religion should take, and the relationship between philosophy of religion and theology. If current trends in philosophical theology and analytical theology continue, these two disciplines may converge. But they may encounter discomfort as they do so for the following reason: that many dilemmas as typically debated within philosophy of religion would look quite different if Trinitarian and incarnational theology were taken into account at a fundamental level.

Christian doctrine is infused with paradoxes of a God who became human, experienced the limitations of mortality and took mortality up into the Godhead. Philosophers of religion debate the omni-qualities of God and the paradoxes which these omni-properties generate in and of themselves (as to whether they cohere), as though many who believe in a God of infinite goodness, power, etc., do not also believe that this God has been made most fully manifest in a form of powerlessness. If the incarnation is made relevant at a fundamental level, as Christian theology would seem to require, then questions of God's goodness, God's interactions with evil and suffering, and God's patterns of forgiveness would be approached through the very way in which this God, as a human being, lived and died.[12] So, if philosophers of religion move more and more in the direction of 'philosophical theology', 'analytical theology' or simply 'theology', much of their treatment of religious belief will need to be reworked.

On the other hand, if philosophers of religion do not deepen the trend of becoming more theological, another problem bites at their heels, *viz*, the problem of 'theism'. While the notion of theism arose principally out of the monotheistic religions, theism is not itself a religion or way of life that has adherents.[13] Therefore, there is a risk that philosophy of religion might concern itself with an abstract form of religion, an uninstantiated 'religion', that has no actual life or followers. The accompanying danger is that it might lose touch with concerns raised by and within religious adherence, and thereby fall into irrelevance.

---

[11]   Ibid., pp. 156–7.

[12]   Cf. Kenneth Surin, *Theology and the Problem of Evil* (Oxford: Blackwell, 1986).

[13]   Cf. Ann Loades, 'Philosophy of Religion: Its Relation to Theology', in Harriet A. Harris and Christopher J. Insole (eds), *Faith and Philosophical Analysis: The Impact of Analytical Philosophy on the Philosophy of Religion* (Aldershot: Ashgate, 2005), p. 136.

The Relevance of Philosophy of Religion

In her chapter for this volume, Victoria Harrison directly addresses the charge that philosophy of religion lacks relevance. She considers this charge from two different quarters. One is John Schellenberg's critique of the narrowly Christian or theistic preoccupations of most philosophers of religion. We have mentioned Schellenberg briefly already and shall come back to him shortly. The other is the challenge posed by Nick Trakakis, that analytical philosophy of religion is irrelevant to the concerns of people outside the subject area.

Trakakis argues that because analytical philosophy is committed to the quest for knowledge and to a scientific understanding of the world, it has abandoned the quest for wisdom. It has forgotten to ask 'how we are to live' or to raise existentially pressing questions about the 'meaning of life'.[14] Trakakis does not expect Continental philosophy to make good this shortfall. He proposes instead that we move towards 'inter-disciplinary, or even non-disciplinary or non-academic, ways of philosophing', by which he means loosening our tongues and following the great poets and visionaries in 'speaking impossible languages'.[15]

This proposal is significantly close to the insight of some theologians, who find that philosophers are not adequately open to theological possibilities. Rowan Williams, for example, describes the activity of prayer as taking us beyond what we can conceive or say and as resisting the urge of religious language to claim a total perspective.[16] We will return to the question of prayer in the next section, for it presents perhaps the greatest challenge to philosophical constraints.

Harrison herself does not run with the notion of loosening our minds and tongues. Instead, she argues that philosophy of religion should be practised across faiths and philosophical traditions far more broadly than is currently the case. Partly, she is embracing Schellenberg's influential proposal that the discipline should be expanded to cover philosophical issues arising from a wide range of religious traditions,[17] but she also argues that this on its own does not go far enough to address the key problem identified by Trakakis – that of the irrelevance of the analytic philosophy of religion.[18] She argues that philosophy of religion needs to draw on developments within other areas of philosophy, especially ethics

---

[14]   Nick Trakakis, *The End of Philosophy of Religion* (London and New York: Continuum, 2008), p. 113. Cf. Harris and Insole (eds), *Faith and Philosophical Analysis.*

[15]   Trakakis, *The End of Philosophy of Religion*, pp. 83, 124.

[16]   Rowan Williams, *On Christian Theology* (Oxford: Blackwell, 2000), pp. 10–14.

[17]   John L. Schellenberg, *Prolegomena to a Philosophy of Religion* (Ithaca, NY: Cornell University Press, 2005); and 'Imagining the Future', *passim*. Cf. Victoria Harrison, 'Philosophy of Religion, Fictionalism, and Religious Diversity', *International Journal for Philosophy of Religion* 68 (2011), 43–58.

[18]   Harrison notes that the supposed irrelevance of analytical philosophy of religion was not a problem Schellenberg himself set out to address.

and metaphysics. Her illustrations are from metaphysics; the rest of this volume could be taken as being illustrative of an engagement with ethics.

The Multi-faith Philosophy of Religion

Harrison answers the charge of irrelevance with effectively two proposals: that philosophy of religion look beyond religion to metaphysics and ethics; and that it look across faiths in seeking to respond to problems concerning religion generated in the world outside the academy.

It is worth saying more about Schellenberg's proposal at this point.

Schellenberg is dissatisfied that so many philosophers of religion treat their discipline as a vehicle for apologetics. His alternative proposal, which he calls 'ultimism', is that philosophers of religion explore the proposition that there is a 'metaphysically and axiologically ultimate reality in relation to which an ultimate good can be attained', through investigation of religions which instantiate this belief.[19] At the very least, he suggests, this proposal will help remind philosophers that there are other religions besides theistic ones.

This reminder is laudable. However, as Schellenberg goes on in his proposal, it is possible to glimpse a downside. He argues that 'we are completely unjustified in believing that the human species or any of its members has *already developed* to the point where either the *truth* ... or the *falsity* of ultimism could become available to our awareness'.[20] He presents this as a new insight and yet arguably it is a new way of phrasing an old insight about the limits of our understanding, an insight that has developed into sophisticated schools of thought within all of the world faiths and within most philosophical schools. It is this insight that leads Trakakis or Rowan Williams to look for impossible languages.

The search for adequate ways of speaking, or for alternatives to speech, is a great challenge to philosophers as it opens the floodgates to all sorts of possibilities, most of which entail some abandonment of cherished methods and criteria. The Jewish philosopher Emmanuel Levinas acknowledged the challenge when he described prayer as 'one of the most difficult subjects for a philosopher' and insisted that 'the Judaism of reason must take precedence over the Judaism of prayer'.[21] There are other philosophers who, when they meet this point of tension, choose prayer and thereby acknowledge limitations to philosophy. The fundamental question left begging is: what induces some ultimately to choose philosophy and others ultimately to abandon it? This question runs deep below the surface of this volume and underlies all practice of philosophy of religion, and it is not finally answered.

---

[19]   Schellenberg, 'Imagining the Future', p. 23.

[20]   Ibid., p. 27.

[21]   Emmanuel Levinas, *Difficult Freedom: Essays on Judaism*, trans. Seán Hand (London: Athlone Press, 1990), pp. 269, 271.

We may move closer to answering it, though, by raising another question, one which is a live issue for philosophers of religion at present: can they best practise their discipline by working across diverse religions and also beyond religious belief or by mining deeply for understanding within a particular religion? Schellenberg is alert to the downfalls of keeping philosophy of religion within a Christian-theistic framework. However, a hazard of spreading out is that we lose the wisdom gained from those deeply familiar with particular traditions, and we lose sight of the ways in which rationality itself is profoundly shaped within traditions.[22] One way forward would be to have philosophers of religion from different religious and belief traditions (and here I would include different versions of agnosticism and atheism) come together more and in ways that: i) deepen without diluting their understanding of their own particular traditions; and ii) enhance their awareness of their rational formation as it has been shaped by their traditions. Philosophers of religion who focus on one faith, who engage in apologetics or anti-apologetics, or in highly specific analytical tasks are developing their knowledge and skills at a deep level. This is fully consistent with their having an accompanying goal for their discipline – that of enhancing conversation with others.

The conviction behind this proposal is that the deeper we go in any one tradition, the more likely that the depths discovered will speak to the depths of other traditions. Multi-faith work amongst theologians is developing in this direction, having found approaches that look for surface common denominators to be unfruitful.[23] Different religious and belief traditions hold up mirrors to one another, but they can do so effectively only when they have adequate images of themselves to present to one another.

Lest this proposal encourage people to take a narrow or parochial attitude towards their own traditions, we might do well to learn from the practice of 'Receptive Ecumenism'.[24] This practice, developed within Catholic theology, holds that the primary ecumenical responsibility is to ask not 'what do the other traditions first need to learn from us?' but 'what do we need to learn from them?'.

---

[22]   An insight promoted by Alasdair MacIntyre and made pertinent to the question of philosophising across religions by Nancey Murphy. See Alasdair MacIntyre, *After Virtue,* 2nd edn (Notre Dame, IN: Notre Dame University Press, 1984) and *Whose Justice, Which Rationality?* (Notre Dame, IN: Notre Dame University Press, 1988); and Nancey Murphy, 'MacIntyre, Tradition-Dependent Rationality and the End of Philosophy of Religion', in Cheetham and King (eds), *Contemporary Praactice and Method in the Philosophy of Religion*, pp. 32–44.

[23]   Cf. Nicholas Adams' account of Scriptural Reasoning in *Habermas and Theology* (Cambridge: Cambridge University Press, 2006), p. 242; and Victoria Harrison's development of Exemplar Reasoning in 'Embodied Values and Muslim-Christian Dialogue: "Exemplar Reasoning" as a Model for Inter-Religious Conversations', *Studies in Interreligious Dialogue* 21 (2011), 20–35.

[24]   See Paul Murray (ed.), *Receptive Ecumenism and the Call to Catholic Learning* (Oxford: Oxford University Press, 2008).

With this open-minded and open-hearted question before our eyes, we are ready to meet others. But we can be of most assistance in the process when we also understand ourselves as best as we are able.

The prospect lies before us, then, of philosophers mining deeply the wisdom of their traditions and finding, at the depths, a meeting place with those of other traditions. Somewhere at this deep level, we may better come to understand why and how people make their ultimate commitments.

I

God, Goodness and Morality

Having suggested the value of working within particular religious and belief traditions, we move on to grapple philosophically with questions about God, goodness and morality.

Within this subject area, philosophers of religion have been less narrowly focused than some their neighbouring philosophers, and more willing to work across disciplines. Most moral philosophers over the past century have had little to say about God or religion. By contrast, philosophers of religion have maintained an interest in goodness and morality.

Their interest falls into two large areas:

1. the relationship, if any, between our sense of morality and a transcendent cause; and
2. the nature of God's own goodness, and whether it coheres with other divine qualities and with the universe God has created.

The main body of this book is divided into two parts to reflect these two areas of interest. Multiple questions arise within each area and this volume does not cover them all. For example, it will strike readers that no author in Part I offers moral arguments for the existence of God and that no-one in Part II devotes a whole chapter to the problem of evil. The remainder of this Introduction sets out what is covered in the each part and how the contributions affect key debates.

It is first worth clarifying that in neither Part I nor II is the existence of God assumed. Rather, most, if not all, arguments within philosophy of religion test the rationality of believing that there is a God. For example, a question behind all of the discussions in Part I is whether the existence of a divine judge, or law-giver, or a divine standard or source of goodness is the best explanation for our moral sensibilities. A question behind the chapters of Part II is whether theories of divine goodness are ultimately incoherent and, if so, whether they thereby count against belief in God's existence. These questions are a sub-text and their presence is more explicit in some chapters than in others, depending on the particular arguments that are being advanced.

Moral Arguments and the Source of Goodness

There are two directions in which philosophers might argue for a connection between our sense of morality and a transcendent cause.

There are what we might call 'bottom-up' arguments, which reason from states of affairs and experiences, towards a transcendent source. Moral arguments for God's existence are of this kind. They include arguments from conscience, arguments from a seeming objectivity or universality of (some) moral values to a common and transcendent source of those values, and Kantian arguments that do not seek to establish the existence of God, but rather propose God as a necessary postulate of morality. The authors in Part I do not take up these arguments. They arrive at hypotheses more subtly, testing whether belief in God helps us to make more sense or less sense of our moral norms and motivations or our theories of goodness. A number of chapters question whether evolutionary theory displaces religious explanations for morality.

In the opposite direction, 'top-down' arguments propose a transcendent source or standard of goodness (God or otherwise), and from there aim better to understand the true nature of goodness and how we might best live a good life.

The authors in this volume do not directly offer 'top-down' arguments either, although John Cottingham's chapter relates heavily to this genre, as do the subsequent chapters on Divine Command Theory and the Euthyphro dilemma.

Many arguments from God to goodness are Platonic in form. In the *Republic*, Socrates says that goodness confers known-ness, reality and being upon things. He says that goodness is not the state of being, but rather surpasses being in majesty and might (509b). The Good is therefore central to ethics and also to metaphysics and epistemology. The Forms, in Plato, are more real than our shadow-like reality, which is devolved from them. Socrates describes the Good as king of the intelligible world, just as the sun-god is king of the visible world. The Good begets this sun-god, and contemplation of the Good is contemplation of something divine or godlike, as opposed to merely human (509d, 508b, 517d).

Therefore, top-down, Platonic arguments propose a transcendent reality (God or Goodness) wherein goodness has its true form, and they understand our sense of goodness or our inclination towards goodness in light of it.[25] The analogy with the sun reveals the shape of such arguments: just as all light proceeds from the sun and can only be understood in light of the sun, so all goodness proceeds from God/Goodness and can only be understood in light of God/Goodness. We cannot look at the sun directly, nor can we look at God directly, so we must expect our comprehension to be partial.

---

[25]   Meta-ethical arguments within this Platonic family include W.R. Sorley's argument in the early twentieth century that moral values have objectivity because God is thinking about them, and Robert Adams' argument that God *is* the transcendent Good. W.R. Sorley, *Moral Values and the Idea of God* (Cambridge: Cambridge University Press, 1918); Robert M. Adams, *Finite and Infinite Goods* (New York: Oxford University Press, 1999).

Cottingham in Chapter 2 offers an argument within this family. He begins with an analogy, imagining a watery world in which different philosophical schools debate the nature and origins of fieriness. The acqualist school proposes that apparent 'fires' can be reduced to aquatic properties. The non-aqualists say fire is a *sui generis*, irreducibly non-acquatic property. The super-acqualists argue for a super-fiery transcendent source which they call 'Sol'.

Two issues immediately arise from the Sol theory. First is the Problem of Darkness, which is analogous to the problem of evil in our world: how could there be both a supremely warm and fiery source of everything, and cold, dark places on the planet? Second is the problem of priority or potential circularity. If Sol is the source of fire, warmth and light, how is Sol an explanation of fire, warmth and light? When we translate this issue into one of God, goodness and morality, the following question arises: is God the source of goodness and, if so, how does this help us to understand the nature of goodness? To say that goodness derives from God who is by nature good seems to bring us back full-circle to our original question 'what is goodness?'.

This quest for an ultimate understanding of goodness relates to Euthyphro-style dilemmas, which we will consider later, for they are the subject of subsequent chapters. Cottingham holds that a quest for ultimate understanding will never be satisfied. In this way he places Euthyphro to one side and makes a different proposal: not that an appeal to God could satisfy a demand for an explanation or understanding of goodness, but that God could be proposed as the source of goodness. Moreover, he argues that proposing God as the source of goodness might make more sense of our world than would positing no external source.

Cottingham then considers what would follow from this in terms of objectivity, particularly in relation to J.L. Mackie's 'error-theory' of ethics. Mackie's challenge was that while it seems to us that moral values have objectivity, we are likely to be wrong about that because: (a) it is not clear how purely empirical properties can have moral characteristics; and (b) we cannot identify a faculty for perceiving these supposed moral features in the universe.[26]

Cottingham proposes that God is the source of goodness in at least two ways. First, he performs actions with good-making qualities, such as supporting the fatherless and widows (Psalm 146 [145]) (or, at least, we might say that scriptures portray God as having especial concern for the vulnerable). Secondly, he creates creatures who themselves perform actions with good-making qualities. Cottingham acknowledges a theodicy question arising from this: why is God not therefore also the source of evil, given that He creates creatures who perform actions with evil-making qualities? This is a question addressed from interesting angles by both Vasil Gluchman and Alicja Gescinska within this volume.

In relation to Mackie's error-theory, Cottingham holds that the pursuit of goodness is not the search for an additional mysterious feature over and above the good-making properties of actions. Rather, the pursuit of goodness involves

---

[26]   J.L. Mackie, *Ethics: Inventing Right and Wrong* (Harmondsworth: Penguin, 1977).

choosing actions and objects which already possess observable good-making features, in that they contain conditional reasons for choosing them. Do they also provide unconditional reasons? Is there, in Mackie's terms, a 'queer' connection between an empirical feature and the strong normative power to require us to act? Cottingham gives a theistic response: if God is by nature merciful, compassionate and just, then when we act in the same way we are drawn closer to God, the source of our being. Good acts command our allegiance in that they draw us closer to home.

Cottingham's proposal includes within it a reason for not offering arguments from morality to God: just as Sol is beyond the grasp of the inhabitants of the watery world, God is a transcendent being beyond our grasp. It also contains a reason why top-down arguments, from God to morality, do not satisfy: just as the invocation of Sol would not provide a plausible scientific explanation of firieness, the invocation of God does not provide a non-circular explanatory theory of goodness. If God can somehow be the explanation for goodness, then the explanation does not work in the ways that we usually expect, such as mapping a sequence of cause and effect, or revealing the inner structure of phenomena. Cottingham comes down firmly in favour of moral objectivity, but by 'objectivity' he does not mean mind-independence; rather, he means a mind-implanted reality. Just as Descartes and other theistic rationalists held that planted within us are the rational patterns that govern the universe, so Cottingham holds that we have a moral awareness implanted in us such that we can orient ourselves towards the good which lies at the heart of reality. His is a rationalist picture of ultimate harmony: that we can choose to conform to an intelligible, rational pattern that was intended for us by a loving transcendent being. But he emphasizes that he offers not a proof but an explanatory hypothesis, the force for which resides in its offering the best explanation for what we can say about goodness, our sense of normativity and the outcomes of good-making behaviour.

Greek and Hebraic Traditions

Within the Greek tradition, virtue is pursued as that which brings us closer to God or the gods. Platonic and Aristotelian traditions are similar in this respect, even though Aristotle rejected Plato's metaphysical theory of Forms, and configured goodness as residing in material objects rather than in a transcendent world. For both Plato and Aristotle, pursuing virtue is a matter of doing what is 'good for us' in the sense of doing what fits our nature, what most enables us to flourish. Cottingham expresses this insight in more Platonic than Aristotelian terms by describing the inclination towards goodness as an inclination towards our own source; we make sense of this inclination because it is an inclination towards 'home'.

Another style of top-down argument is that contained in Divine Command Theories (DCTs). These theories propose that some, or all, of our moral imperatives come by divine command. As such, they argue from a God to our moral systems.

The Hebraic tradition is usually understood as a Divine Command tradition. The Hebrew God commands the world into being and then commands the human beings he has made. In this respect, Yhwh seems significantly unlike the God of Aristotle who 'is not a superior who issues commands, but is that for the sake of which wisdom issues commands' (*Eudemian Ethics* VII, 15, 1249b12f).[27] A corollary of this contrast is that whilst within Greek tradition, virtue is pursued because it is good for us and brings us closer to God, in Hebraic tradition, virtue is pursued in obedience to divine law, as a matter of duty.

At least, this is how the Greek-Hebraic distinction is usually drawn. Jaco Gericke in this volume calls for an important revision of our understanding. We shall consider his modifications in due course. For now, it is helpful to have a sense of the influence of the seeming contrast between Greek and Hebraic traditions on Western moral thought.

Elizabeth Anscombe, who has been a central figure in the twentieth-century revival of virtue ethics, argued in the 1950s that a Christian emphasis on duty, bringing with it a legal conception of ethics from the Torah, undermined the Greek virtue tradition.[28] Her point was that a divine command ethic instills in us notions of obedience, disobedience and guilt, which move us a long way from the insights and motivations of the Greek tradition. Anscombe did not take adequately into account the development of Christian tradition or the ways in which Greek and Hebraic strands have interacted within it. Nor, as regards her conceptual analysis, did she consider Jewish and Christian notions of mercy and grace, without which 'law' cannot be properly understood.[29] But her thesis is a good example of the way in which goodness-as-well-being and goodness-as-obligation can be put into opposition.

Indeed, one way of interpreting the fundamental disagreement between Roger Scruton and Herman Philipse in this volume is precisely in terms of the tension between obligation and well-being. Scruton holds that we have a deep-seated sense of obligation and he asks what grounds it. Philipse is oriented in the well-being direction and offers evolutionary grounds for morality. He formulates moral truth as that which enables human life, particularly societal life, to flourish. A question that presents itself is whether evolutionary theories of ethics naturally incline in a well-being direction. For example, some philosophers have sought to relate evolutionary ethics to a naturalistic reading of Aristotelian tradition

---

[27]   This contrast is drawn by John E. Hare, 'Goodness', in Taliaferro and Meister (eds), *The Cambridge Companion to Christian Philosophical Theology*, p. 68.

[28]   G.E.M. Anscombe, 'Modern Moral Philosophy, reprinted in Roger Crisp and Michael Slote (eds), *Virtue Ethics* (Oxford: Oxford University Press, [1958] 1997), pp. 26–44.

[29]   Harriet A. Harris, 'Ambivalence over Virtue', in Jane Garnett et al. (eds), *Redefining Christian Britain: Post-1945 Perspectives* (Norwich: SCM, 2006), pp. 210–21.

along the lines that the pursuit of our natural inclinations is what is good for us.[30] But presumably a nuanced evolutionary theory could seek to accommodate the sense many of us have that there are duties that sometimes challenge our natural inclinations. A follow-on question is whether Western moral thought has made too much of a dichotomy between duty and well-being, a dichotomy that insights from evolutionary theory might help to undercut.

However, before we turn to the chapters on evolution, there is much to understand about the Divine Command tradition and the issues it raises.

Divine Command Theories and Euthyphro Dilemmas

DCTs provoke a question about priority: which comes first, God or the goodness that God commands? Does God command things because they are good or are they good because God commands them? Although DCTs are more pertinent to Judaeo-Christian culture than to Greek culture, this question is often referred to in short-hand as 'the Euthyphro dilemma' because it resembles a question posed in Plato's dialogue the *Euthyphro*.

In this dialogue, Socrates debates with a religious professional. He enquires not about goodness but about piety or holiness, because he is about to face a charge of impiety, on which he is subsequently found guilty and condemned to death. Euthyphro says that piety is loved by the gods. But Socrates asks whether it is loved by them because it is holy or whether it is holy because it is beloved of the gods (*Euthyphro* 10a–11b). His own answer seems to be the former, if we can interpolate from *Euthyphro* 7e, where Socrates says that the gods love what is beautiful, good and just, and hate their opposites. However, despite Socrates seeming to favour one side to the dilemma, the dilemma remains. The question is changed and is raised again and again within philosophy of religion: are things good because God commands them – in which case anything might count as good simply by virtue of God commanding it – or does God command things because they are good – in which case God is subject to some standard outside of God.

We can see already that this is a Christianized version of the dilemma, for Socrates did not have the Judaeo-Christian notion of a God who commands. But within the Christianized version, the dilemma calls into question not only whether goodness can be ultimately comprehended but whether the concept of God can be defended. Robin le Poidevin suggests the following 'meta-ethical argument for atheism':

1. we can make sense of the goodness of God, and of God willing us to do what is good, only if goodness is defined independently of God;

---

[30]   See particularly Larry Arnhart, *Darwinian Natural Right: The Biological Ethics of Human Nature* (Albany, NY: SUNY Press, 1998). John E. Hare finds Arnhart's naturalistic reading of Aristotle implausible: *God and Morality: A Philosophical History* (Chichester and Oxford: Wiley-Blackwell, 2009), pp. 65–72.

2. if goodness is defined independently of God, then God does not explain the existence of moral values.

Therefore, theism contains an inconsistency.[31]

Robin Le Poidevin acknowledges a way out of the inconsistency if we argue that 'God is good precisely because his existence explains the existence of moral value' (p. 85). But then other problems dog the theist regarding the objectivity of moral values, how we perceive them and why we disagree over them. Le Poidevin concludes that atheism presents fewer problems than theism when it comes to making sense of morality, a position that pitches him most directly against John Cottingham and Roger Scruton in this volume, and aligns him most strongly with Herman Philipse.

Meanwhile, three other authors in this volume raise significant questions about the so-called 'Euthyphro dilemma'. Timothy Chappell, Jaco Gericke and Anders Kraal explore, respectively, whether the Greeks, the ancient Hebrews or modal logic can free us from the supposed 'dilemma'.

Timothy Chappell tells us that the dilemma is not in the *Euthyphro*, for there the debate is about what the gods love, not about what they will. Moreover, the point at issue for Socrates is one of definition: that 'what the gods love' cannot serve as a definition of 'what is holy'. This definitional or conceptual question is perhaps distinct from a question about ontological priority, though we would need to show how to separate out the conceptual from the ontological issues. In his chapter, Cottingham puts Euthyphro-style questions to one side precisely because he believes that the quest for an ultimate definition of goodness cannot be satisfied.

Chappell goes on to argue that the so-called 'dilemma' is not a dilemma, for theists can choose one or other horn, or else refuse both horns. He shows with great succinctness that any of these three routes is open to theists and each can be argued with plausibility. He directly challenges the assumption that we must choose an order of priority between God and goodness: why cannot each entail the other, just as equilaterality in triangles determines equiangularity in triangles and vice versa? This is the nature of solution tested in Chapter 5 by Anders Kraal.

But there is a different, and in Chappell's view more interesting, question relating to the *Euthyphro*, which is the question of Socrates' own disposition towards the divine. Arguably, naturalistic readings of the Greeks are implausible, as John E. Hare argues in relation to Aristotle[32] and as Chappell argues here in relation to Socrates. Socrates has often been assumed to discount the supernatural in favour of employing our own reasoning. But Chappell argues that it is clear from both Plato's and Xenophon's evidence that Socrates believes in supernatural guidance as something separate from the guidance he gets through his own careful thought. A sense of divine commands within Socrates' thought runs throughout

---

[31]   Robin Le Poidevin, *Arguing for Atheism: An Introduction to the Philosophy of Religion* (Abingdon: Routledge, 1996), p. 85.

[32]   Hare, *God and Morality*, pp. 7–72.

Chappell's chapter, which may question the strong disjunction implied by Anscombe between Greek and Judaeo-Christian notions of morality. Socrates seems sometimes to feel himself commanded by *theos*. He takes note of dreams, visions and voices. If nothing else, Chappell argues that this discounts claims that the *Euthyphro* is an attack on divine commands. He also suggests that Plato may be providing a context in which divine commands can be acceptable, by showing a preference for an ethical theism over chaotic polytheism. If so, what happens to the disjunction that Anscombe had proposed? To carry his point, Chappell has to navigate through the many and varied places in Plato's dialogues, where Plato seems sarcastic or principled in his rejection of inspiration from a divine source. But he finds in Plato a position that we have already canvassed, in discussion of Trakakis and Schellenberg: that since we are creatures of imperfect knowledge, we cannot expect to attain perfect truth by our own rational efforts and so should not neglect the possibility of attaining truth by less rationally pure routes.

Chappell ends on a note similar to that of Cottingham – a note wary of too much effort to systematize or to provide a fully cogent theory. He warns us not to overrate the value of a system at the cost of overlooking the possibility of epiphany.

DCTs are often characterized by reference to parts of the Hebrew Bible, such as the giving of the Ten Commandments. Jaco Gericke in Chapter 4 challenges the assumptions behind such characterizations. While he argues that there are elements of DCT in the Hebrew Bible, this is not all that the Hebrew Bible conveys concerning the relationship between divinity and morality. He finds evidence of belief in an independent moral order against which Yhwh is judged to be good and is also sometimes judged to be wrong. In the Hebrew Bible, Yhwh is sometimes held responsible not only for natural evil but also for moral evil; ancient Israel not debating theodicy as we do. As Gericke points out, the possibility that some divine commands can be judged not-good complicates efforts to equate divine commands with 'the good'.

Gericke's contribution is unique in providing not only a philosophical approach to ancient Israelite religion but also metaethical reflection on the Hebrew scriptures. When Gericke speaks of 'Moral Realism', he means that goodness has a reality independent of Yhwh, so far as the religion of ancient Israel is concerned. It is important to distinguish his meaning from a more conventional use of 'moral realism' to mean that moral statements possess a truth-value. Even the strongest DCT, and one which supports the notion that God is the very standard of goodness, is realist in the more conventional sense. A strong DCT would hold that the statement 'it is wrong to kill' has a truth-value that is derived from the command 'thou shalt not kill' issuing from God. All DCTs are 'realist' in the conventional sense, either because they accept an independent order of morality, against which God's commands can be judged, or because God chooses or is the standard of goodness. Either way, moral statements will have a truth-value.

Gericke's point is that the Hebrew Bible cannot be drawn on in support of strong DCTs. Just as Chappell has exposed some false assumptions about the thought of Socrates and Plato, Gericke has challenged assumptions about the religious world-view of ancient Israel. He shows that ancient Hebrews believed in a God who mediates rather than creates divine commands, whose will (usually) corresponds to what is good, and whose nature instantiates rather than defines the property of goodness. Gericke judges the 'Euthyphro dilemma' to be a non-issue for the ancient Hebrews because they, unlike later Christian theologians who had been influenced by Platonic thought, did not regard goodness as an essential part of the divine nature. Rather, they regarded Yhwh as their moral instructor or guide, because their underlying moral epistemology was the view that humans need good gods to tell them what the good life is.

The God of ancient Israel in Gericke's account, seems not so very different from God or the gods of Socrates in the *Euthyphro* in Chappell's account. It seems not to be the case that the Hebrew God/gods command whilst the Greek God/gods do not. Nor is it the case that deities in the world-view of the Hebrews or of the *Euthyphro* are thought to create moral norms and define goodness. (The *Republic* is a different matter, for therein the doctrine of the Forms is developed and from there the idea, taken up by Augustine, emerges that a fall away from goodness is by the same token a fall away from being.) According to the chapters by Chappell and Gericke, at least, the gods of the *Euthyphro* and the God of the Hebrews are thought to mediate moral values and instantiate goodness.

In Chapter 5, Anders Kraal therefore addresses a different world: one in which the Euthyphro dilemma has currency because of the way in which theology has developed. Notably, Kraal moves us from Gericke's world in the Hebrew Bible,to the world of the New Testament, in which Jesus is quoted as saying 'There is only One who is good, that is, God' (Matthew 9:17). Within Christian thought, God has come to be identified with goodness itself. At least two elements are crucial in the making of this identification. One is concern to secure divine sovereignty, such that God is subject to no standard beyond Godself; not even the standard of goodness. Another is the way in which contemplation of the divine nature took theologians towards a doctrine of divine simplicity, according to which the divine being is identical to the divine attributes. If God is simple rather than complex, and is therefore indivisible in nature, goodness comes to be seen as an essential part of the divine nature.

Augustine, as influenced by the Platonism of Plotinus, was crucial in this development. Augustine came to agree with the Platonic philosophers that God is at once the author of all things, the illuminator of truth and the giver of happiness (*City of God*, 8. 5). He distinguished between three natures or kinds: bodies, which are mutable in time and place; souls, which are incorporeal but mutable in time; and God, who is incorporeal and immutable (*De Genesi ad Litteram*, 8. 20. 39). He argued that God makes everything, and all that God makes is good. Badness is therefore not created but arises when created things decay or fall away from being. So, as in Platonic thought, goodness and being are equated.

Aquinas saw in the doctrine of divine simplicity a resolution to the 'Euthyphro dilemma': for good is neither independent of God's will nor existent because God wills it; rather, God and goodness are identical. Furthermore, if God is by nature good, worries about divine arbitrariness in the case that God defines goodness are soothed.

However, there are critics, notably Alvin Plantinga, who argue that a doctrine of divine simplicity is confused.[33] If it is confused, resolutions of the 'Euthyphro dilemma' cannot reside therein. Plantinga's famous objection is that if God is identical to each of God's properties, then those properties are identical to each other, such that God has only one property. Moreover, God is identical to that one property. That God is a property is, Plantinga says, incompatible with classical Christian doctrine.

Kraal tests some systems of formal logic and finds a system which he believes can save the doctrine of divine simplicity and thereby save us from the 'Euthyphro dilemma'. His method of philosophizing by formal logic is the most strongly analytical in this volume and, as such, would seem to be the most vulnerable to charges that the analytical philosophy of religion is irrelevant. Perhaps the most fitting response to that charge is to point out that relevance is in the mind of the beholder. Many philosophers of religion are engaged in methods of contemplating the divine. Formal logic, for those trained and informed by it, serves this end. Kraal is an example of a philosopher who digs deep into at least two traditions – Christian thought and analytical philosophy – to develop an argument whose conclusions will strike a chord with others digging in the same or in neighbouring wells.

Grounding Morality

In the first half of Part I, the chapters are about the source of goodness, because they have reasoned downwards from speculation about a transcendent source. The second set of chapters in Part I takes up the question of priority differently – 'from the ground up', we might say. They consider our nature as evolved beings and, in the case of Scruton's chapter, the ways in which our social practices are bound up with our deepest concerns. If we start from where we are with our sense of morality, we ask what grounds it.

While the quest for a 'source' primarily concerns origins and derivation, a quest for 'grounds' carries with it connotations of justificatory explanation or valid reason. Scruton believes that evolution has no or little significant explanatory power in relation to our deepest moral concerns, whilst Attfield and Philipse ask what sort of explanatory role evolution might play in relation to our moral values, given that evolutionary theory explains much about how we come to be as we are.

---

[33]　Alvin Plantinga, *Does God Have a Nature?* (Milwaukee, WI: Marquette University Press, 1980).

Piety Revisited

The term 'piety', which is usually substituted by 'goodness' when philosophers of religion discuss the Euthyphro dilemma, is central to Scruton's chapter. That the word and its meaning are old-fashioned is partly his point. He finds modern moral and political philosophy, with its focus on contract, justice, equality and rights, inadequate in addressing our ultimate concerns. Anthropologists realize, he says, that the concepts of piety and impiety, sacred and sacrilegious, and pure and impure are central to the belief systems and behaviours of peoples. Using the example of orthodox Christians and Muslims, he argues that these concepts are part of the *a priori* endowment of human beings. 'Indeed, for the believer', he writes, 'there is no clearer proof of God, than the fact that we can make sense of our moral experience only by employing concepts like those of the pious, the sacrilegious and the sacred, which point beyond this world to its transcendental ground.'

Scruton's argument rests not only on the experience of believers but on experiences arguably common to all people. What matters to people about sex, he says, are issues of dirt and cleanliness, purity, pollution and violation. Notions of consent and contract barely touch these concerns. It is not surprising, he thinks, that we flounder around in our attempts to relate religion to morality, given that it is experiences articulated in terms of piety, purity and the sacred that constitute religion's main input into the moral life of human beings. Scruton's analysis chimes, perhaps, with that of Jurgen Habermas, who has recently argued that every discipline must rethink its philosophical core if it is to accommodate religion and religious issues in our analyses of late modern societies.[34]

Despite suggesting that a transcendental orientation to our moral experience provides proof of God for the believer, Scruton is not himself offering a proof. Like Cottingham, he is providing a line of reasoning with which he purports to make the most sense of our moral experience. His point is that a belief in God enables our moral experience and concepts to hold together by providing for them a transcendental ground. Behind this proposal lies a question: what happens when we try to ground morality scientifically, with no transcendental reference, as evolutionary psychologists may try to do?

If evolution can offer a sufficient explanation for morality, then no matter what story we might tell about a transcendental source of goodness, that very act of trying to trace its genealogy is itself in principle explicable in terms of evolutionary processes. Scruton is engaged in a fundamental struggle with those who believe that evolution can adequately account for morality. He holds that wholly scientific accounts leave untouched that which enables us to make most sense of goodness

---

[34]   Jurgen Habermas, responding to questions at the 'Religion in the Public Spheres' International Conference, University of Aarhus, Denmark, May 2008. I am grateful to Grace Davie for alerting me to Habermas' pronouncement.

and morality, and he sees it as one of the primary tasks of philosophy of religion to give a transcendental deduction of the validity of our core moral concepts.

Evolutionary Theories

Scruton's argument is against entirely adaptationist accounts of evolution. But not all theories of evolution are wholly adaptationist. Robin Attfield takes us towards non-deterministic and probably non-adaptationist accounts of evolution, in order to account, within our theories of evolution, for non-reciprocal altruistic behaviour.

The proposal Attfield most strongly wishes to make is that evolutionary theory cannot supply sufficient conditions of human behaviour. His success will depend on whether the category of human choice can be adequately accommodated within the theory of causation he adopts. This question has larger ramifications within debates over free will and determinism, and within debates over how we adjudicate between our natural desires when they conflict with one another or with some sense of duty. So, like Scruton, Attfield is looking for something over and above an evolutionary explanation in order to make sense of morality.

Herman Philipse, by contrast, argues that evolutionary theory may itself be able to provide an ultimate explanation of the content of some fundamental moral truths. To make this case, we need to rethink meta-ethics.

Philipse's meta-ethical proposal directly addresses the question of adaptation in evolution. He contrasts two alternatives: 1) that the evolution of our moral convictions tracked the truth, in which case the evolutionary origin of our moral convictions is compatible with strong meta-ethical realism; or 2) our moral convictions evolved adaptatively, regardless of their truth, to promote reproductive success, in which case evolutionary explanatory ethics may undermine strong meta-ethical realism. Philipse follows Sharon Street in regarding the adaptive-link account of the evolution of our moral sense as superior to the truth-tracking account. If adaptation can explain many of our emotionally based moral beliefs, then strong meta-ethical realism becomes superfluous as an explanation. Strong meta-ethical realism may be true even so, despite being apparently superfluous as an explanation. However, then we would have the following possible scenario: that 'whatever objective morality may truly dictate, we might have evolved in such a way as to miss completely its real essence', which would be counter-intuitive.[35]

In rejecting truth-tracking accounts of evolution, Philipse denies the plausibility that natural selection favoured ancestors who were able to grasp objective (in the sense of mind or person-independent) moral truths. Ultimately the question between Philipse and Scruton is whether scientific theories can address transcendental matters. Scruton insists that evolutionary theory leaves meta-questions unaltered, while Philipse holds that evolutionary theory renders obsolete any reference to a transcendent ground for morality.

---

[35] Philipse quoting Michael Ruse, 'Evolutionary Ethics: A Phoenix Arisen', *Zygon* 21 (1986), 108.

The case against a transcendent ground, as made by Philipse and Street, is by nature not decisive. It rests on the oddity highlighted by Ruse and already quoted: that 'whatever objective morality may truly dictate, we might have evolved in such a way as to miss completely its real essence'. Their argument seems essentially to be this: that it would be odd to hold that our moral evaluations fit us for survival and at the same time to hold that we have grounds in reason to distrust these evaluations. Put this way, their point sounds very like that of the common sense philosopher Thomas Reid, who argued in the eighteenth century that it would be odd to believe that our reason and our perceptive and moral faculties would all fit us for life on this earth and yet would point in conflicting directions, i.e. that our perceptive and moral senses would enable our survival, whilst our reason would lead us to distrust these senses.[36]

Behind Reid's epistemology and moral philosophy lay the conviction that we have one Author who has equipped us perceptively, rationally and morally. He did not offer a top-down argument to this effect, and his philosophy can stand without reference to God. His point is that we make our way through this life trusting the compatibility of our senses and reason. However, his philosophy is a good example of how exploration of what fits us for survival is compatible with a belief in a meta-reality, an appeal to which makes sense of the compatibility between our perceptions, our moral evaluations and our other reasoning.

Reid's approach may suggest the ongoing philosophical possibility of a fit between our human development and a divine Author, but Philipse takes a different route. Following David Copp and others, he explores a 'society-centred theory' of meta-ethical realism.[37] In Copp's theory, a stable society needs to be governed by shared norms or standards, which, when internalized widely enough, will induce its members to behave in a cooperative, society-sustaining manner. On this account, the 'truth-grounding status' of a moral standard is that it best serves a society in enabling it to meet its need. Moral realism is maintained because moral statements have a truth-value: they either correspond or fail to correspond to the relevant truth-grounding status. In such a theory, adaptations that enhance social stability will also tend to approximate to truth, because the criterion of truth is correspondence to the moral code that best serves societal needs. Hence, truth-tracking is not rendered obsolete.

Philipse concludes that the only forms of meta-ethical realism that could survive evolutionary explanations of our moral sense are versions like Copp's, in which truth criteria are linked to what is adaptive for humans. He calls this the 'Thesis of Adaptive Truth'. A question remains: is a meta-ethical theory that

---

[36] Reid argues this position throughout his works *An Inquiry into the Human Mind on the Principles of Common Sense*; *Essays on the Intellectual Powers of Man*; and *Essays on the Active Powers of Man*. For access to all three, see the abridged *Inquiry and Essays*, Ronald E. Beanblossom and Keith Lehrer (eds) (Indianapolis: IN: Hackett, 1983).

[37] David Copp, 'Darwinian Skepticism about Moral Realism', *Philosophical Issues* 18 (2008), 186–206.

complies with the Thesis of Adaptive Truth able to ground adequately the deep-seated concerns that Scruton highlights, or do questions about piety, purity and the sacred, which imply a transcendent referent, have the truth-value 'false'?

II

The Goodness of God

In Part II of this volume, we turn to consider the nature of God's own goodness, and whether it coheres with other divine qualities and with the universe God has created. The authors in Part II are primarily focused on the coherence of the concept of God. They do not directly pursue theodicy questions about the goodness or otherwise of creation,[38] although all discussion of divine goodness has a bearing on theodicy, and the final two chapters consider the nature of sin and its entry into the world.

Dan O'Brien opens with a chapter on the limits of divine attributes. He tests the limits of God's goodness against the limits of omniscience: if God is omniscient, would not God need to understand evil, but if God were to understand evil, would not that compromise God's goodness? Behind this question lies another: what is involved in 'understanding' motivations and thoughts to which one does not subscribe or which one does not oneself harbour? O'Brien, through a thoughtful exploriation of empathy, raises the challenge that if God is omniscient, He must be able to understand sinful thoughts, otherwise He would not understand us and there would be a large area of creation that is incomprehensible to Him. If God can understand sinful thoughts, God, whilst not harbouring or subscribing to sinful thoughts, must be able to imagine them: He 'must be able, in his imagination, to have morally imperfect thoughts'. However, it is reprehensible, O'Brien asserts, to propose that God has morally imperfect thoughts. Therefore, omniscience and moral perfection are incompatible and the traditional God of Christianity cannot exist.

In order to salvage the prospect of God's existence, O'Brien explores a theory devised by Yujin Nagasawa called the 'Maximal God Thesis'. Nagasawa's proposal is that 'God is the being that has the maximal consistent set of knowledge, power and benevolence'.[39] This is a new and significant departure within philosophy of religion, and is worthy of some introduction here.

Nagasawa's starting point for the Maximal God Thesis is the God of Anselm: the being than which no greater can be thought. According to most Anselmian

---

[38]   As taken up, for example, by Hugh Rice, *God and Goodness* (Oxford: Oxford University Press, 2003) and Mark Wynn, *God and Goodness: A Natural Theological Perspective* (London: Routledge, 1999).

[39]   Yujin Nagasawa, 'A New Defence of Anselmian Theism', *Philosophical Quarterly* 58 (2008): 577–96.

theists, that God is the being than which no greater can be thought entails that God is omniscient, omnipotent and omnibenevolent. For the last 900 years or so, however, critics of Anselmian theism have tried to show that there does not exist an omniscient, omnipotent and omnibenevolent being by advancing numerous distinct arguments, such as the argument from evil, the paradox of the stone and the argument from God's inability to sin, each of which challenge the coherence of divine omni-qualities. Defenders of Anselmian theism have responded to each argument on a case-by-case basis. Nagasawa argues that this approach is uneconomical, particularly if one's ultimate goal is to defend Anselmian theism. He proposes a radically new and more efficient defence, which undercuts almost all the existing arguments against Anselmian theism at once.

Nagasawa claims that arguments against OmniGod Theism are not arguments against Anselmian Theism. If the being than which no greater can be thought is not omniperfect (because of the contradictions inherent in holding together various perfections), but rather maximally great, one could be an Anselmian theist whilst relaxing on one or more of the perfections. Nagasawa proposes that philosophers of religion be open to the possibility that God is not an omniscient, omnipotent and omnibenevolent being, but rather a being who best holds together an optimum set of qualities.

Philosophers and theologians do, as Nagasawa points out, already explore the possibility of modifying omni-qualities, especially in relation to the problem of suffering and evil. The most commonly recurring proposal is that God, by virtue of creating, and perhaps by choice, has undergone a reduction in power in order to give freedom to creation. Process philosophers and theologians go furthest in modifying divine power. They regard God as imminently bound up in the evolving processes of creation and as vulnerable to the directions in which creation may go. Such attempts would be examples of what Nagasawa calls case-by-case responses to the challenge of OmniTheism.

Dan O'Brien takes up Nagasawa's proposal for a general modification of the OmniGod thesis, and turns his particular attention to the modification of omniscience. 'God may be the greatest being of which we can conceive', he writes, 'and one way to articulate his greatness is to accept that he is limited in his understanding of some of his creation, yet he is morally perfect.' Significantly, O'Brien takes up the matter alluded to earlier, of the mystery of the divine. He proposes a mutual unknowing between ourselves and God: God's ways are mysterious to us and ours are not fully comprehended by God. This is an interesting proposal to explore in terms of the freedom God extends to creation. It would have a knock-on effect for spirituality and for those religious practices in which believers position themselves before God as the one who knows even the secrets of their hearts.

Whilst O'Brien explores the extent of God's knowledge, Nicholas Wolterstorff explores the nature of God's love. In his book *Justice: Right and Wrongs*, Wolterstorff provides a theistic account of natural human rights, and roots our intuition about human rights in the Hebrew and Christian scriptures (and decidedly not in Greek and Roman philosophy).[40] He now turns his attention to the relationship between justice and love. His chapter in this volume takes up an idea in Anselm's *Proslogion* that forgiveness undermines justice.

Forgiveness is by its very nature something 'given'. It is an act of generosity. Wolterstorff focuses on gratuitous generosity and asks what makes it sometimes unjust. He takes two of Jesus' parables – the labourers in the vineyard and the prodigal son – as providing examples of gratuitous generosity. We usually associate God with the owner of the vineyard and with the father of the son. If in making these associations we understand the parables rightly, then Wolterstorff is questioning the justice of God when he questions the justice of those actors in the parables.

In the parable of the labourers in the vineyard, the vineyard owner comes at different hours of the day to contract casual labourers to work. The last labourers that he employs, towards the end of the day, work for only one hour. The first labourers, whom he employs at the start of the day, work all day long. At the end of the working day, the owner pays all the workers the same amount: a daily wage. When those who have worked longest complain, the owner explains that he has paid them what they earned and expected. He rebukes them for being envious at his generosity. In the parable of the prodigal son, the son who takes and squanders family money is welcomed back by his father and is treated to a feast with the fatted calf. The elder son is aggrieved because he has stayed and worked for his father throughout his younger brother's shameful absence and has never been given so much as a goat for a feast with his friends.

Within the parables, the actions of the vineyard owner and father cause grievance, but are they unjust? Wolterstorff is not content with theological claims that these acts of spontaneous love and generosity render justice obsolete. He is wary of the notion that justice might ever be obsolete, and asks whether the Aristotelian paradigm of a fair distribution of goods can pinpoint where, if at all, an injustice has occurred.

According to the Aristotelian paradigm (as mediated by Joel Feinberg), injustice arises when there is a departure from equal treatment without good, i.e. morally relevant, reason. Wolterstorff finds this paradigm inadequate to distinguish just from unjust behaviour in a number of cases, let alone in cases of generosity. Sometimes, for example, a benefactor might choose some charities over others in an arbitrary way because all are equally worthy, and morally relevant factors cannot clinch the decision. This does not render the benefactor unjust. But what if an employer pays workers the same amount of money for unequal amounts of the same work? Whether or not this is unjust, Wolterstorff argues, depends on whether the prior rights of the employees have been met. If the prior rights are taken care of, such as that everyone is paid what was agreed, then no-one's rights are violated if additional payment is made out of the employer's generosity. This is because

---

[40]   Nicholas Wolterstorff, *Justice: Rights and Wrongs* (Princeton, NJ: Princeton University Press, 2010).

generosity does not generate new rights. By the same token, if two sons are both treated equally as sons, to throw a party for one because he has returned does not violate the rights of the other or generate a right for him also to have the fatted calf.

In arguing that generosity does not generate new rights, Wolterstorff rejects the Aristotelian paradigm; according to that paradigm, if landowners or parents distribute gifts generously to some recipients, they must, unless there is morally relevant reason not to, give equally generously to all similar parties. In other words, on the Aristotelian paradigm, generosity does generate new rights. The religious import of this challenge to the Aristotelian paradigm is that God's generosity does not transcend justice by rendering it obsolete, but rather by doing what justice requires and more. Thus, Wolterstorff has gone some way in resolving the tension raised by Anselm between justice and forgiveness. Forgiveness, such as that shown to the prodigal son, may feel unjust to others who are close to the situation. But all forgiveness, precisely because it is a gift, is unearned. Is it thereby unjust? Not, Wolterstorff argues, if the prior rights of all relevant parties have been properly met. If all such rights have been met, forgiveness is pure gift, with no detraction.

The doctrine of hell is a provocative topic to follow a discussion of divine forgiveness, and throws into question the goodness of God from the opposite direction. In juxtaposing the chapters by Woltestorff and Ioanna-Maria Patsalidou, we arrive at the following questions: how could one and the same God be both generously forgiving and able to condemn people to eternal suffering?; and are the doctrines of forgiveness and of hell so mutually conflicting as to render the traditional concepts of God incoherent?

Patsalidou takes up a question raised by Eleonore Stump: how is divine love shown to any mortal who receives unending suffering for finite evils? Stump argues, in relation to Aquinas' notion of love and Dante's vision of hell, that the creation and utilization of hell flows out of God's nature. Patsalidou tests this theory in relation to a currently popular notion that instead of condemning people to hell, God allows their annihilation. The annihilation thesis takes as a premise the apparent futility of eternal punishment.

Annihilation would result in the complete removal of being. Stump holds that this would be unloving, because love desires the goodness of things, and 'being' and 'goodness' are identical. As such, a removal of being would, by the same token, be a removal of goodness. An alternative would be for to God prevent people from acting contrary to divine will, such that no-one need suffer eternal damnation. But then God would be acting contrary to the free will of his creatures and would to that extent be destroying their nature as human beings. Loss of being and hence of goodness entailed by preventing them from acting in evil ways is a greater loss of being than whatever loss may be incurred by the evil God permits. Stump argues that God shows that He loves His human creatures by preserving them in being in hell, and by allowing them to express as much of their vicious dispositions as possible, which have, through their own free choice, become a *second nature* to them.

Patsalidou argues against this verdict. Her point is that the damned in hell would not be maintained in a state of being that they had chosen. Instead, they would become worse and, by that token, would decrease in being. Although Aquinas holds that a total lack of being would be an absolute evil, he also holds that non-being is desirable where it reduces suffering. Hence, Patsalidou, following this point, argues that annihilation rather than eternal suffering would be the option most consistent with God's love. Her argument, rooted as it is in Aquinas, bolsters the annihilationist cause against those who regard it as a 'philosophical dead end'.[41]

Human Autonomy and the Greater Good

In light of a philosophy that relates evil to non-being, it is interesting to encounter a thinker who finds many benefits in sin. Such a thinker is Augustin Doležal, a Lutheran pastor and theologian of the Slovak Enlightenment, introduced to us in this volume by Vasil Gluchman.

In his work *Tragoedia* (1791), Doležal was influenced by the optimistic outlook of Leibniz's *Theodicy* (1710), according to which greater good ensues where there is evil to overcome. In various ways, Doležal interprets the sin of Adam and Eve in a positive light, emphasizing the benefits that have ensued for humankind. These benefits include: diversity of employment, because of the diversity of needs that have arisen due to sin; virtues that are exercised in overcoming evil; a growth in knowledge due to the curiosity and desire for autonomy that prompted the first sin and also due to the need, occasioned by the consequences of sin, to better understand nature. Indeed, Doležal thinks up an ingenious number of benefits that follow from our ancestors' original misdemeanour. Though he never fully says so, he implies that 'thanks' to the primary sin or desire for knowledge, for the discovery of the new and unknown, human beings develop their knowledge and skills, and realize their full potential.

The suggestion that sin might yield benefits to those committing it, because it can enhance self-realization, seems to run counter to the philosophical tradition that unites being with goodness. Yet, it may be that Doležal is expressing the Leibnizian view that the best possible universe will contain the highest levels of power, knowledge, happiness and goodness in created things that the universe could allow. Leibniz understands the best possible world to combine the maximal possible complexity with the maximal possible order. Complexity is achieved by monads, notably human minds or souls, reflecting the world from an infinite number of unique perspectives, such that the universe is replete with an infinite number of different representations of God's works. When Doležal emphasizes the opportunities and complexity that develop because of the doors opened by sin, he

---

[41]   Claire Brown and Jerry L. Walls, 'Annihilationism: A Philosophical Dead End?', in Joel Buenting (ed.), *The Problem of Hell: A Philosophical Anthology* (Farnham; Burlington, VT: Ashgate, 2010), pp. 45–64.

seems to be saying that sin is a product of the human quest for realization, which is part of what makes our world gloriously replete. If this heavily Leibnizian interpretation of Doležal is along the right lines, then sin is taken up into the greater good of helping creation manifest the fullness of God.

A hundred years on from Doležal, the German Catholic, and post-Catholic, theologian Max Scheler shared a similar emphasis upon human knowledge and self-realization. Alicja Gescinska recalls our attention to Scheler's work and recovers the reputation of his later, metaphysical writings, which are often regarded as disappointingly inconsistent with his earlier work in ethics. Gescinska traces the continuities in Scheler's thought, but also brings to the fore a kind of Process Theology evident in his later work, in which God is regarded as incomplete and as dependent on humankind for fulfilment. The earlier Scheler regards humankind as responsible for realizing the Good, while the later Scheler holds humankind responsible for realizing God.

Thus, Scheler places enormous responsibility upon human autonomy. His philosophical struggle, Gescinska writes, is a struggle against nihilism, moral indifference, relativism and passivity, all of which are forms of moral slavery. It is through moral responsibility and autonomy that we break free from moral slavery, that we live out the responsibility to be. Thus, in Scheler's work, we discover a different route back to our starting point: the question of identification between being and goodness, God and the Good. There is a Platonic relationship between being and goodness in Scheler's thought, and an accompanying hierarchy: a hierarchy of knowledge which maps onto a hierarchy of values, such that the highest knowledge motivates us to the highest and most beautiful of moral values – the bringing into being of God. The crucial difference is one of direction. Rather than Goodness and Being emanating from the Form of the Good, or from God, God is realized through moral goodness. If, in Doležal's works, moral autonomy assists creation in its full realization, in the later works of Scheler, it assists the realization of God.

Theism, as typically debated by philosophers of religion, casts God as the omnipotent, omnibenevolent Creator. Scheler moves from this perspective in his later works. He develops a theology infused by Hegelian notions of an immanent God whose being flows out into creation, a notion also taken up by Process Theologians and others who find much fruit in the suggestion that not only do we depend on God for our being but that God somehow also depends upon us.

That would be a topic for another volume.

Chapter 1

What's the Use of Philosophy of Religion?

Victoria S. Harrison

Increased attention to the theoretical and methodological issues underlying the current practice of analytic philosophy of religion indicates that this discipline is currently undergoing some dramatic changes. Moreover, much in the recent literature suggests that many hold the discipline to be in a state of crisis. Not only is there widespread disagreement about its aims, scope and method, there are also many who argue that it has become irrelevant to all but the few specialist practitioners actually working within the field.[1] This last concern has taken on particular importance given the research impact agenda currently under discussion in universities the world over. Here I consider the charge of irrelevance and argue that, despite arguments to the contrary, analytic philosophy of religion does have a valuable contribution to make to our understanding of issues of vital public importance.[2]

In a recent book, ominously entitled *The End of Philosophy of Religion*, Nick Trakakis presents a detailed argument for the irrelevance of analytic philosophy of religion.[3] I have chosen to focus on the argument of this book here because it seems to be representative of a view that is increasingly widely held. Trakakis claims that analytic philosophy of religion is largely irrelevant to the concerns of people outside the subject area. While taking up this charge, I will question aspects of Trakakis' account of what has caused this situation and his proposed solution to it.

Trakakis' Account of the Problem

We can define analytic philosophy as that style of philosophy which emphasizes conceptual analysis, and analytic philosophy of religion as an instance of this style of philosophy applied to issues arising from religious beliefs and practices.

---

[1] For a sample of diverse approaches to philosophy of religion, see David Cheetham and Rolfe King (eds), *Contemporary Practice and Method in the Philosophy of Religion: New Essays* (London: Continuum, 2008).

[2] Elsewhere I have discussed the issue of disagreement concerning the aims, scope and method of the discipline. See Victoria S. Harrison, 'Philosophy of Religion, Fictionalism, and Religious Diversity', *International Journal for Philosophy of Religion* 68 (2011), 43–58.

[3] Nick Trakakis, *The End of Philosophy of Religion* (London and New York: Continuum, 2008).

A philosopher of religion himself, Trakakis charges the discipline with having become almost completely cut off from the concerns of ordinary people, even those having interests in religion. What analytic philosophers of religion do, he argues, has quite simply become irrelevant to the concerns of anyone outside the discipline.

Trakakis holds that the problem currently facing analytic philosophy of religion is just one instance of a fundamental problem affecting all analytic philosophy. In modelling itself on the natural sciences, Trakakis argues, the whole tradition of analytic philosophy has made itself irrelevant because the subject matter of philosophy cannot be adequately addressed by the methods of the natural sciences.[4] In pursuing a chimerical ideal of scientific objectivity, analytic philosophers have allowed their work to become more and more detached from experience. As a consequence, it has less and less to contribute to our understanding of meanings and values. Applying this conclusion to philosophy of religion, Trakakis argues that it is no surprise to find that analytic philosophers of religion are unable to make a useful contribution to the understanding of religion and that they fail to address the urgent questions that actually trouble people outside the academy.[5]

Comparing the often dry, scientific prose of analytic philosophers of religion to the freshness characteristic of the writings of Continental philosophers of religion and certain novelists, Trakakis argues that the latter writings are capable of conveying genuine insight and, at best, are evocative of religious experience. By modelling their style of philosophy on the literary arts rather than on the natural sciences, Continental philosophers work in a medium that is more in touch with experience – or so Trakakis claims.[6] Analytic philosophy of religion, on the contrary, does not facilitate religious experience or incite one to prayer. Moreover, according to Trakakis, it usually fails to satisfy those who turn to it for a deeper understanding of religious matters. He also complains that analytic philosophy of religion is not personal enough. Analytic philosophers of religion do not speak from the heart but wrap up their work in dense jargon-filled prose that fails to inspire. Given this account of the current state of the discipline, the following question arises: what is the use of analytic philosophy of religion? Trakakis' answer is that it is of no use to anyone. If an analytic philosopher of religion wants to make a genuine contribution to religious understanding, he or she should give up analytic philosophy and turn to literature.[7]

Furthermore, in Trakakis' view, the fact that analytic philosophy of religion is based on a method that is entirely unsuited to its subject matter is not the only

---

[4]   Ibid., pp. 47–8.

[5]   Believing that the same fundamental problem plagues the whole of analytic philosophy, Trakakis deploys philosophy of religion as a test case to establish his conclusions. He holds that analytic philosophy is in what we might describe as a Catch-22 situation: the better its practitioners get at it, the more irrelevant it is doomed to become. See ibid., Chapter 3.

[6]   See ibid., Chapter 4.

[7]   For an example of how this might be done, see ibid., Chapter 5.

problem it faces. He argues that a further problem has also contributed to the current irrelevance of analytic philosophy of religion. This additional problem arises from the professionalized academic context within which analytic philosophy of religion is now practised. By rewarding specialization, the academy has reified boundaries between subjects of study to the extent that they have become stifling of intellectual engagement. He argues that this has further undermined the relevancy of philosophy by isolating its practitioners from their peers working within other subject areas.

On the basis of his characterization of the current state of analytic philosophy of religion in particular and analytic philosophy in general, Trakakis proposes that a key part of the solution is to remove philosophers from philosophy departments, thereby forcing them to interact with those working in other subject areas. He views the division of subjects within academia, and the intensively competitive specialization this has engendered, as an invidious force which has emasculated philosophers by encouraging them to ignore what goes on outside the increasingly narrow confines of their own specialist area. In particular, he argues that philosophers of religion would benefit from being thrust into the company of colleagues engaged with theology and religious studies. Pushing this idea to its conclusion, he recommends that disciplinary boundaries within university institutions should be abolished and that philosophers should find new ways of practising philosophy within this new, more open institution framework.[8]

Trakakis is surely correct that analytic philosophy of religion can seem irrelevant to the concerns of people outside the academy, as indeed it can to scholars in other disciplines within academia, and that it often fails to satisfy those who come to it looking for religious insight. His proposed solution to the irrelevance of philosophy of religion follows from his conviction that it is the method of analytic philosophy itself, along with the academic environment that has legitimatized its practice, which has generated the irrelevance. But, as we shall see, a different analysis of the root of the irrelevance will suggest a different remedy. Below, I outline a different account of the current state of analytic philosophy of religion and suggest an alternative response to the criticism of irrelevance. Before explaining my approach, though, a very brief summary of how the discipline got to where it is today is required.

Background to the Current State of the Discipline

It is well known that philosophy of religion grew out of the critiques of religion advanced by philosophers during the European Enlightenment. It is also well known, although less often brought to our attention, that all of the key figures formative of the modern Western philosophical tradition – John Locke, David Hume and Immanuel Kant being prominent examples – were concerned with questions

---

[8] These issues are discussed in ibid., Chapter 6.

raised by religious belief. Indeed, in the early modern phase of this philosophical tradition, all of the thinkers who are now regarded as being at the forefront of philosophical development in their day were interested in religious questions. In most cases, their philosophy was so profoundly shaped by their approaches to these religious questions that it would not be an exaggeration to claim that theism formed the backdrop against which their philosophical views emerged.[9]

As the Western philosophical tradition evolved, it diversified into several distinct areas, key amongst which are metaphysics, ethics and philosophy of religion. As time passed and philosophers became increasingly specialized, it became harder to find examples of significant new philosophical work cutting across these boundaries.[10] One result of these divisions within philosophy was that religious questions came to be treated exclusively within philosophy of religion and often without reference to other areas of philosophy. Moreover, those philosophers specializing in ethics or metaphysics became increasingly detached from the questions that preoccupied philosophers of religion. Alongside this development, religious studies evolved as a separate discipline covering the empirical study of religion, and this served to further constrict the scope of those specializing in philosophy of religion. I will return to the issue of philosophical specialization below, but before doing so I will briefly explain a separate, although related, factor that has also shaped the way that much of philosophy of religion is practised today.

Because philosophy of religion emerged from the interaction of Western philosophy and Western religion, from the outset it was profoundly shaped by theism in the specific form of Abrahamic monotheism. It inherited much from the heavily intellectualized theological tradition typical not only of Western Christianity but also of certain forms of Judaism and Islam that had flourished in Western Europe. By the time of the European Enlightenment, there had already been a long tradition of theological reflection on religious faith. Key examples of this earlier tradition include the two Christian scholar-monks, Anselm of Canterbury (1033–1109) and Thomas Aquinas (1225–74). There were individuals of comparable stature within Islam, such as Averroës (also known as Ibn Rushd, 1126–98), and within Judaism, such as Moses Maimonides (1135–1204). Each of these figures made a profound and lasting contribution to the tradition of theological philosophy which fed into the later discipline of philosophy of religion. Given this background, and the lack of engagement with non-monotheistic religious traditions, it is unsurprising that philosophy of religion came to be dominated by reflection on the concept of God. Over time the focus on this concept, which was undoubtedly appropriate to the age that gave rise to it, came to be another factor in narrowing the scope of study occupying philosophers of religion.

---

[9]   On this, see Charles Taliaferro, *Evidence and Faith: Philosophy and Religion since the Seventeenth Century* (Cambridge: Cambridge University Press, 2005), Chapters 1–5.

[10]   It is plausible to suggest that the last examples of this are to be found in the early twentieth century in the work of the British Idealists and the American Pragmatists.

The concerns of philosophy of religion, which were inherited from the monotheistic theological traditions that dominated European intellectual history until relatively recently, still shape the discipline in the twenty-first century. Despite the increasingly attenuated links between Christianity and culture that are apparent today, even now most of philosophy of religion remains focused on philosophical puzzles generated by the concept of God.[11] Nevertheless, there is growing recognition that an exclusively theo-centric approach to philosophy of religion is unsuitable for today's multicultural environment.[12]

Part of the pedagogical difficulty involved in teaching philosophy of religion today is that the traditional philosophy of religion defined itself and its subject matter against the context of Western religion at a time when that religion was a powerful shaping force within Western culture as a whole. Even if people were not themselves religious, they could still be expected to resonate with the issues and topics covered by philosophy of religion because of their taken-for-granted cultural background. This is no longer the case in most of the West.[13] Students taking philosophy of religion classes in modern universities increasingly expect more than a tour of the traditional theo-centric philosophical problems. Moreover, students today may come into a philosophy of religion class with no relevant experiential background or cultural knowledge that would prepare them for the material. Many lack all but the most superficial understanding of, and acquaintance with, the concept of God. It is also common to find that many students simply assume that science has made the idea of God irrelevant. Trakakis is right to point out that there is little within philosophy of religion, as it is traditionally construed and currently practised, to which students such as this can relate. More worrying still, it seems likely that these students can be taken as representative of a very large segment of the population. Under these circumstances, the focus of philosophy of religion on the concept of God surely contributes to its inability to engage fully with the range of religious questions and concerns that face many people today.

Now, despite the loss of an overtly religious cultural background, briefly alluded to above, it can be argued that religion continues to play an important

---

[11] The enduring popularity of Brian Davies' *Introduction to the Philosophy of Religion* (Oxford: Oxford University Press, 2004, first published 1982) as an undergraduate textbook is an indication of this.

[12] This is evident in the steadily increasing number of books aimed at undergraduates taking seriously ideas and arguments concerning a range of different religious traditions. Some of the best examples are: Charles Taliaferro, *Contemporary Philosophy of Religion* (Oxford: Blackwell, 1998); Keith Yandell, *Philosophy of Religion: A Contemporary Introduction* (London and New York: Routledge, 1999); Gwen Griffith-Dickson, *The Philosophy of Religion* (London: SCM, 2005) and *Human and Divine: An Introduction to the Philosophy of Religious Experience* (London: Duckworth, 2000).

[13] This is clearly an over-simplification. A more nuanced analysis would make careful distinctions between what is the case in the UK, different parts of Europe, Israel, the USA, Canada and Australasia.

role within all the cultures of the world and that its influence in the West does not seem to be waning (as had been predicted in the last century by proponents of the secularization thesis).[14] Consequently, it seems that philosophers of religion really ought to have a lot to say to students and others who are interested in religion.

More than ever, there is an urgent need in our rapidly globalizing environment for deep and sustained philosophical thought about religion; philosophers of religion can position themselves to make an important contribution to this process. In my view, it is of critical importance that they do so.[15] Philosophy of religion needs to be re-envisioned so that it can both better serve the needs of people dealing with issues raised by religion outside the academy and contribute to research within and across traditional disciplinary boundaries.

A Possible Way Forward

One way forward has been suggested by John Schellenberg. He argues that rather than focusing on the concept of God, the central concept of philosophy of religion should be 'religion'.[16] The traditional domain of philosophy of religion, he points out, had only covered one instance of this broader phenomenon.[17] He welcomes the fact that making 'religion' the organizing concept in philosophy of religion will involve a radical reconfiguration of the discipline.

Like Trakakis, Schellenberg is critical of the way in which much of analytic philosophy of religion is currently practised. He goes so far as to claim that much of it is not genuinely philosophical because it is not inspired by curiosity, which he regards as one of the hallmarks of genuine philosophy. Instead of being curious, most philosophers of religion, he argues, generally just assume that they know

---

[14]   See Victoria S. Harrison, *Religion and Modern Thought* (London: SCM, 2007), Chapter 10.

[15]   Religious fundamentalism is a growing force in many parts of the world and I have argued elsewhere that one reason for this is that people are becoming increasingly unequipped to deal with the intellectual issues at the heart of religious traditions. Consequently, they are more willing to be satisfied with intellectually thin forms of religion which offer immediate emotional security and psychological certainty. In its concentration on narrow technical issues, philosophy of religion is doing little to alleviate this situation. See Harrison, *Religion and Modern Thought*, Chapters 10–11.

[16]   For a concise account of his position, see John L. Schellenberg, 'Imagining the Future: How Scepticism Can Renew Philosophy of Religion', in Cheetham and King (eds), *Contemporary Practice and Method in the Philosophy of Religion*, pp. 15–31.

[17]   Putting Schellenberg's main idea in other words, we might say that monotheistic religion is one token, whereas the type is 'religion'. Schellenberg emphasizes that it is artificial for a philosopher of religion to think that the discipline should only focus on one token of religion – that which has been historically dominant in the West. If a philosopher is serious about the questions raised by religion, he or she should not artificially limit the set of data used in his or her inquiry.

in advance which religious tradition is most likely to be correct and focus all their attention on small technical problems within that tradition. In this respect, Schellenberg singles out Richard Swinburne and Alvin Plantinga for particular criticism.[18] It is not a coincidence that Trakakis uses the same two philosophers to illustrate that form of philosophy of religion which he thinks has come to the end of its days.[19] Schellenberg points out what he clearly regards as a critical lacuna in the work of Swinburne and Plantinga, one that Trakakis does not comment on, namely that neither of them (and this is typical of practitioners of the philosophical tradition they represent) has shown any interest in the religions or philosophies of non-Western cultures. Indeed, few analytic philosophers of religion have seriously considered the claims made by Islam, let alone looked as far afield as the religious traditions of India or China.

Perhaps because Schellenberg is concerned with what he regards as the failure of most analytic philosophers of religion to extend their inquiries beyond the scope of their own tradition, his proposal for the future development of philosophy of religion is much more constructive than that of Trakakis. Schellenberg outlines a way forward for philosophy of religion that makes full use of the intellectual tools of conceptual clarification and critical reasoning that analytic philosophers are specially trained to use. While Trakakis claims that the analytic philosopher's toolkit is useless and may as well be discarded, Schellenberg does not underestimate the value of the tools in the philosopher's kit; rather, he suggests that they might be put to more varied uses than most of those currently employing them have hitherto imagined. In Schellenberg's vision for the future of philosophy of religion, nothing needs to change with respect to the analytic methods used by philosophers; the only change necessary is in the discipline's scope.

The subject matter to be included within philosophy of religion will be determined by how the question 'what is religion?' is answered.[20] It is a positive sign that many of the most recent books on the subject take this question seriously.[21] This move, which would have been almost unthinkable in philosophy of religion even 20 years ago, provides an example of a place where the concerns of philosophers of religion directly converge with the concerns of people outside this field of study. Philosophers have sought to define religion, but so have lawyers, government policy advisors and a host of others. This is clearly an important issue

---

[18]   See Schellenberg, 'Imagining the Future', p. 22.

[19]   On Plantinga, see Trakakis, *The End of Philosophy of Religion*, pp. 37–40, and on Swinburne, see pp. 61–2.

[20]   Schellenberg has written on this question, as have a number of other philosophers of religion. See, for example, John Schellenberg, *Prolegomena to a Philosophy of Religion* (Ithaca, NY: Cornell University Press, 2005), Chapter 1; and Taliaferro, *Contemporary Philosophy of Religion*, Chapter 1.

[21]   For example, Charles Taliaferro, *Philosophy of Religion: A Beginner's Guide* (Oxford: Oneworld, 2009).

with many practical ramifications and it is one to which philosophers of religion have already made a significant contribution.[22]

I do not intend to answer the question 'what is religion?' here.[23] Suffice it to say that taking that question seriously as the starting point for philosophy of religion inevitably yields a discipline that cuts across the traditional boundaries separating the philosophies of the world's religions. Any definition of religion that is likely to command wide assent would have to recognize that Buddhism, Hinduism, Taoism and Confucianism, at least in many of their forms, fall under the concept of religion. If that is the case, then they, and the philosophical traditions associated with them, provide appropriate subject matter to be included within the broadened scope of philosophy of religion. Just as philosophers of religion have traditionally been concerned with exploring the philosophical implications of the religious beliefs and practices of Western religion, so now they can widen the scope of their interests to include the philosophical dimensions of the range of religions practised across the globe. But the philosopher of religion does not have to start from the beginning with respect to philosophizing about the religious traditions of India and China. Each of these has already been the subject of long and rich traditions of philosophical exploration. These have hitherto been the exclusive domains of scholars of Chinese philosophy and Indian philosophy, but surely philosophers of religion today can include them within their remit.

The proposal to regard 'religion' as the central organizing concept of philosophy of religion thus has far-reaching consequences, in that carrying it through will involve the transgression of familiar and comfortable academic boundaries between Western philosophy, Indian philosophy and Chinese philosophy.[24] This is only appropriate in today's multicultural environment in which we surely need to draw on the intellectual resources of all the world's philosophical traditions to confront the problems that face our global community.

Schellenberg's proposal dramatically to expand the scope of philosophy of religion is a welcome one and it is being taken seriously by a growing number of philosophers in that field. It can certainly contribute to making the discipline more relevant within a multicultural environment. Nevertheless, it should be noted that there is nothing inherent within Schellenberg's approach to prevent philosophy of religion remaining as irrelevant to the problems generated by religion faced by people outside the academy as it was as before its scope was extended. A philosopher

---

[22]   See the discussion of this in Griffith-Dickson, *The Philosophy of Religion*, Chapter 1.

[23]   For my answer to this question, see Victoria S. Harrison, 'The Pragmatics of Defining Religion in a Multi-Cultural World', *International Journal for Philosophy of Religion* 59(3) (2006), 133–52.

[24]   There is significant evidence to suggest that these academic boundaries are artificial creations that have served to conveniently excuse us from engaging with the complex histories of intellectual exchange that have shaped these traditions of thought. See Thomas McEvilley, *The Shape of Ancient Thought: Comparative Studies in Greek and Indian Philosophies* (New York: Allworth Press, 2006).

of religion working away on some technical issue within Indian philosophy may have as little to contribute to genuine religious understanding as someone working away on some technical aspect of the inductive argument from evil.

Trakakis and Schellenberg both address important issues currently facing philosophy of religion as an academic discipline, although the issues that concern them are different. Schellenberg targets parochialism within philosophy of religion and he seeks to correct the tendency for philosophers of religion to concern themselves with only one religious tradition. As we have seen, Trakakis targets the irrelevancy of philosophy of religion to the majority of people outside the disciplinary boundary and he proposes to remedy this by abandoning the method of analytic philosophy, as well as by changing the institutional context within which philosophy of religion is practised.

I agree with Schellenberg's proposal that philosophy of religion should focus on the concept of religion, not on the concept of God.[25] However, I suggest that his proposal be deployed within the context of an even broader conception of what philosophy of religion is and of what a philosopher of religion does. This approach, I believe, can provide a way to respond to Trakakis' worries about the irrelevance of analytic philosophy of religion. Philosophers of religion need to rediscover, on the one hand, the vital connections between what are usually regarded as distinct areas of philosophy and, on the other hand, the connection between philosophy of religion and the real-world matrix which generates the problems raised by religions which people actually confront.

Addressing the Real Problem with Philosophy of Religion

Karl Popper famously declared: 'Genuine philosophical problems are always rooted in urgent problems outside philosophy, and they die if these roots decay.'[26] This claim provides an important clue to the origin of the irrelevance of much of analytic philosophy of religion to people who are not themselves philosophers of religion. In short, the charge is that many philosophers of religion have lost touch with the practical contexts which generate the problems to which their work might otherwise be expected to respond. Developments within philosophy of religion tend to be responses to new argumentative moves within familiar and well-defined branches of the subject (a new move in the ontological argument, for example). Such developments may, of course, be significant. But if Popper's claim is correct, philosophers of religion should also be responsive to problems encountered by

---

[25] Such broad disciplinary focus would not preclude individual philosophers of religion from working exclusively on some aspect of the philosophy of one religious tradition. However, on the current proposal, being conversant in the philosophy of more than one religious tradition would be the norm rather than the exception.

[26] Quoted in Eberhard Herrmann, *Scientific Theory and Religious Belief: An Essay on the Rationality of Views of Life* (Kampen: Kok Pharos, 1995), p. 15.

those practising religion and by those dealing with the (sometimes tense) interface between religious belief and other areas of public life. If they seek to respond to these problems that are actually keenly felt by people both within and without the academy, then surely their work will be of real potential benefit to a much broader audience than has hitherto been the case.

The tendency of philosophers of religion to look 'inward' towards the minutiae of the discipline rather than 'outward' in seeking problems to address is related to a difficulty, briefly considered above, that is inherent in the way in which the discipline is currently configured. As Trakakis points out, following the model of natural science has led analytic philosophers to become increasingly more specialized. A philosopher of religion typically is an expert in just this one area of philosophy, and within this area they are a specialist on one particular topic. Because of this finely-honed and artificial specialization, it has become especially difficult for philosophers of religion to see the wood for the trees (or, perhaps, even the leaves on the trees). Working on a narrow research area, which they approach using highly technical philosophical vocabulary, it is often hard for them to see a connection between their work and the bigger picture formed by philosophy of religion as a whole. Moreover, many seem to have lost a sense of how the questions that concern them relate to what occupies their colleagues in other branches of philosophy.

To make matters worse, philosophers within each area of philosophy have been encouraged to make their work as distinctive as possible and not to be seen to borrow too much from other areas. In the contemporary jargon, borrowing is regarded as merely 'consumptive', while the real work of philosophy is supposed to be 'productive'. This compartmentalization would have been alien to the philosophers of an earlier era, whether Western, Chinese or Indian, and many regard it to be deeply problematic.

While disagreeing with Trakakis' conclusions, I agree with his claim that a new understanding of philosophy of religion appropriate for today should both emphasize the discipline's relevance to problems generated in the non-academic world and address the excessive specialization characterizing it. Trakakis is correct that artificial academic boundaries need to be broken down, although I believe that he has targeted the wrong boundaries for dissolution. The boundaries between different broadly defined areas of study (such as that between religious studies and philosophy), which Trakakis proposes to remove, are those which help to preserve philosophy's peculiar techné. This would be lost under Trakakis' proposal, as the analytical philosopher's toolkit is judged to be lacking in real value. Thus, far from improving on the current situation, Trakakis' proposal to dismantle the disciplinary boundaries seems likely to undermine philosophy's ability to contribute anything distinctive at all to issues of wider public concern.

Rather than these disciplinary boundaries constituting the problem, I suggest that the real problem – at least as far as philosophy is concerned – is the artificial separation between different areas *within* the discipline. As the twenty-first century marches forward, those working within each area of philosophy are being put under increasing pressure to demonstrate the public 'impact' of what they do. Not surprisingly, many philosophers have been at a loss to show how their work contributes to a measurable public good. Trakakis claims that breaking down the boundaries separating philosophy from other disciplines will alleviate their difficulty in this respect. But surely it is more urgent to reconsider the relationship between individual areas within philosophy. This should facilitate a clearer view of what these areas might contribute both to each other and to problems generated by the non-academic world. Philosophers of religion might fruitfully work more closely with those practising other branches of philosophy, particularly metaphysics and ethics.

Metaphysics is usually considered by those who specialize in it to lie at the very heart of philosophy. Its practitioners claim that it addresses the most fundamental questions of concern to philosophers: questions about the ultimate nature of things, the existential status of universals, the nature of space and time, the relationship between truth and language, etc. Metaphysicians examine and create theories dealing with very abstract questions that have few obvious practical applications. This focus on abstract questions made metaphysics particularly amenable to being moulded to the model of mathematically-based scientific inquiry. Nevertheless, those practising this branch of philosophy typically find it excruciatingly difficult to demonstrate any practical importance to their work.[27] Faced with the contemporary impact-driven research agenda, metaphysicians have been compared to deer caught in the headlights.

Why is this the case? One might answer that for the most part, and with certain key exceptions, the philosophical problems dealt with by metaphysicians are, in a sense, nobody's problems. Most people do not have difficulty individuating objects or classifying the various ways in which things exist. So, on the whole, the problems dealt with by metaphysicians do not count among those that are keenly felt by people struggling to make sense of their experience outside the academy. It is unsurprising, then, that metaphysicians stand to lose most if impact is used to measure the worth of their research.[28] However, it seems to me that despite the lack of direct impact, the work of metaphysicians might have an indirect impact that is easily overlooked. This is because the answers they provide to the questions that nobody asks are often presupposed in the work of philosophers of religion and moral philosophers.[29] Thus,

---

[27]   Peter Simons' intriguing work on the ontology of aeroplane parts is a notable exception.

[28]   The claim that impact should be used as a measure of the value of research in the humanities is not one I wish to defend. My argument merely takes it for granted that this is the measure currently being promoted.

[29]   I focus on metaphysics, philosophy of religion and ethics because, due to their intermeshed history, the relationship between them is easy to identify. A more elaborate exposition of my position would take into account the other areas within philosophy that seem to have defined for themselves unique subject areas, such as the philosophy of the mind and aesthetics.

the work of metaphysicians might make an important contribution to wider debates through its deployment by philosophers of religion and moral philosophers. For this reason, it seems ill-advised for metaphysicians to complain if philosophers working in these other areas are 'consumptive' of their work rather than themselves being 'creative' of new metaphysical theories. In engaging with problems that real people do have, philosophers of religion and moral philosophers have an opportunity to put the work of metaphysicians to good use.

To cut a long story short, a number of different pressures have contributed to the current division of philosophical labour and have forced these three areas of philosophy further and further apart (see Figure 1.1). We are now in a situation in which philosophers who specialize in any one of them are likely to have only a sketchy knowledge of what goes on in the other two. Surely, such a lack of contact between these core areas of philosophy is to the detriment of the subject as a whole. Moreover, it does not seem unreasonable to suggest that it is a key factor preventing recognition of the ways in which philosophers can make a real contribution to the public good by engaging with the problems experienced by people in the non-academic domain (see Figure 1.2). Philosophers of religion and moral philosophers would be better placed to respond to the complex problems generated by the world outside the academy, which does not always recognize a neat distinction between ethics and religion, by pooling their resources. Drawing on the work of metaphysicians could be expected to allow them to muster more comprehensive and deeper contributions to issues of public debate. This in turn might seed a revivification of analytic philosophy as a whole by connecting it more firmly with, as Popper put it, its roots in 'urgent problems outside philosophy'.[30] Moreover, recognizing that the boundaries between these areas of philosophy are more fluid than they have often appeared in the age of specialization opens the way for fruitful work that explores possibilities of cross-fertilization between them.

Another entrenched boundary which we would do well to re-examine if philosophy of religion is to become explicitly responsive to problems generated outside the academy is the one separating the philosophical traditions of the West from those with origins in other cultural and religious traditions. This boundary

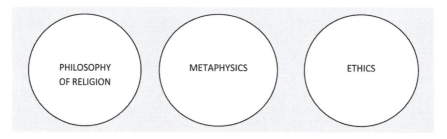

Figure 1.1   The artificial separations within philosophy

---

[30]   See note 26, above.

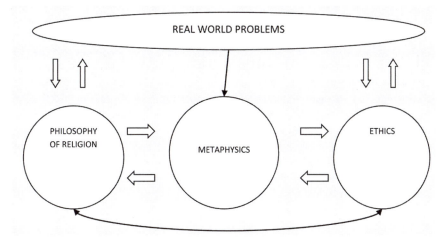

Figure 1.2   A fuller picture of the connection between different areas of philosophy

can prevent us from seeing the significant areas of overlap between the concerns of 'Western' and 'Eastern' philosophies. A genuinely globally-relevant philosophy of religion should be able to draw on the resources available within a number of philosophical traditions (see Figure 1.3). Which traditions are drawn upon in responding to any particular problem should be determined by the nature and context of that problem rather than on whichever tradition a particular philosopher feels most at home in.

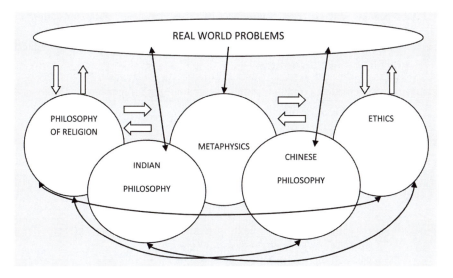

Figure 1.3   A globally responsive model of philosophy

Indeed, crossing this boundary also opens up a fertile way of engaging with ethics. Part of Trakakis' critique of analytic philosophy is that it does not regard philosophy as a way of life. Wisdom, which was the preoccupation of philosophers in antiquity, has fallen out of the picture.[31] Philosophers today, he laments, do not stand out as figures to be emulated for their wisdom in public life. However, it may be that what Trakakis is looking for can be found in the Chinese philosophical tradition where the figure of the sage has always played a central role in the philosophical imagination.[32] Indeed, the portrayal of the sage within classical Chinese philosophy seems to have much in common with the ideal of the philosophical life that Trakakis finds lacking in the modern Western tradition. Drawing on these elements of the global tradition of philosophy, we might find a way to redress this imbalance.

Some Proposals

I have argued that if philosophy of religion is to be relevant to the concerns of people who are not themselves philosophers of religion, it must be responsive to problems generated by religious belief and practice outside the academy. I have sketched out some broad proposals which, if implemented, would position philosophy of religion to respond effectively to such problems. It is time now very briefly to consider what some of these problems might be. Here are some possibilities:

1. Problems arising from tension between religious belief and science. Disputes concerning the nature of evidence, the status of naturalism, etc.
2. Problems arising from interaction between people of different religious traditions.
3. Problems concerning how to explain religious faith within a twenty-first-century intellectual context.
4. The problem of religious conviction motivating terrorism.
5. Problems concerning how to educate young people about religious traditions responsibly.

My view is that analytic philosophy of religion can respond to these kinds of problems and that by doing so it can be of genuine practical use. Problems in categories 1–3 above already fall clearly within the generally acknowledged

---

[31]   See Trakakis, *The End of Philosophy of Religion*, p. 2.

[32]   For a study of some different conceptions of sageliness in the Chinese tradition, see Stephen C. Angle, *Sagehood: The Contemporary Significance of Neo-Confucian Philosophy* (Oxford: Oxford University Press, 2009).

scope of philosophy of religion.[33] However, the problems listed above do not only concern the religious domain but also the ethical and the metaphysical. Thus, to address them effectively, the philosopher of religion, the moral philosopher and the metaphysician will need to join forces. Within academia there is a relatively clear division between the domains of ethics, philosophy of religion and metaphysics, but this distinction does not seem to be mirrored in the outside world. Similarly, within academia we currently have sharp and clear divisions between Western, Chinese and Indian philosophies, but again the complex world within which we live does not always respect these distinctions. The problems to be addressed by philosophers arise within different cultural contexts and sometimes from the inter-penetration of these different contexts, so it is surely appropriate to draw on a range of philosophical traditions in responding to them.

I have outlined an ambitious programme for the future development of philosophy of religion. It seeks to enable the discipline to regain its relevance, within and without the academy, by making a real contribution to the understanding of religious questions arising from the shared public world. But my vision of the future for philosophy of religion does not stop there. I believe that the discipline can do more than merely respond to the problems actually generated by religious belief and practice. Paying attention to such problems can disclose the extent to which religious traditions are constantly evolving in response to a range of pressures from within and without. A philosopher of religion needs to be sensitive to the way that the problems he or she is addressing are themselves constantly being reconfigured in rapidly changing cultural environments. Philosophers of religion can contribute to this evolution, rather than just seeking to understand the way things currently are in some religious tradition or other. Today religious traditions are subject to negotiation to what is perhaps an unprecedented degree. Philosophers of religion (along with moral philosophers and metaphysicians) can contribute constructively to this process.[34] Philosophy of religion need not be the conservative discipline that it was during much of the twentieth century; instead, it has the potential to become a source of innovative religious thinking.[35]

---

[33] This suggests that current analytic philosophy of religion is not quite as irrelevant as Trakakis believes.

[34] This will require specific knowledge of the details of religious belief and practice that is informed by theology and religious studies.

[35] I am indebted to Rhett Gayle for comments on an earlier draft of this paper and to Fiona Macpherson for her comments and helpful suggestions about the visual representations. I am also grateful to the Department of Public and Social Administration at City University, Hong Kong, for the opportunity to present and discuss the ideas presented here with an excellent group of practically engaged philosophers and scholars.

PART I
Goodness, Morality and Transcendence

Divine Commands and the
Source of Goodness

Chapter 2
The Source of Goodness

John Cottingham

Fire and the Sun

Let me begin with a fable. (I claim no great originality for it, since there is a long tradition going back to Plato, which explains the idea of a source of goodness by using the symbol of the sun.) Suppose there is a planet – let us call it Oceana – which is surrounded by an impenetrable luminous watery mist. The inhabitants believe, arguably with good reason (since there is no evidence of anything other), that they inhabit a 'closed' cosmos: that their world, and its surrounding atmosphere, is the universe, comprising everything that exists. Their world is a watery world – they live, reproduce and move around in a marine-style environment. In addition to the faint luminosity which enables them to find their way around, their world contains *fires* – strange burning islands of what we would call wood, which float around on the ocean, giving out light and heat. The expert scientists of Oceana have mapped out with great mathematical precision and accuracy the laws which govern all the watery phenomena of their ocean and their atmosphere. But the workings of the 'fires' do not seem to be derivable from, or explicable in terms of, any of the natural watery phenomena that their science has so successfully investigated.

Some of their philosophers, the *aqualists*, propose that, despite appearances, the 'fires' must after all be reducible to some kind of watery interactions and that it is just a matter of time until they are explained in terms of standard aquatic science. Others (highly respected for their philosophical profundity) say that fire is a *sui generis*, irreducibly *non-aquatic* property. But (though the jury is out) neither aqualism nor non-aqualism has so far completely carried the day. There is, however, a third group, the *super-aqualists*, who maintain that the fiery phenomena derive ultimately from a super-fiery transcendent source, a source that is wholly other than the universe comprising Oceana and its atmosphere. They identify this source with Sol, a traditional object of worship since time immemorial, which is supposed to be the source not just of fieriness but of everything that exists.

There are, of course, many objections to the Sol theory from the aqualists and even from the non-aqualists. If Sol, supremely warm and fiery, is the source of everything, how come there are parts of the planet that are cold and dark? This is known as the Problem of Darkness. But quite apart from such general objections, a further, more specific criticism of invoking Sol as the source of fieriness is commonly put forward, namely that it fails as an explanation. For if we are puzzled by the existence of fieriness in the ordinary world (so runs the objection), it surely does nothing to assuage our puzzlement to be told that it derives from something, beyond the world, that is *itself* fiery – precisely the property we sought to explain in the first place.

I will pause with the science fiction before it becomes too laboured; however, the cluster of Euthyphro-type problems associated with theistic accounts of goodness will already have begun to be visible in the guise of our fable if we substitute goodness for fieriness. The dilemma posed in Plato's *Euthyphro* was (in updated and simplified form): is something good because God ordains it or does God ordain it because it is good? I will here assume (what I take to be pretty clear) that the first horn of the dilemma is a very unpromising one for the theist to take: even God cannot arbitrarily make something good just by ordaining it (if He could, then wanton cruelty would become good if so ordained, which is absurd). In any case, most theists will want to say that God would never issue such repugnant commands: because He is essentially good, He would only ordain good things. This suggests we should take the second horn of the dilemma – that things are ordained by God because they are already, as it were, good. But then we face, in effect, a *vicious regress*. Very crudely, we wanted to be given some account of this mysterious property called goodness which things have; we are then told it derives from God, who is Himself good, and from His ordaining things because they are themselves good. But that does not appear to get us any further from an explanatory point of view. The *explanandum*, the self-same phenomenon of goodness that we were seeking to explain, is re-imported and served up again: it pops up in the *explanans* and we are no further forward.

I hope the parallel in our fable is reasonably clear. Fieriness, which was our explanandum phenomenon, reappears as a property of Sol, the very entity that was invoked to provide an explanation for fieriness in the first place. The threat of a regress of this kind has a long history. In the *Parmenides*, Plato famously canvasses an objection to his theory of Forms which has subsequently become known as the 'Third Man' argument: if what makes something *F* is participation in the Form of *F*, and every Form of *F* is itself *F*, then we have an explanatory regress: we still have not really explained what makes the Form itself count as *F*, unless we posit a further, 'third' entity, in which the previously posited Form and its instances all partake – and so on ad infinitum.[1] For our purposes in this chapter, for *F*-ness read goodness. If we block the regress by saying that the Form of the Good, or God, is just good in virtue of its nature or in a way that requires no further explanation, then it is not clear that our initial puzzlement about what makes for goodness has really been assuaged.

Are regresses always vicious? No. If I want to know how or why my house and my neighbour's house are on fire, then it will, in one way, be a perfectly good explanation to say that they were struck by a fiery meteorite from above. I

---

[1]   Plato, *Parmenides* (c. 360 BC), 132a–b. The argument concerns the form of largeness; Aristotle's reference to this type of argument as 'the third man' occurs in his *Metaphysics* (c. 325 BC), 990b17.

have explained a given object's possession of a particular property by invoking its 'participation' in a property coming from outside, or by the property having been transmitted from a supra-terrestrial body which itself possesses the relevant property of fieriness. As far as explaining the particular phenomenon I started with is concerned, this is fine. But if I want to explain how fieriness *in general* comes about, or what fieriness consists in, invoking a further fiery object, however exalted, does not seem to do any useful work.

For all the reasons just given, it seems that the scientists of Oceana are perfectly justified in being impatient with those who invoke the supposed fiery body Sol as a putative explanation of fieriness. And if we cash out the fable and apply it to theism and to the invocation of God as the source of goodness, then it seems that those who object that this explains nothing about the nature of goodness are in one way perfectly correct. Indeed, I am inclined to think (though I cannot argue this out here) that the same applies to any attempt to explain problematic features of reality by invoking a transcendent source which is itself supposed to incorporate the relevant features. In my view (as I have argued elsewhere), God is not, and cannot be invoked as, an *explanation* in anything like the way in which explanations are understood in a scientific context. For God's transcendence means that he is wholly outside the normal chain of events and causes. As Anthony Kenny has aptly put it: 'God is not a part of any of the explanatory series which he is invoked to account for.'[2]

Yet for all that, and notwithstanding these difficulties, it seems to me that we can perhaps glimpse (at least by analogy) how a transcendent God might be responsible for our world, or even certain aspects of it. Let us go back to the world of Oceana. With respect to this world, we who have created or imagined the story have, so to speak, a window on the transcendent. We are in the fortunate position of being outside the limiting framework within which the unfortunate scientists of that planet had to operate, given their impermeable atmosphere. From the point of view of our privileged perspective, we can see that their world is *not* a closed cosmos and that the luminosity of their atmosphere does in fact derive from its being exposed to the light of a star, to something in some ways similar to what the super-aqualists imagined as the transcendent deity Sol (though of course this is only an analogy, since, for us, stars and suns are not transcendent items but part of our natural universe). Again from our privileged perspective, we can also see that their positing of Sol as the source of the fieriness of their islands was in a certain sense correct. It is not that their sun somehow transmitted fieriness to the floating wooden islands either causally or in virtue of some mysterious fiat; nor indeed is it true that Sol is itself fiery in anything like the same sense as the flaming wooden islands (the working of a solar nuclear furnace being radically different from the combustion of wood). Instead, the sun (as we privileged observers know) is the source of fieriness in a quite different sense, which the isolated scientists and philosophers of Oceana could not possibly conceive of: it is the source of

2   A. Kenny, *What is Faith?* (Oxford: Oxford University Press, 1992), p. 111.

that energy without which their planet could have contained no life, no plants, no photosynthesis and therefore no trees or bushes of any kind able to store the energy later released on the burning wooden islands. The mysterious phenomenon of the combustion of wood, wholly outside the scope of any of their laws for aquatic phenomena (accurate and complete though these laws were, as far as they went) – this mysterious and apparently anomalous phenomenon, the manifestation of energy accompanied by heat and flame, was indeed (as we privileged external observers can see) made possible by virtue of a vast and to them inconceivable extra-planetary source of energy. A supreme fire – fiery, albeit only by analogy with the ordinary fires they observed – was indeed the ultimate source.

Could God be the source of goodness in our own world in something like that way? I will not claim that our fable has made such a view more plausible. However, I think it does suggest that the possibility cannot be dismissed out of hand – unless, of course, we are prepared to follow the dogmatic naturalist metaphysicians of Oceana and insist that the cosmos we inhabit must be a closed cosmos, that the total set of objects and events occurring since the Big Bang comprises all the reality that there is.

God as Source

Having completed this (perhaps rather protracted) preliminary softening-up process, let me turn directly to theistic accounts of goodness. God, the God who is the object of worship in the Judaeo-Christian and Islamic traditions, is conceived of as the source of truth, beauty and goodness. He is, as the Epistle of James puts it, the giver of 'every good and every perfect gift'; in the words of the seventeenth-century Cambridge philosopher Peter Sterry, the 'stream of the divine love' is the source of 'all truths, goodness, joys, beauties and blessedness'.[3] For the worshipper, involved in the praxis of daily or weekly liturgy, this idea is pretty much central, the basis of the sense of joy and exaltation experienced as one turns to God in praise and thanksgiving.

But once we are out of the church (synagogue or mosque) and back in the study, particularly in the cold and unforgiving light of the analytic philosopher's study, questions arise as to what exactly it can mean to say that God is the source of truth, beauty and goodness. Well, I suppose one of the most important things it implies, to begin with, is a firm denial of relativism. If an eternal, necessary being, existing independently of us, is the source of truth, then this rules out pragmatic and relativistic conceptions according to which truth is simply what works for

---

[3]   Epistle General of James (c. AD 50), 1:17: '*pasa dosis agathê kai pan dôrêma teleion anôthen esti, katabainon apo tou patros tôn phôtôn*' ('Every good and every perfect gift is from above, coming down from the father of lights'). Peter Sterry, *A Discourse of the Freedom of the Will* [1675]; reprinted in C. Taliaferro and A.J. Teply (eds), *Cambridge Platonist Spirituality* (Mahwah, NJ: Paulist Press, 2004), p. 179.

us or what is currently accepted in our culture circle. And, similarly, beauty, if stemming from God, cannot not simply be 'in the eye of the beholder' – just a function of the subjective tastes of various human beings. Moreover, goodness, and value generally, cannot be dependent merely on our personal or societal preferences, let alone something we can create or invent by our own magnificent acts of will, as Friedrich Nietzsche maintained.[4] All these things, truth, beauty and goodness, must, on the contrary, be objectively based.

In addition to underwriting *objectivity* and *non-relativity*, the idea of a divine source for truth, beauty and goodness also implies a certain kind of *authority*. This seems to connect with the notion (by no means confined to theists) that truth, beauty and goodness exert some kind of normative pull on us. Truth is *to be believed*; beauty is *to be admired*; and goodness is *to be pursued*. These imperatives in a certain sense constrain us, whether we like it or not. We can of course deviate from them, and often do, but that does not seem to alter their validity. They are, to use an apt metaphor employed by Gottlob Frege in a rather different context, rather like 'boundary stones which our thought can overflow, but not dislodge'.[5]

The Oxford philosopher John Mackie famously put the point, or something close to it, by observing that there is something 'queer' about goodness and other moral properties. They have a magnetic quality, a kind of inbuilt 'to be pursuedness', and Mackie pointed out that it is hard to see how such normativity could be a function of merely the empirically observable features of things. In effect, he noted that there is an unexplained connection involved in the transition from 'this action wilfully inflicts distress' to 'this action is bad/wrong', or from 'this helps someone in distress' to 'this is good/right'.[6] Establishing this 'synthetic connection', as he put it, was the kind of thing that might be done by God. Mackie himself was of course a convinced atheist and was also a subjectivist about value (he followed the Humean line that goodness is simply a projection of our own inclinations and desires). However, in his book *Ethics: Inventing Right and Wrong* he concedes that if there *were* such a thing as objective goodness, then it might provide a good argument for theism. If objectivism were true, he argues, then there would have to be some objective relationship (in the jargon, a 'supervenience' relation) between a natural empirical property (for example,. an action's alleviating suffering) and the property of its being good: 'If we adopted moral objectivism, then we should have to regard the relations of supervenience which connect values and obligations with their natural grounds as synthetic: they would then be in principle something that god may conceivably create; and since they would otherwise be a *very odd*

---

[4]   Friedrich Nietzsche, *Beyond Good and Evil* [*Jenseits von Gut und Böse*, 1886], trans R.J. Hollingdale (London: Penguin, 1973), §203.

[5]   G. Frege, *The Basic Laws of Arithmetic* [*Die Grundgesetze der Arithmetik*, vol. I, 1893], trans. M. Furth (Berkeley, CA: University of California Press, 1964), p. 13.

[6]   There are of course differences between 'good/bad' and 'right/wrong', but important though these are, they will be ignored for present purposes, since they do not affect the general structure of the argument we are considering.

sort of thing, the admitting of them would be an inductive ground for admitting also a god to create them.'[7]

So far, perhaps, so good. But *how* exactly does God create these connections? Or, more generally, how does God function as the 'source' of truth, beauty and goodness? God does not, surely, 'create' these things by some arbitrary act of will or preference – that would merely be a sort of subjectivism or relativism transposed to the celestial realm. Instead, in the case of truth, first of all, one must presumably envisage God as the source of truth insofar as he establishes those objective features of reality in virtue of which the propositions that rational beings assert can be true or false. God, in other words, does not 'create truth', whatever that would mean, but creates the *truth-makers*, as it were. He creates (as the first verse of Genesis has it) the 'heavens and the earth', in other words, the universe (how – in what stages or via what evolutionary process – need not concern us here); in consequence of the coming into being of the resulting properties and configurations of stars, planets, plants, molecules, atoms, etc., certain beliefs or propositions now have the property of being true or false. That seems (relatively at least) quite straightforward. There may be a more complex account to be told of the kind of truth enjoyed by the eternal and necessary truths of logic and mathematics (and theists differ amongst themselves about what exactly is God's relation to them), but for present purposes we may leave this to the experts in modal logic to sort out.

What about beauty? Perhaps the simplest picture would be to think of God creating beauty analogously to the way in which a human creative artist is responsible for it – namely by creating beautiful objects. When an artist paints a beautiful picture, he does so by endowing it with beauty-making properties – harmony of colour, symmetry, rhythm, proportionality, etc. Again, it is not beauty itself that is created, whatever that would mean, but rather those objects or entities with their relevant properties and qualities in virtue of which they are beautiful. The Andromeda galaxy, seen though a telescope, is extraordinarily beautiful – a coruscating spiral of millions of blazing stars of different hues, wheeling around in an infinitely complex gravitational dance. The Psalmist of the Hebrew Bible could not of course see these features, but he could see (as most us sadly no longer can because of pollution) the awesome splendour of what we now call our own 'local' galaxy. So affirming the beauty and wonder of God's creation, referring to the various observable properties in virtue of which it is glorious or beautiful – all the natural properties visible in the diurnal cycle of the sun and stars – he wrote 'the heavens declare the glory of the Lord, and the firmament shows his handiwork' (Psalm 19 [18]).

Thus, beauty, like truth, is relatively easy for the believer to see as divinely sourced, in the sense explained above. But what about goodness and, in particular, moral goodness? Following the kind of model adopted so far, we will want to say that God creates goodness by performing actions with good-making properties

---

[7] J.L. Mackie, *The Miracle of Theism: Arguments For and Against the Existence of God* (Oxford: Clarendon, 1982), p. 118, emphasis added.

– for example, he 'protects strangers and supports the fatherless and the widow' (Psalm 146 [145]). He is the source of goodness in this sense; in addition, of course, he brings into existence creatures who themselves have the power to perform such actions. They may not always do so because they are free to refrain (or even to do things with bad-making properties). But when they do what is good, they are fulfilling one of the purposes for which God created them. In this sense, then, God may be said to be the source of the goodness not only of His own acts but of that which pertains to the acts of His creatures. (An interesting question, which is beyond the scope of this chapter, is why God is not also the source of the evil acts performed by humans; there are, of course, many responses familiar from the theodicy literature, most hinging on the idea that God does not create anyone with the intention that they should perform such evil actions, albeit foreseeing that they may do so.)

Now, if we adopt the above picture, we seem to be implicitly favouring a so-called 'buck-passing' account of goodness of the kind that has become fashionable among moral philosophers in recent years.[8] The focus, in such accounts, is not on goodness itself but on the various good-making properties in virtue of which something counts as good. So, if we start with a non-moral example, to say that a knife is good is not to refer to some special property it has in addition to its ordinary empirically observable properties; rather, 'the buck is passed' and the goodness devolves down to the ordinary properties (sharpness, strength, durability) that make it fit to be chosen as a cutting implement. In creating a knife with these ordinary, natural properties, a human craftsman has automatically thereby made a good knife. And similarly with moral goodness, by enacting beneficent actions (such as helping the fatherless) or by creating humans who can perform beneficent actions, God automatically qualifies as a source of goodness in the world. Nothing more, as it were, is needed. This is consistent, incidentally, with the first chapter of Genesis, where it is said of God, looking on His creation, that He 'saw that it was good' – not that He decided it was good or ordained that it should qualify as good. God does not have to enact any additional decrees in order to create goodness; rather, He creates the world as it is, with all its various good-making properties, and then (so to speak) He can just see, in virtue of those created properties, that it is good.

However, now the following question arises. If the goodness devolves down to the various observable good-making properties in this way, then do we not have to say that it exists in the world *whether or not the world was created by God*? And does not that cast serious doubt about the idea of God as *the* source of goodness? For as we look around us (the atheist may urge), there *are* the good-making properties already existing in the ordinary empirical features of the world; flints are sharp and are therefore apt for cutting; people sometimes choose to perform actions which help other people – these relevant good-making features indisputably exist, whether or not the world was created by God or whether instead it arose by chance

---

[8]   T. Scanlon, *What We Owe to Each Other* (Cambridge, MA: Belknap, 1998), pp. 95ff. Cf. P.J. Stratton-Lake, *Ethical Intuitionism* (Oxford: Clarendon, 2002), pp. 15f.

or some other impersonal mechanism. Thus (it might be argued), does that not make God, in a certain sense, redundant? In other words, we do not need God as the putative 'source' of goodness; we just need the relevant purely natural features in virtue of which things count as good – and that is that.[9]

I think there is something right about this move but also something that it leaves out. It is right that our pursuit of goodness is not a matter of seeking some mysterious extra quality in addition to the observable features of actions and objects, but rather involves choosing actions and objects which already possess these observable good-making features. So, the atheist and the theist are, as it were, on an equal footing when it comes to assessing what objects and actions are good or bad: the available tools are not some hotline to a special, divinely-sourced property of goodness, but ordinary human observation of the natural world, and ordinary human reasoning about the features of this world and their observable effects and qualities. Ethics is a matter of human inquiry, just like science. It is a subject of rational debate, in which proper reasons for and against certain courses of action need to be marshalled using our ordinary human capacities, as well as our ordinary human perception of the various natural features of objects and actions which make them good or bad. So much, I think, is entirely correct (and is, incidentally, a welcome result, since the cause of rational and constructive discussion in ethics is furthered when theists and atheists see themselves as being on an 'equal footing' in this way when it comes to debating moral questions).

Despite this, I think that there must, for the theist, be something questionable about the implication that God is, as it were, redundant when it comes to questions of goodness or that God has no special role to play as the source of goodness. To begin with, the theist will of course want to say that even if the account that passes the buck to the ordinary natural good-making features is correct, God still retains an all-pervasive general role, since His action was still required to create the world with all its natural features in the first place. God still performs the mysterious metaphysical act which (as Herbert McCabe puts it) makes the difference between its existing and not existing.[10]

However, with that important proviso in place, should the theist then go on to concede that once the world is in existence, the goodness or badness of things can be 'read off', as it were, from their ordinary natural features, without any need for reference to God as its source (except insofar as He is regarded as the source

---

[9]   Interestingly, one of the most prominent of theistic philosophers, Richard Swinburne, despite regarding God as *a* source of moral obligation (since 'his command to us to do some action makes it obligatory to do that action when it would not otherwise be obligatory'), considers that God is not *the* (sole) source of goodness or of obligation, since 'many truths of morality hold whether or not there is a God'. He cites the cases of feeding the starving and keeping promises: the first is clearly good, while the second clearly obligatory, and these truths hold 'independently of God'. See *Was Jesus God?* (Oxford: Oxford University Press, 2008), p. 11.

[10]   Herbert McCabe, *Faith within Reason* (London: Continuum, 2006), pp. 75–6.

of the universe existing at all)? In some ways this is a tempting option. It would mean that the theist and the atheist will see themselves as inhabiting exactly the same cosmos, a cosmos which naturally possesses some good-making and some bad-making features, but that the theist merely(!) adds the extra metaphysical claim that the world was divinely created.[11] Possibly this is as far as the theist should go. Yet, without being wholly sure about it, I am inclined to think that, tempting as it may be, this view (as I suggested a moment ago) leaves something out. What I think it leaves out is any explanation of *why* certain features of actions or agents should be good-making features, not merely in the weak sense that they provide conditional reasons for choosing such actions, but in the stronger sense that they provide a *conclusive* or *unconditional* reason for choice,[12] one that requires our compliance.

In a random or impersonal universe, why should the fact that an action oppresses the weak and helpless be a reason – a conclusive reason – against performing it? Or why should the fact that an act is one of forgiveness towards someone who is sincerely sorry for having caused injury be a reason, a conclusive reason, for performing it? How can such descriptions of things have this compelling, action-guiding force, this especially strong version of the magnetic quality that we noted earlier, this conclusive built-in 'to-be-doneness'. For many atheists (such as Mackie), the 'queerness' of such supposed conclusive reason-giving force will be taken as a reason for concluding that genuine objective moral properties do not really exist – that they are in the end specious, a mere projection of our own preferences. That is a radical position, which faces many philosophical problems, but at least it has the courage of its convictions. But for those who do not want to take this radical subjectivist route, for the increasing number of moral philosophers, even of an atheist stripe, who are drawn to objectivism in ethics, some account is surely required of *how* certain features of things are endowed not just with provisional or instrumental but with unconditional or categorical action-guiding force. How is it that the fact that something involves the deliberate infliction of distress provides a conclusive reason not to do it, and one that is applies whatever

---

[11] Compare McCabe: 'So far as the kind of world we have is concerned, the atheist and the theist will expect to see exactly the same features': ibid., p. 76.

[12] Compare Immanuel Kant's famous distinction between various types of imperative in his *Grundlegung zur Metaphysik der Sitten* [1785], Chapter 2, nicely summarized in H.J. Paton's edition as follows: 'some objective principles are *conditioned* by a will for some end; that is to say, they would necessarily be willed by an agent *if* he willed that end ... Some are *unconditioned* ... and have the form "I ought to do such and such" without any *if* as a prior condition' (*Groundwork of the Metaphysic of Morals*, trans. H.J. Paton (London: Hutchinson, 1948), p. 27). Kant called the first type of imperative 'hypothetical' and the second 'categorical', but the term 'categorical imperative' is now so overlaid with complications arising from Kantian scholarship that I prefer to avoid it in the present chapter. (It is worth noting that Kant added an intermediate class of imperative, a 'pragmatic' imperative, which is technically hypothetical, since it is dependent on willing an end, but where the end is one that 'every rational agent wills by his very nature' – such as one's own happiness.)

aims or projects I happen to have chosen? How is it that the property of helping the weak and afflicted provides (assuming there are no prior claims on my resources) a conclusive reason to perform a given action? What establishes this weird or 'queer' (in Mackie's phrase) connection between an observable feature of the natural world and this kind of strong normative power to require us to act?

For the theist, there is an answer. If God himself is in his essential nature merciful, compassionate, just and loving, then when we humans act in the ways just mentioned, we are drawn closer to God, the source of our being and the source of all that is good. Such acts command our allegiance in the strongest way, since they bring us nearer to the 'home' where our true peace and fulfilment lies; conversely, in setting our face against them, we are cutting ourselves off from our true destiny, from the ultimate basis of joy and meaningfulness in our lives. If, on the other hand, there is no God, if God is 'dead', then there might (as Nietzsche frighteningly suggested) be conclusive reasons to steel ourselves *against* impulses of love and mercy, to harden our hearts against compassion and forgiveness, since such sentiments might get in the way of our will to power, our passion for self-realization or some other grand project we happen to have.[13] Only if those features we call good-making point us towards the true goal of our existence will we be able to make sense of their having, in addition to their observable aspects, a normative force which commands our allegiance whether we like it or not, independently of our own contingent inclinations. Only if the universe has a moral teleology behind it will moral goodness or righteousness really exist – as something we have conclusive reason to choose – rather than merely dissolving away into features that are suitable for furthering whatever projects we may happen to have adopted or whatever purposes we may happen to have set ourselves.

Problems and Conclusions

In this final section, let me try to draw some threads together and canvass some problems.

First, a summary of some of the more important conclusions about the relation of God to goodness – points which I take to be illustrated in part by our earlier discussion of the 'closed world' of Oceana: 1) Just as the invocation of Sol did not succeed in providing a plausible scientific explanation of fieriness, so theistic accounts cannot provide non-circular 'explanatory theories' of goodness: they cannot provide explanations of the features of things in anything like the way ordinary scientific theories do – for example, by placing them in a sequence of causes or investigating their inner structure. 2) Just as Sol and its properties were beyond the grasp of the inhabitants of Oceana, so God is a transcendent being who cannot properly be comprehended from our limited perspective on things. As Paul's letter to Timothy puts it, He dwells in 'light inaccessible, whom no

---

13   See, for example, Nietzsche, *Beyond Good and Evil*, §37.

man hath seen or can see' (I Timothy 6:16) and, hence, the goodness of God is understandable, if at all, only by analogy. 3) Nevertheless, in the analogy offered in our fable, we can glimpse how something beyond the closed world studied by science might be responsible for our human world and all its natural features. 4) In this sense at least, the theist may maintain that God is the source of goodness, insofar as He is the creative force that brought the world, with all its natural good-making features, into existence.

These are our minimal conclusions. Now for some more specific points with respect to goodness: 5) Just as the fiery floating islands of the fable are *supported* by the waters of the ocean, so goodness depends or 'supervenes' on the ordinary natural properties of things. 6) However, just as the fiery properties could not be derived from the aquatic properties studied by the scientists of Oceana, so moral goodness is not wholly reducible to those natural features which underpin it. 7) In particular, goodness has a normative or magnetic force, and in the moral domain, certain natural features of actions or agents seem to provide conclusive and authoritative reasons for choosing them or commending them. 8) A theistic metaphysics seems to provide an interpretive framework for accommodating all these aspects of goodness.

Now for some problems and questions. Even if it were conceded that a theistic metaphysics provides *a* viable framework for understanding value, many will ask why we should suppose it is the only viable framework, let alone the best one. In our fable, there were the aqualists, and the non-aqualists, both of whom had alternative accounts to the 'super-aqualist' account of fire; so what of their counterparts in contemporary moral philosophy, the various naturalist and non-naturalist theories of goodness which reject supernaturalism? Obviously, this is not the place to examine, let alone try to refute, all the sophisticated contenders in the field. But at least some general points can, I think, be made. Naturalism, at least in its crude reductionist form, seems unlikely to work, since, as already suggested, it does not appear to have the resources to explain how purely empirical features of reality can have magnetic or normative force – at least in those cases where we take the normativity to be conclusive and unconditional. Non-naturalism takes us outside the domain of the empirical, but simply doing this does not in itself solve the problem of normative force; moreover, there is a further problem about how these mysterious *sui generis* moral properties are related to natural properties and what sort of existence they enjoy. (It will hardly dissolve the obscurity to declare, as one recent ethicist has put it, that such properties are 'part of the furniture of the universe'.)[14] But the more sophisticated kind of buck-passing account mentioned earlier does seem in a stronger position than either crude naturalism or bald

---

[14]   E.J. Wielenberg, *Value and Virtue in a Godless Universe* (Cambridge: Cambridge University Press, 2005), p. 52. Cf. R. Shafer-Landau, *Moral Realism* (Oxford: Clarendon, 2003): moral standards 'just are correct'; they are 'a brute fact about the way the world works' (pp. 46, 48). In fairness, Shafer-Landau is candid enough to acknowledge that such bald ethical realism is a theory with 'very limited explanatory resources' (p. 48).

non-naturalism, for it is able to construe the natural features of things as having the second-order property of providing reasons for action by virtue of their ordinary natural properties.

As already indicated, I think that such buck-passing accounts are true, but incomplete. In the moral arena, they do not tell us *why* certain features of actions provide conclusive reasons for choosing to do them. Ultimately, in a godless universe, what I have reason to do will depend merely on the set of contingent desires I happen to have developed, and the set of inclinations and preferences I and my society happen to have evolved to possess. Ethics, in short, will be subject to what Bernard Williams called a 'radical contingency'.[15]

Yet is this really so troubling? Some contemporary philosophers who are drawn to objectivism in ethics have recently pointed out that, notwithstanding the contingencies of personal and social development, reasons for action remain objective and external, not personal or subjective. For example, what gives me reason to thank you for doing me a good turn does not hinge on what contingent beliefs or desires I have, but instead is a perfectly objective or external matter: the plain external fact that you did me a service. This may be true, but one still wants to ask the following question: how do such so-called objective or 'external reasons' get their normative force? The moral philosopher John Skorupski has recently given the example of a character, Tom, who has been helped by Mary but who simply has no sense of gratitude – he simply doesn't 'get' what it is all about. Do we want to say that Tom has reason to thank Mary? Skorupski argues that our response to this question is 'interestingly uncertain'. On the one hand, we want to say: 'Of course he does – look what she has done for him!' But, on the other hand, we can understand the basis for answering 'no' – namely that Tom simply does not see the reason-giving force of the fact that she has done him a good turn. Thus, Skorupski concludes that 'only considerations which the agent has the ability to recognize, for him or herself, "from within", *as* reasons, can *be* reasons for that agent'.[16]

The upshot of this argument, in my view, is that the objectivity of ethics is indeed undermined by the 'radical contingency of the ethical'. The possibility that people and societies might have developed – or might still develop – different evaluative outlooks, depending on their evolving dispositions and preferences, undermines any confidence that certain features of actions *must* always provide objective and conclusive reasons to choose them. I think that such radical contingency means, in the end, that there is ultimately no room in ethics for the idea that, in our attempts

---

[15]   Bernard Williams, *Truth and Truthfulness* (Princeton, NJ: Princeton University Press, 2002), p. 20.

[16]   John Skorupski, 'Internal Reasons and the Scope of Blame', in A. Thomas (ed.), *Bernard Williams* (Cambridge: Cambridge University Press, 2007), pp. 73–103, at p. 88.

to pursue the good, we have got something right, in the way that we believe can get things right (or at least make progress towards getting things right) in science.[17]

From a theistic perspective, this alarming contingency of the ethical, the threat to objectivity and the disturbing gap between the kinds of knowledge we can have in science and in ethics are all avoided. In science, as Descartes and other theistic rationalists maintained, we can gain an insight, through the mathematical awareness innately implanted in us, of the rational patterns which govern the physical universe; similarly, in ethics, in the light of the fundamental moral awareness implanted in us, we are able to orient ourselves towards the good which lies at the heart of reality. The strongest kind of objectivity in ethics is secured, just as it is in science (although this does not of course mean that ethical questions have quick and easy answers any more than is the case with scientific questions).

A further reason why a theistic metaphysics is fundamentally hospitable to the idea of genuine objectively normative standards like rationality and goodness (hospitable in a way I believe secular world-views are unlikely to be) is that ultimate reality, on the theistic view, is *personal* and *purposive*, rather than blind, irrational, neutral, random or blank – which is in the end what an alternative atheistical world-view must take it to be. Thus, the two features of God that are prominent above all others in the Christian Gospels (especially in the fourth and most metaphysical of the Gospels) are reason, *logos*, and love, *agape*. These are features that are very closely connected with attributes (intelligence and loving concern) that are irreducibly personal and, indeed, in the Christian picture, are supremely manifested in a particular person, the person of Christ.

Humans are (on any showing) an imperfect species and are clearly not always disposed to conform their lives to reason and to love; however, if the cosmos ultimately reflects a divine teleology or goal-directedness, our lives, because of the way we were created, cannot flourish without them. That rationality and love are the sources behind the cosmos is not something that could be established by ordinary scientific inquiry. Because of the 'transcendence' of God (the fact that the Creator is taken to be wholly 'other' than His creation), a long theological tradition maintains that we cannot even properly grasp these qualities (such as reason and love) as they exist in the divine nature. And as for the Christian claim that their human face has been disclosed to us in a way we *can* grasp, in the person of Christ – this is a matter of revelation, and therefore of faith, rather than philosophical reason. The extraordinary claim of this cosmic intrusion of the divine into our

---

[17] See Bernard Williams, *Ethics and the Limits of Philosophy* (London: Fontana, 1985), Chapter 8; see further Adrian Moore, 'Realism and the Absolute Conception' in Thomas (ed.) *Bernard Williams*, pp. 24ff. There are of course sophisticated subjectivists who claim they can still make room in their theories for our ordinary ways of talking whereby moral judgments can be said to be 'correct' or 'true'. But even if such moves work, there will still be a gap between such 'truth' in ethics and that which obtains in science, since the former will turn out, in the end, to be wholly internal to the prevailing norms or preferences of our culture circle.

human world is nonetheless made with unmistakable clarity in the Fourth Gospel: the title of *to phôs tôn anthrôpôn* (the 'light of humankind'), applied to the *logos*, the divine creative intelligence, in John 1:1–5, is directly appropriated by Christ, when he claims 'I am the light of the world' (*ego eimi to phôs tou kosmou*, John 8:12). In this context, the *ego eimi* ('I am') is the ancient signature of divinity, recapitulating God's self-disclosure to Moses as the source of the moral law.[18] Traditional theism has always insisted that there is an eternal source of goodness, truth and beauty behind the visible cosmos; in its Christian form, it insists that this source, though transcendent – dwelling in 'light inaccessible' – is made manifest in human form, full of 'grace and truth', dwelling amongst us and visible to human sight (John 1:14).

Because of the gap between transcendent reality and any manifestation accessible to human understanding, the idea of a divine source of goodness (or indeed of truth or of beauty) is not, I think, something that can be fully explained philosophically. The gap can only be closed by revelation and faith. But the idea of such a divine source is at least strikingly consistent (so the theist will maintain) with what we can establish philosophically about goodness (and indeed the rest of reality). And, crucially, it provides a framework that frees us from the threats of contingency and futility that lurk beneath the surface of supposedly self-sufficient and autonomous secular ethics. It offers us not a proof but a hope: that the cave of our human world is not sealed and closed, but that our flickering moral intimations reflect the ultimate source of all goodness (just as our logico-mathematical and aesthetic intimations reflect the ultimate source of truth and beauty). The unqualified, unprovisional and non-contingent good-makingness of the ordinary good-making features of actions arises from this. By choosing such actions and continuing to choose them, we conform to an intelligible, rational pattern, the pattern that a being of surpassing love and benevolence intended for us. To so believe may partly be a matter of faith, but it may also reflect a more rational and coherent conception of the nature of goodness than anything else that is on offer.[19]

---

[18]   Exodus 3:14 (compare John 8:58).

[19]   Some parts of this chapter are taken from Chapter 2 of my book *Why Believe?* (London: Continuum, 2009). Earlier versions of the paper were presented at a colloquium in honour of Gerry Hughes at Heythrop College, University of London in December 2008, and at the Conference of the British Society for the Philosophy of Religion Conference on 'God and Morality', held at Lady Margaret Hall, University of Oxford, in September 2009; I am grateful for helpful comments received from participants on both occasions.

Chapter 3

Euthyphro's 'Dilemma', Socrates' *Daimonion* and Plato's God

Timothy Chappell

I

The commonest use that most philosophers today make of Plato's *Euthyphro* is as the citation for what they call 'the Euthyphro dilemma', which is supposed to be 'an intractable difficulty' (to quote one of many instantly Googlable sources) or 'a fatal objection' (to quote another) to 'divine-command morality', which is said to be the view that what is good or right is what God loves or wills or commands. The usual story is that the sceptical Socrates meets the credulous Euthyphro, a rather sanctimonious divine-command theorist, and sets him the following question: 'Is what is good good because God wills it? Or does God will it because it is good?' But Euthyphro – so the usual story goes – cannot take the first alternative, that what is good is good because God wills it, for if that were true, then the content of the good would be set by God's willing it, which would make the nature of the good arbitrary. Nor, however, can Euthyphro take the second alternative, that God wills what is good because it is good, for then the nature of goodness is already set before God's will comes into the picture, and so God is not sovereign but subordinate to morality and we do not need God's commands to know what goodness is.

This interpretation, it seems to me, has just two flaws. First, 'the *Euthyphro* dilemma' is not in the *Euthyphro*. Secondly, 'the *Euthyphro* dilemma' is not a dilemma. Let me take these flaws in turn.

'The *Euthyphro* dilemma' is not in the *Euthyphro*, because Socrates and Euthyphro are not talking about 'what God wills'. Rather, they are talking about 'what the gods love': two crucial differences, since willing is obviously different from loving and since, as Socrates points out (7b), different gods might love different things. Also, they are not talking about 'what is good' but about 'what is holy (*to hosion*)' – a crucial difference because, as Socrates highlights (7e), 'the holy' is only one kind of goodness or virtue. There are other kinds, for instance, 'the just' and 'the honourable', and the relation of 'the holy' to these and to the good or virtue itself is central to Socrates' inquiry (see, for example, 12a). (Still less are Socrates and Euthyphro talking about 'what is morally right'. Their argument is not concerned with the *orthotês* (rightness) of Euthyphro prosecuting his father, but with its *hosiotês* or *eusebeia* (holiness or religious propriety). As many commentators have pointed out, it is anachronistic to read our concept of 'the *morally* right' back into Plato.) Finally, Socrates is not arguing that 'what is holy' is *not* 'what the gods love': at *Euthyphro* 10e–11a he explicitly allows that it can be, provided the gods agree, and at *Euthyphro* 11b1 he calls 'being loved by the gods' a *pathos* (a true description) of 'what is holy'. The point of his argument is that the mere description 'what the gods love' cannot serve as a *definition* of 'what is holy'. But then Socratic definition is a notoriously demanding business, so this may not be a very great restriction. In any case, it is certainly not a restriction that prevents it from being true that what is holy is loved by the gods.

Secondly, 'the *Euthyphro* dilemma' is not a dilemma in the sense of an insoluble problem, because theistic ethicists can and do take either horn or else refuse both horns. They can affirm with some plausibility that God's will (or, better, love) determines the nature of the good, provided that they do not also say that God's love is what we would call arbitrary (which any intelligent and civilized theist is hardly likely to say anyway). On this view it is true that *if* God had willed that infanticide was a good thing, then infanticide *would* be a good thing. But it does not matter: though we are in a way very much at the mercy of His divine pleasure, God is good and trustworthy, so we may be sure that infanticide is *not* His will.

Or theists can with equal plausibility affirm that the nature of the good determines what God loves, provided that they do not also say that this makes God subordinate to morality in some sense that undermines His sovereignty. On this view it is true that God has no more freedom to make infanticide a good thing than He has to make $2 + 2 = 5$ or create a stone so heavy that He cannot lift it. But it is of no consequence: God is not in the least impaired by these formal restrictions from doing anything that He actually wants to do.

Better still, theistic ethicists can refuse both horns: they can reject the whole idea that they need to choose between the God-to-good and good-to-God orders of determination.[1] If someone asks 'Does equilaterality in triangles determine equiangularity in triangles, or is it the other way around?', we do not expect geometricians to accept this as the first line of a proof by dilemma that equilaterality and equiangularity cannot be connected features of triangles. Rather, we expect them to reject the question. One should not imagine that triangles *first* being equilateral and *then*, as a result of this, become equiangular as well. We could say something

---

[1]   Another possibility: Robert Audi has suggested a distinction between the command*ed* and the command*able* right, in 'Divine Command Morality and the Autonomy of Ethics', *Faith and Philosophy* 24(2) (2007), 121–43. All sorts of things might be possible commands of God because they are *prima facie* morally right, while only some things are actual commands of God and therefore morally right *sans phrase*. The nature of the good determines the commandable right; God's choice determines the commanded right. This is not my picture, since it does seem to involve us in accepting antecedent determinants of God's will, but it is another way out of the dilemma.

Again, could theists resist the dilemma by reading 'because' in different senses of 'because', e.g. constitutive vs. causal, in 'It's right because God commands it' and 'God commands it because it's right'? Perhaps, though I find this combination hard to make sense of.

parallel in the theological case: that one should not imagine God's will existing *first* and *then* shaping or creating morality; or morality existing first and then shaping God's will. All such conceptions are misconceptions. When they put them aside, theistic ethicists will probably come to agree with the 'dilemma's' proponent that, in truth, neither horn can be affirmed. But not for the reason he or she thinks.

II

'But surely there is *some* dilemma about divine commands and ethics in the *Euthyphro*, even if it isn't the one that is usually supposed to be there. Doesn't *Euthyphro* 10a1–2 set a dilemma? And can't we call that the Euthyphro dilemma?'

We can *call* it what we like. But Socrates' famous question at 10a1–2 ('Is the holy loved by the gods because it is holy, or is it holy because it is loved?'), while it certainly offers Euthyphro two options to choose between, is not very well described by calling it a dilemma. A true dilemma is, so to speak, a *modus tollens* with a disjunction in it: if p, then either q or r; but not q; and not r; so not p. But there is no suggestion that both of the alternatives in front of Euthyphro are impossible for him to accept. On the contrary, Socrates shows Euthyphro which horn of the alleged dilemma to grasp. What Euthyphro should say – and confused and disgruntled though he is throughout the discussion, and ultimately discomfited at its end,[2] he never shows any clear sign of disagreeing with this – is that the holy is loved by the gods because it is holy and not vice versa.

So, if we insist on speaking of a dilemma, we should say that Socrates here grasps its second horn, 'subordinating' (if that is the word) the gods to what is holy. However, to 'subordinate' *the gods* to what is holy is not to subordinate *God* to what is holy or to what is good in general. Contrast *Republic* 597b, where we are told that God (*theon*) makes the Forms: an apparent subordination of the Forms to God. Thus, for Plato the *gods* may be on the second horn of the dilemma, but when we consider how the dilemma applies to Plato's *God*, apparently the right option to take would be the third one sketched in section I above – that the whole dilemma should be rejected.

---

[2] Mark McPherran, in 'The Aporetic Interlude and Fifth Elenchos of Plato's *Euthyphro*', *Oxford Studies in Ancient Philosophy* 25 (2003), 32–5, interestingly raises the question of where Euthyphro goes at the end of the *Euthyphro*. He departs in a hurry (15e4–5): to proceed with the prosecution of his father? He does not say so, as we might expect him to. Rather, it seems that Euthyphro, so to speak, gives up his 'place in the queue' at the door of the court: unlike Socrates, he no longer *diatribei peri ten tou basileôs stoan* (spends his time around the King's Porch) (1a2–3). Evidently, he lacks the constancy of character to bring an unjust prosecution, while Socrates does not lack the constancy to face one. So, part of the irony of Socrates' *Hoia poieis, ô hetaire?* (What are you doing, my friend?) (15e6) is that Euthyphro's flight may be bad news and a big disappointment for one old gentleman, but is good news, and an unexpected reprieve, for another.

Therefore, neither Euthyphro nor Socrates is at a loss as to how to choose between these two alternatives, as we would expect in a true dilemma. Nor does Socrates suggest that his argument has refuted the whole idea of a divine-command ethics. Certainly, it has refuted Euthyphro's attempted definition of the holy. However, as pointed out above, Socrates does not argue by dilemma: he does not force Euthyphro to choose between two equally unpalatable alternatives, where the impossibility of both disproves Euthyphro's initial claim. Rather, he refutes Euthyphro's definition by insisting, not entirely explicitly, on two familiar Socratic doctrines, both closely connected with his own rather specialized notion of definition. One is what we might (with what I hope is a harmless anachronism) call the logical priority of essence over accident and of activity over passivity (10b–c). The other is the doctrine that definitions must refer to the essences of things, not merely to their accidents or affections:

> And it looks, Euthyphro, as if – when you were asked, about the holy, exactly what it is (*ho ti pot' estin*) – you were unwilling to make its essence (*ousia*) clear to me. Instead, you told me about some affection (*pathos ti*) pertaining to it – something that this 'the holy' has undergone, namely to be loved by all the gods. But its *being* (*ho de ti on*) you have not yet spoken. (*Euthyphro* 11a8–b2; I use my own translations throughout)

The point is not the downfall of any possible system of divine-command ethics. It is not even that what is holy might not be truly described as 'what the gods love'. It is simply that what is holy cannot be *defined* as 'what the gods love' because 'what the gods love' is a term in the wrong logical category to do this defining work. If we know only that the gods love something, we still need to know *why* they love it. It is only as we begin to get answers to that sort of question – if we do – that we can begin to get any sense of the real nature of what is holy.

But, of course, if the gods disagree on what they love (8d–e), then they will be little better as authorities about what is holy than Euthyphro's own warring family (4d–e). Taking views about what is holy will then be no more than taking sides in a feud, and our interactions with the gods will remain at the lowly level where Euthyphro's clearly are – the level of an *emporikê technê* of bartering temple-sacrifice for protection, perhaps even protection from other gods. The implied critique of Euthyphro's own beliefs about what the gods command, and of the popular religious ethics of Socrates' own day that they no doubt represent, is obvious.[3] It is much less obvious that we are being told by Plato that *any* ethical

---

3   Though Xenophon manages, with even more than his usual obtuseness, to present Socrates as a conventionally-minded defender of this *emporikê technê* (marketplace skill): *khrê oun mêden elleiponta kata dunamin timan tous theous tharrein te kai elpizein ta megista agatha* ('so we should leave no part of religious duty out, honouring the gods as much as we can, being of good heart and hoping for the greatest goods') (*Memorabilia* 4.3.17). It is quite an achievement to make Socrates' views sound so dull.

beliefs based on divine commands, or *any* religious ethics, should be rejected. On this evidence, the moral of the *Euthyphro* might equally be the very different point that, in order to formulate an adequate divine-command ethics, we need a more adequate theology than Euthyphro's.

III

There is another obvious reason why it was paradoxical to follow the usual reading of the *Euthyphro* and see Socrates as an opponent of divine-command ethics. This reason is that, as Euthyphro himself reminds us right at the start of the dialogue, Socrates himself lives by divine commands (*Euthyphro* 3a10–b5):

EU.   What things does [Meletus] say you are doing that corrupt the young?
SOC.   My fine fellow, they are absurdities, or at least they sound absurd. For he says that I am a maker of gods; that I make new gods, and do not respect the old ones. He has indicted me on behalf of the old gods, or so he says.
EU.   I understand, Socrates; it is because of the daemonic sign (*to daimonion*) that you say comes to you every now and then.

What is this 'daemonic sign'? As Socrates very famously puts it in the *Apology*:

The explanation of this [Socrates' way of life] is what you have so often heard me tell you about in so many contexts: it is that something divine and daemonic (*theion ti kai daimonion*) comes to me, the very thing that Meletus makes fun of me for in his indictment. From my childhood on it has come to me as a sort of voice (*phônê tis*), and whenever it comes, it always holds me back from something that I am about to do – it never pushes me forward ... (31c10–d6; cp. 40b, *Phaedrus* 242c1, *Euthydemus* 272e)

We may contrast the directness of Socrates' 'voice' with the most direct way in which, so far as we know, Euthyphro hears from the divine (5e–6b):

EU.   See, Socrates, what a great proof (*mega tekmêrion*) I give you that the law really stands this way – one which I have given others already ... The fact is that men themselves believe that Zeus is the best and most just of the gods, and they agree that he chained up his father because he [Cronos] devoured his children, contrary to justice, and Cronos had mutilated *his* father [Ouranos] for other crimes of this sort. Yet they find fault with me for prosecuting my father when he has acted unjustly! So they are contradicting themselves in what they say about the gods and about me.
SOC.   And isn't this, Euthyphro, the very reason why I am being prosecuted – that when someone tells me this kind of story about the gods, I find it

> rather hard to accept?[4] ... Yet what shall we say, we who confess that
> we know nothing about them [*autôn*: could equally refer to the stories
> or the gods]? But tell me – in the name of the god of friendship [Zeus]
> – do you really believe that these things happened like this?

EU.   Yes, and even more amazing things than these ...

Euthyphro's rather boastful claim (5a2) to a unique level of accurate (*akribôs*) knowledge about everything to do with holiness is shown up here. Despite his confession of ignorance, it is clear that Socrates knows more about holiness and the gods than Euthyphro does.[5] Euthyphro is a sort of fundamentalist of the Greek myths. The basis of his belief that the gods command him to prosecute his father is that the myths say that Zeus did something horrible to his father because his father had done something even worse. And Euthyphro just accepts these myths as providing him with examples to justify his own actions by. It is hard to imagine a more rickety and secondhand basis for ethics. The central problem with Euthyphro's way of thinking is not so much that it commits him to relying on divine commands as that he cannot give us any reason to agree with his belief that the bizarre and savage myths that he mentions here should have anything like the status of commands or examples for anyone. Of course, Socrates too is not above appealing – in a rather more controlled fashion – to the Greek myths while considering ethical questions (see for example *Apology* 28c–d, praising Achilles' fearlessness of death). However, Socrates in the *Republic* explicitly and directly bans his hearers from providing a pretext for their own misdeeds by appealing to the gods' misdeeds, in a passage where Plato quite clearly alludes to *Euthyphro* 4b: 'When a young man is listening, it is not to be said that it is nothing special

---

   [4]   Compare *Phaedrus* 229e–30a, where Socrates rejects the (Anaxagorean?) project of seeking rationalizing explanations for stories of the gods, and even says that he does accept traditional theology: 'I cannot yet know myself, in compliance with the Delphic inscription, and it seems ridiculous to me to inquire into unrelated matters when I am still ignorant about that. And so I pass by these questions about the gods, *and accept the conventional view about them* (*peithomenos de tôi nomizomenôi peri autôn*); as I said just now, I don't investigate them myself.' Similarly, he says at *Apology* 35d7 'I believe in the gods as none of my accusers does': *nomizô ... hôs oudeis tôn emôn katêgorôn*. There is an obvious double entendre in *hôs*: Socrates' theism differs from Meletus' not just, as it were, in quantity, but in quality too. (Thanks to Mark McPherran for discussion of this. For his views on this issue, see further Mark McPherran, 'Recognizing the Gods of Socrates', in M. McPherran (ed.), *Wisdom, Ignorance and Virtue: New Essays on Socrates, Apeiron*, Supplemental Volume 28 (1997), 125–39.

   [5]   *Cratylus* 396dff. has Socrates claiming to have been inspired by his recent conversation with Euthyphro. However, this is obviously ironic. The *Euthyphro* says nothing about etymologies, which is what Socrates is here claiming to speak about with inspiration. Nor is there any sign in the *Euthyphro* that Socrates learns anything at all from his conversation with Euthyphro. The passage proves little except that the *Cratylus* was written after the *Euthyphro*, which presumably we expected anyway.

for someone to do the very worst kind of injustice, or again to punish his father's injustice in the extremest possible way, because it is no more than what the greatest and first of gods have done already' (*Republic* 378b1–5). Moreover, Socrates also knows something directly of the gods, by inner experience.

Does Euthyphro too hear directly from God in his inner experience, as well as being an expert in the myths? Apparently he does claim to hear from God; he certainly claims to foretell the future (3c) and it looks as if such claims were at least often based on claimed direct experience of a 'divine voice' or some such experience. However, notice this: at *Euthyphro* 3e, Socrates invites a prophecy of how his and Euthyphro's cases will go, and Euthyphro (3e3) replies *all' isôs ouden estai, o Sôcrates, pragma, alla su te kata noun agôniei tên dikên, oimai de kai eme tên emên* ('But no doubt there will be nothing to it, Socrates, and you will fight your case according to wisdom, as I think I will mine'). So, the only time in the dialogue that Euthyphro actually gives us a prophecy, he apparently gets it spectacularly wrong – certainly about Socrates' case and probably about his own too.[6] To be more precise: either Euthyphro's experiences of divine guidance are wholly illusory, unlike those of Socrates, or else he fails in the attribute he most boasts of, *akribeia*, by failing to be an accurate *hermênês* of his own numinous experiences. Since (we might say) Socrates will indeed conduct his case *kata noun,* perhaps Euthyphro does have hold of something genuine. But that something genuine is also something Delphic, and Euthyphro misunderstands the ambiguous phrase *agônisthai kata noun* ('fight your case according to wisdom').

The evidence could hardly be clearer that Socrates' report of his *daimonion* is a report of a direct religious experience of being divinely commanded. We should not follow some recent writers in attempting to naturalize the *daimonion* into no more than a moral or rational hunch (as Vlastos says), or the voice of reason within him[7], or into the voice of Socrates' own subconscious.[8] Of course, if you are a philosophical naturalist, then (from an external, *de re* standpoint) you will want to

---

[6] There again, Socrates makes a false prophecy too: that Isocrates will turn out a philosopher (*Phaedrus* 279b). Perhaps the point there – I admit that this suggestion may be a bit of a stretched one – is that Isocrates *would* have turned out a philosopher had he not ignored the divine within (and Socrates) – so that, as it were, it is not Socrates' prophecy which was wrong but Isocrates' choice to ignore it.

[7] Martha Nussbaum, 'Commentary on Edmunds', in John Cleary (ed.), *Proceedings of the Boston Area Colloquium in Ancient Philosophy*, vol. 1 (Lanham, MD: University Press of America, 1985), p. 234.

[8] Roslyn Weiss, *Socrates Dissatisfied.* (New York: Oxford University Press, 1997/8), p. 19: 'The *daimonion* is not ... a voice independent of Socrates' own thinking and intuition that instructs him to contravene their guidance but rather a voice inspired by Socrates' thinking and intuition, by beliefs that are for the moment "subconscious" – if the reader will forgive the anachronism – a voice that gives him the strength to implement these "subconscious" beliefs when he is tempted to do otherwise. Indeed, when there is no tension between Socrates' imminent act and his deeper sense of what is right, when Socrates has no reservations, no qualms, about the course he is about to pursue, his *daimonion* is silent.'

naturalize Socrates' *daimonion* somehow. Be that as it may, there are no grounds for the corresponding internal, *de dicto* claim that *Socrates himself* saw his own *daimonion* this way. As Vlastos[9] puts it, we have here to face

> a fact about Socrates which has been so embarrassing to modern readers that a long line of Platonic scholarship has sought ... to explain it away: Socrates' acceptance of the supernatural ... If we are to use Plato's and Xenophon's testimony about Socrates at all we must take it as a brute fact – as a premise fixed for us in history – that, far ahead of his time as Socrates is in so many ways, in this part of his thought he is a man of his time. He subscribes unquestioningly to the age-old view that side by side with the physical world accessible to our senses, there exists another, populated by mysterious beings, personal like ourselves, but, unlike ourselves, having the power to invade at will the causal order to which our own actions are confined ... how they act upon us we cannot hope to understand. But the fact is that they do and their communications to us through dreams and oracles is [*sic*] one of the inscrutable ways in which they display their power over us.[10]

Two quick comments on this: 1) the embarrassment that Vlastos identifies here is an embarrassment that he seems at least partly to share. Vlastos seems to see Socrates' supernaturalism as a failure on Socrates' part to transcend his own culture. *Ad hominem*, I observe that this is strange given that Vlastos was a Christian, and so presumably a supernaturalist, himself; and 2) Vlastos speaks here of Socrates' supernaturalism as 'unquestioning' and wholly traditional. Not *ad hominem,* I reply that even the earliest evidence, as far back as Meletus' indictment as cited above, says clearly that Socrates' theism had become in important ways very untraditional, precisely as a result of Socrates' own questioning. (Contrast *Phaedrus* 229e–30a, cited in Note 5 above, for Socrates' willingness to leave traditionalism alone on the grounds of ignorance, with *Timaeus* 40d7ff. (cited below), for Plato's much less irenic attitude to traditional beliefs.)

At the level of Socrates' own self-understanding, it is perfectly clear, both from Plato's and Xenophon's evidence,[11] that Socrates takes the voice of the *daimonion* to be a form of supernatural guidance quite separate from the guidance that any of us might get, and that Socrates himself obviously sometimes gets, from doing

---

[9]   Gregory Vlastos, 'Socratic Piety', in Gail Fine (ed.), *Plato 2: Ethics, Politics, Religion, and the Soul* (Oxford: Oxford University Press, 1999), p. 57.

[10]   Cf. Mark McPherran, *The Religion of Socrates* (University Park, PA: Pennsylvania State University Press, 1997), p. 6: 'by [Socrates' religious language] he is [on one line of interpretation] simply referring surreptitiously in the language of "the many" to the "divine" inner promptings of his utterly secular, completely human powers of ratiocination ... In my judgement, this portrait of Socrates is the result of slighting and misinterpreting the evidence of our texts.'

[11]   Xenophon on Socrates' *daimonion*: *Memorabilia* 1.2–5.

some careful reasoning or from trying to plumb the depths of our own minds. For if the *daimonion* were not, on Socrates' own conception of it, explicitly supernatural, what could be the point of his argument at *Apology* 27c that, since he believes in *daimonia*, he must also believe in *daimones* and so cannot be accused by Meletus of atheism?

This restraining voice is not 'virtually worthless' from a rational point of view,[12] and in any case, the restraining voice is not the only supernatural voice that Socrates hears. If we take *au pied de la lettre* his last remark just quoted – that his *daimonion* always speaks negatively, to forbid, and never positively commands – then the voice that Socrates talks about a little later in the *Apology*, as positively commanding him to philosophize, must be a different voice, or voices:

> This task [of philosophizing], as I say, has been commanded for me by (the) God (*tôi theôi*), both by oracles, and by dreams, and by every way there is of commanding a divine destiny (*theia moira*) for any man. (*Apology* 33c5–8; cp. 37e6)

('For any man': notice the generality of this. Socrates tells us at *Republic* 496c2–4 that he doubts that many others have experienced *to daimonion sêmeion* – though perhaps a few have. Even if the *daimonion* is almost unique to Socrates, the other sorts of religious experience and divine guidance that he also claims to have had hardly are. Thus, I doubt we should infer, with Pierre Destrée,[13] that Plato depicts Socrates as uniquely divinely guided because he is the only true philosopher. For one thing, Plato does not think that Socrates *is* a true philosopher: what Socrates has is the right way in to the true philosophy, Platonism, but not Platonism itself.)

It is not obvious that this *theos* who commands Socrates is straightforwardly Apollo, whose ambiguous oracle Socrates interprets as telling him to begin his

---

[12]   *Pace* Thomas Brickhouse and Nicholas Smith, *Socrates on Trial* (Princeton, NJ: Princeton University Press, 1989), pp. 253–4: 'Once we notice how little information Socrates gets from a daimonic alarm, we can see why Socrates could never be made wise by his *daimonion's* alarms. After all, when the *daimonion* tells Socrates that he should desist from what he is about to do, he can be completely certain that he must not continue what he was about to do. But this information tells him nothing about what it is that is wrong, when it is wrong, why it is wrong, and what it is to be wrong. The god does not lie to Socrates, but does manage to tell him next to nothing through the *daimonion*. What Socrates gets from his sign, therefore, is virtually worthless for the pursuit of the sorts of truth Socrates seeks philosophically – truth that explains and defines, and which thus can be applied to judgments and deliberations required for the achievement of the truly good life for men.' For more about this implicit contrast between seeking truth *philosophically* and in other ways, see towards the end of this chapter.

[13]   Pierre Destrée and Nicholas D. Smith (eds), *Socrates' Divine Sign: Religion, Practice, and Value in Socratic Philosophy*. Special issue of *APEIRON: A Journal for Ancient Philosophy and Science* 38(2) (June 2005) (Kelowna, BC: Academic Printing and Publishing, 2005).

quest for a wiser man than himself (*Apology* 21a–3b). For one thing, texts like *Euthyphro* 6a6–9 give us good reason to doubt that Socrates believed in the traditional Apollo at all and hence would have seen oracular utterances from an 'Apollonian' source as really messages not from that Apollo, but at least from Apollo non-traditionally conceived, and/or from the being whom Socrates calls *ho theos*, which we may translate either 'God' or 'the god'. Thus, at *Apology* 21b7, Socrates asks himself what 'the god can mean' by the oracle (*ti pote legei ho theos*) and takes it for granted that the god cannot be lying – 'for that would be against his nature' (*ou gar themis autôi*). But a host of texts and traditions which Socrates must have known prove that lying and deception, like the rest of the anthropomorphic characteristics condemned in the *Republic* (for example, at 378d and 379e), are not against *Apollo*'s nature, not at least on the traditional conception of Apollo: see Aeschylus, *Agamemnon* 1228ff. for a start, where Cassandra recounts how she double-crossed Apollo and he double-crossed her back. Again, it may have been Apollo's oracle that started Socrates' quest, but we have no decisive evidence that Socrates thought that the many other portents that he mentions here were from Apollo, not at least if that means an Apollo anything like Aeschylus' Apollo.[14]

What Socrates did think is that these dreams, visions and voices came (more or less directly: perhaps the *daimonion* is an intermediary) from God and that they came to him as divine commands. That makes it as certain as it could be that, whatever else the *Euthyphro* is meant to be about, it cannot be intended as an attack on divine-command ethics. It is better understood, I suggest, as part of Plato's campaign against contemporary Athens' dominant theology of (as we might call it) chaotic polytheism and in favour of something more like the ethical monotheism that is familiar to those of us who live in cultures shaped by the Abrahamic religions. Thus, even when Socrates speaks of gods plural in the *Euthyphro*, what he says of them is that *ouden gar hêmin estin agathon, ho ti an mê ekeinoi dôsin* (15a1; cp. *Stm* 273b8) – almost like the Anglican Eucharistic affirmation that 'all that we have comes from you, and of your own do we give you'. The dialogue's deepest moral is not that divine-command ethics should be rejected, it is that Plato's ethical theism is preferable to chaotic polytheism because it gives us the only possible context in which divine-command ethics can be sustained. For only if God is good can it be reasonable to hope that what God commands will converge with what is morally right.

Might we go even further and describe Socrates and Plato not just as ethical theists but as ethical monotheists? Almost, but not quite. When he is speaking of his own beliefs, Plato's Socrates seems usually to prefer to speak of *ho theos*

---

[14]   For a different view, see Mark McPherran, in ibid., pp. 13–30. As McPherran has reminded me, Socrates is at least orthodox enough to compose a hymn to Apollo in prison (*Phaedo* 60dff.), though both Cebes and Euenus seem rather astonished to hear that he is doing this.

than of *hoi theoi*.[15] However, he also apparently believes that there is more than one divine being, even if one of these is clearly distinguished, for example, at *Stm* 272e8, as the 'greatest', the others as *hoi kata tous topous sunarkhontes tôi megistôi daimoni* (the spirits who in this place or that rule alongside the greatest spirit). Further, he believes that alongside what he calls *daimones* ('spiritual beings'), there are *daimonia* ('spiritual messengers' or 'angels'?), among them his own *daimonion* (*Apology* 27c1). Likewise, Plato can speak both of gods (for example, at *Phaedrus* 248a1), and also of one necessarily unique unmoved mover (*Laws* 894e ff.; cp. *Timaeus* 28a), the *dêmiourgos* of the *Timaeus,* whom he calls *ho theos* (44e4, 46c8, 53b7). *Timaeus* 40a1 tells us that the *dêmiourgos* created a 'heavenly race of gods'; *Timaeus* 40d7ff. suggests that this *ouranion theôn genos* is quite different from the traditional Olympian pantheon, 'of which there is neither cogent nor even suggestive proof', and about which Plato, with obvious disingenuousness, confesses that 'it is beyond our powers to speak of them or know their coming to be'. Overall, the evidence is that both Socrates and Plato are insistent on the supremacy of one God over all other beings that might be called gods. The latter are created beings, and so could not, strictly speaking, be called gods at all in a Judaeo-Christian context. But that is no bar to calling them gods in a Greek context.

'But surely Plato can't give any respectable place in his thought to anything like Socrates' *daimonion*! Whatever the historical Socrates (or any other Socrates distinguishable from Plato) may have thought, *Plato's* sarcastic dismissal of *manteia*, inspiration, prophecy, and the like is one of the most frequent themes in his canon. How could Plato of all people, austere rationalist as he is, possibly retain such a relic of primitive religious irrationalism in his philosophy? Mustn't there be too much irony in his reports of Socrates' supposed religious experiences for us to take them seriously?'[16]

Briefly, my answer is No. I explain this answer in the next section.

---

[15] Though admittedly traditionalists like Ion can also speak of *theos* singular: for example, *ean theos ethelêi* (*Ion* 530b2).

[16] Or, as Vlastos ('Socratic Piety', p. 6), puts it: 'For Socrates diviners, seers, oracle-givers, poets are all in the same boat. All of them in his view are know-nothings, or rather, worse: unaware of their sorry epistemic state [unaware that they do not have the requisite sort of understanding], they set themselves up as repositories of wisdom emanating from a divine, all-wise source. What they say may be true; but even when it is true, they are in no position to discern what there is in it that is true. If their hearer were in a position to discern this, then *he* would have the knowledge denied to them; the knowledge would come from the application of *his reason* to what these people say without reason.' Note the conflict between this Socrates-as-rationalist and the Socrates-as-traditionalist of the Vlastos quotation at note 6 above.

IV

At *Apology* 22b2–c8 Socrates is explaining to the judges at his trial how he discovered, to his surprise, that the poets were not wiser than him:

> I took in hand what seemed to me to be the most carefully thought-out productions of the tragedians, dithyrambists, and the other poets, and I questioned them on what these works meant, so that I might learn from them too. And – well, I am embarrassed to tell you the truth, gentlemen justices, but it must be told: you might say that pretty well anyone present could explain those poems better than the very men who wrote them. I soon recognised that the thing about the poets was that they too [like the orators] did not do what they did by wisdom (*sophiai*). Instead they did it by some sort of natural instinct and by divine indwelling (*physei tini kai enthousiazontes*), like prophets or soothsayers (*theomanteis kai khrêsmôidoi*): who also say many fine things, but do not know anything of what they are talking about (*isasin de ouden hôn legousin*) … Their poetic gifts made them think that they were the wisest of all men in other things besides poetry as well; but mistakenly.

This is just the sort of passage that is easy to read as Plato engaging in a 'sarcastic dismissal', as I called it above, of the claims of any sort of inspiration or revelation. There are plenty of other passages like it: *Ion* 533c–34e, for instance. The most strikingly similar – at times it is almost a doublet of the *Apology* passage – is in the conclusion of the *Meno* (99b–e):

> it was not by wisdom (*sophiai*), nor by being wise, that men like these led their cities – men such as Themistocles and his circle, and those whom Anytus here mentioned just now … So if it was not by knowledge (*epistêmêi*), it must have happened by the only alternative, well-founded opinion (*eudoxiai*). That is what these politicians used to direct their cities; in respect of rational understanding (*pros to phronein*), their condition was no different from that of soothsayers and prophets (*khrêsmôidoi kai theomanteis*). For these too say many true things, but do not know anything of what they are talking about (*isasin de ouden hôn legousin*) … those soothsayers and prophets whom we have just mentioned – and all who are artistically inclined (*poiêtikous*) as well – succeed in many great things in what they do and say, even though they lack mind (*noun mê ekhontes*). For this reason, we could rightly call them divine (*theious*). And we should say that the politicians are no less divine and divinely-indwelt, being inspired and possessed by god (*theious, enthousiazein, epipnous, katekhomenous ek tou theou*) … So if our search and discussion has been right, virtue would be neither natural nor taught, but something that comes upon us by a divine dispensation without mind (*theiai moirai paragignomenê aneu nou*).

It is easy to read passages like these two as constituting clear and decisive evidence that Plato (or Socrates, or early Plato – take your pick) has no sympathy at all for the idea that anything might be learned from special experiences of apparently direct inspiration or revelation, whether these supposed revelations are religious, ethical or aesthetic. Since inspiration is just a kind of stumbling around in the dark, the 'praise' of Themistocles and his circle that Socrates offers here is obviously (on this reading) no more than a veiled condemnation of them and their methods. They do not work by knowledge but at best by true opinion – and, as the *Republic* shows at length (the reading continues), there cannot be a clearer condemnation of their ways than that. One deservedly influential recent interpretation of Plato, that of Nussbaum in her celebrated 1986 essay 'Madness, Reason, and Recantation in the *Phaedrus*',[17] takes as read this early hostility to claims of inspiration and assumes that it is Plato's uniform and consistent attitude until the time of the dialogue she focuses on, the *Phaedrus*, where Socrates' famous 'recantation' (242dff.) introduces a rather less austere and rationalistic approach to such claims.

But, in fact, even the earliest evidence is much more equivocal than such a reading suggests. For instance, the two passages I have cited above, one from a central early-period dialogue, the *Meno*, and the other from what may be Plato's very first philosophical publication, the *Apology*, are not, on a closer reading, merely 'sarcastic dismissals' of the claims of inspiration. There are passages in Plato where it is right to hear sarcastic dismissiveness as the tone of the text. This is true, for instance, of Socrates' exchanges with Thrasymachus, and with Callicles and Polus – indeed, it is true of both sides in both exchanges. But the sense of these passages from the *Meno* and the *Apology* is more nuanced.

The first point to note about both passages is their contexts. Socrates at *Apology* 22b–c cannot be concerned only with dismissing with sarcasm the very idea that divine inspiration or revelation could have any authority. There is no way of squaring that reading with Socrates' own appeals to inspiration throughout the *Apology*. Two are most notable. One is his own prophecy of Athens' future at 38c. Of course, as far as that passage goes, we might be right to read it as Plato's retrojection of words into Socrates' mouth in the light of hindsight. But even if that is correct, Plato is still committed by this passage to the claim that this was *the sort of thing* that Socrates said. This we see anyway from the other most notable appeal to inspiration in the *Apology*, which introduces this very passage: at 22a4, he tells us that his examination of the poets was itself prompted by a divine command.

Similarly, Socrates' aim in the *Meno* 99b–e cannot just be to mock politicians, poets and priests for their dependence on the illusions and fatuities of supposed divine inspiration. This is because what is arguably the deepest and most important teaching of the *Meno* itself is introduced by a passage in which it is possible to see Socrates himself as being overcome by a divine inspiration (81aff.). Even on the most modest interpretation of this passage, Socrates here appeals to the authority

17   Martha Nussbaum, 'Madness, Reason, and Recantation in the *Phaedrus*', in *The Fragility of Goodness* (Cambridge: Cambridge University Press, 1986), pp. 200–233.

of certain priests and priestesses 'about divine matters' (*akêkoa gar andrôn te kai gunaikôn sophôn peri ta theia pragmata*, 81a4–5). It is quite impossible to square this way of proceeding with Plato's alleged 'austere rationalism'. (These wise ones have, intriguingly enough, succeeded in their studies of their own enterprise to a point where they are able to 'give an account' of it. Tantalizingly, however, this is an account which Socrates does not pass on to Meno and us.)

Similar structural and contextual remarks can be made about other early-period texts which ought, on a reading like that of Vlastos or Nussbaum, to be straightforward exemplars of a high-minded rejection of the claims of inspiration. Euthyphro's initial attitude to Socrates (3c) is to see him as a kindred spirit; if Euthyphro is laughed at for offering prophecies in the *ekklêsia*, the kind of things that bring Socrates too the Athenians' derision and slander do not seem to him very different. Even the *Republic* has at least one myth in it (614bff.) and even the *Crito* (44b) reports a prophetic dream of Socrates', while the *Phaedo* (60e–61b) reports multiple dreams and a divine command to him – a command, moreover, to practise poetry.

Turning from their contexts to the two quoted passages themselves and taking the *Apology* passage first: notice Socrates' embarrassment (*aiskhunomai*, 22b6) at relating his discovery about the poets. Is his talk of embarrassment here mere affectation of what he does not actually feel, a clumsy attempt to make what he is saying more acceptable to his listeners? That is how we must read it if we think (like Vlastos) that Socrates' real point here, ironically concealed, is merely that poets talk a lot of irrational rubbish, which true philosophers in their superiority will shun. On that reading, similarly, when Socrates says that the poets *legousi polla kai kala* (say many and fine things) (22c4; cp. *Euthyphro* 13e12), we will have to take these words as nearly the reverse of his real view. It is surely more natural to take both remarks at face value. Socrates really is embarrassed and the source of his embarrassment is that he really does think the poets' works fine productions, yet he cannot square their admirable qualities with the chaotic and irrational way in which, it seems to him, all poetry comes to be.

Similarly, with *Meno* 99b–e, the point of equating poetry (and the political and priestly arts) with *eudoxia* (well-founded belief) as opposed to equating them with *epistêmê* (knowledge) is not at all to dismiss poetry, politics and priestcraft as completely worthless. Rather, the point is the same as the point of the famous comparison between knowledge and true belief – the image of the road to Larisa – that Plato's Socrates has just offered us at *Meno* 96e–8b. Knowledge and true belief can produce the same good results; the difference between them lies not in their results but in the *unaccountability* of the good results of true belief. With mere true belief, there is by definition no *explaining* how we get the good results we do; we just *do* get those results, and that is all we can say (*Symposium* 202a4–9). This difference between knowledge and true belief may have grave consequences in some areas – for example, as the *Meno*, *Protagoras* and *Laches* all stress, it is a difference that makes true belief impossible to convey to another by teaching, or at any rate by rational teaching. But it does not abrogate from the genuine admirability, indeed, the divine quality, of the good results that true belief can have. Both Socrates' mission in the *Apology* and Themistocles' political skill in the *Meno* come *theiai moirai* (by divine allotment). So, when Plato's Socrates describes politicians such as Themistocles as *theious*, he is not merely being snide. His admiration for their achievements is perfectly sincere. What complicates his attitude to them is not an undertone of sarcasm but of puzzlement at how they can be so divine in their achievements and yet so innocent of any touch of real understanding of what they are about.

Compare Socrates' puzzlement, in the *Ion*, about how Ion can be (as he himself says he is: 532c) so expert in understanding and expounding *Homer*, yet so dozy and incompetent when it comes to *Hesiod*. The answer is that his understanding of Homer is a *theia dunamis*, not a *tekhnê* or *epistêmê*: *Ion* 533d2 (it too comes *theiai moirai*: *Ion* 534c1). And the present point generalizes in a way that shows up something wrong in W.R.M. Lamb's comment in his introduction to the *Ion* in the Loeb edition,[18] that in that dialogue Plato insists 'that no art ... can be of real worth unless it is based on some systematic knowledge'. The point is rather that art like Homer's *is* clearly of real worth – there is no irony in Socrates' description of Homer as *aristos kai theiotatos tôn poiêtôn* (*Ion* 530b10) – *even though it is not* based on systematic knowledge. The puzzle, and it is a deep one, is how this can be.

Of course, we might feel the same puzzlement about Socrates himself. How can Socrates' philosophical inquiries have such remarkable results, when he himself knows nothing? Famously, Socrates' own explanation is that he is a sort of midwife of ideas: he produces no children of his own but he helps bring others' conceptions to the light (*Theaetetus* 148c–51d). Then (we could speculatively ask) might not something similar be true of Themistocles' sort? Might not they too be able to bring about in others a knowledge or expertise that they cannot attain to themselves? The trouble with this suggestion is that Socrates, for all his looking, never finds anyone who actually possesses any such *politikê tekhnê*. Come to that, never in the early dialogues do we see Socrates' midwifery bring about any successful labours. Given that so many of those dialogues end in *aporia*, it is hard to see who Plato thinks are Socrates' successful patients. (Perhaps he has his own philosophical school in mind;[19] more about that suggestion later.)

Given the scant results of Socrates' own rationalistic endeavours, the dialogues' attitude to politicians like Themistocles is generally not one of simple denunciation, but is more nuanced. It is summed up by the question posed by the *Meno* quotation above: how can they be so 'divine' (*theious*) when they are also 'lacking in mind' (*noun mê ekhontes*)?[20] And this use of the word *nous* seems not

---

[18]   W.R.M. Lamb and H.N. Fowler, *Plato: Statesman, Philebus, Ion.* (Loeb Classical Library. Cambridge, MA: Harvard University Press, 1925), p. 403.

[19]   David Sedley, *The Midwife of Platonism* (Oxford: Oxford University Press, 2005).

[20]   In the Ion, God not only bypasses but actually takes away the nous of rhapsodes: *ho theos exairoumenos toutôn ton noun* (God takes mind away from these people) (534c9–10).

to be an accident, since both for Socrates in the *Phaedo* (97c1) and for Plato in the *Timaeus* (39e8) and *Laws* (897c6, d9), Mind, *Nous*, is apparently a name of God. Its use here presses what struck Plato as a forceful paradox.

V

What is the paradox? The parallel may seem outlandish, but it is almost Pascal's: *le cœur a ses raisons que la raison ne connaît point.*[21] It is that inspiration, revelation or intuition seems to be a possible route to the truth – as it clearly is for Socrates, for instance. Yet we cannot rationally explain *how* it gets us to the truth. By all the stern rules of philosophical rationality, that can only make inspiration suspect. Plato (and Socrates) can be read as regarding its directness and certainty as a kind of *cheat*: when we should be earning our certainties by the long and arduous road of the dialectical education that the *Republic* lays out for us, simply to claim to *see* the truth has all the advantages of theft over honest toil. We might say, with a second and even more outrageous parallel, that it is as bad as getting a computer to find the meaning of life for you:

> 'You just let the machines get on with the adding up,' warned Majikthise, 'and we'll take care of the eternal verities, thank you very much. You want to check your legal position, you do mate. Under law the Quest for Ultimate Truth is quite clearly the inalienable prerogative of your working thinkers. Any bloody machine goes and actually finds it and we're straight out of a job aren't we? I mean what's the use of our sitting up half the night arguing that there may or may not be a God if this machine only goes and gives us his bleeding phone number the next morning?'[22]

Unlike Majikthise, Plato takes no pleasure in prolonging intellectual struggle and bewilderment for its own sake (still less for cash). However, he is convinced that we cannot claim real knowledge unless we cannot only see the truth but also explain what makes it the truth, and how each truth connects to the others. If we are so lucky that intuition or revelation or inspiration *gives* us the truth, we should not be ungrateful for that, but we should not be satisfied either. Beyond true belief, there is still the long road of justification to travel. And Plato is justly famous for thinking that what we are likely to have by the end of this journey is so different from what we started with that we should not speak of knowledge as simply an

---

[21]   *Le cœur a ses raisons, que la raison ne connaît point. On le sent en mille choses. C'est le cœur qui sent Dieu, et non la raison. Voilà ce que c'est que la foi parfaite, Dieu sensible au cœur* – Blaise Pascal, *Pensées*, IV.277, p. 458 in L. Brunschvicg (ed.), *Blaise Pascal: Pensées et Opuscules* (Paris: Classiques Hachette, 1961).

[22]   Douglas Adams, *The Hitchhiker's Guide to the Galaxy* (London: Pan, 1979), pp. 129–30.

upgraded version of true belief at all. Most obviously in the *Republic* and the *Theaetetus*, knowledge is apparently so different from true belief or perception that true belief and perception are not even ingredients of it.

However, as Plato apparently comes to see in those two dialogues, there is a further twist of paradox in the tale. The twist is, of course, that the ultimate aim of the *Republic*'s dialectical education is itself described by Plato again and again as a sort of direct, revelatory perception, acquaintance or intuition: 'True Being ... is visible (*theatê*) only to *Nous*' (*Phaedrus* 247c8; cp. *theôrôn* at *Symposium* 210d4). Thus, we find Plato apparently denouncing this-worldly perception in almost the same breath as he exalts the perception of the Forms (*Rep* 517b1–9):

> Compare the prison-house of the cave to the realm of visual appearance; compare the light of the fire in the cave to the power of the sun ... and take it that the prisoner's journey to the upper world, and his contemplation (*thean*) of what is up there, stands for the soul's journey up into the intelligible realm ... in the realm of the known, what is seen last of all – and with difficulty (*teleutaia ... kai mogis horasthai*) – is the Universal of the Good.

Knowledge, as the *Theaetetus* insists, is not perception in any ordinary or mundane sense; however, at the end of the philosopher's laborious ascent, by way of reasoning and hard thought and logical work, what we find is that the ultimate knowledge is itself something so extraordinarily like perception in its directness, immediacy and non-discursive simplicity that Plato never finds a better or more illuminating image to describe it by.

The worry lurking behind Socrates' Dream at *Theaetetus* 201e–2d is precisely about this similarity. The worry is that, for all the disanalogies between Plato's own view and the empiricist theories that (on my reading, which is controversial, but not to be defended here)[23] the *Theaetetus* is devoted to attacking, still there is a deep structural parallel between empiricism and Platonism. Both rest all discursive, propositional and rational knowledge on a foundation of non-discursive, non-propositional, surd acquaintance. Thus, both raise the paradox that the ultimate objects of what we would like to call knowledge are themselves not *reasoned about* or *known* but *perceived.* In the words of what I take to be the most important sentence in the whole *Theaetetus* (202b6–7): *houtô dê ta men stoikheia aloga kai agnôsta einai, aisthêta de* (thus the elements are without accounts and unknowable, but they are perceptible).

Of course, given the differences between physical and intellectual perception that Plato also stresses, these parallels between the two kinds of perception would not amount to a revalidation of physical perception and other less-than-ideally-rational forms of intuition, such as inspiration and religious experience, were it not for this small point about the vision of the Form of the Good: it is impossible. Or at least – more accurately, perhaps – that vision is an ideal limit of the understanding.

---

[23]   Timothy Chappell, *Reading Plato's Theaetetus* (Indianapolis, IN: Hackett, 2005).

It is what all our mortal, body-imprisoned attempts at knowledge and wisdom strive towards. But we have little reason to think that any of us can actually *reach* the godlike state of contemplation of the Form of the Good that Plato urges us to imitate (*Theaetetus* 176b2, *Timaeus* 90b–c) so long as we remain in this life, or that we can know beyond all possibility of error that we have reached it even when we have.

Certainly, *Socrates* – whether that means the historical one, or Plato's character – makes no claim to have attained this state. On the contrary, he explicitly disavows any such knowledge (*Rep* 506c1):

> 'What then?' I said, 'do you think it justice for someone to speak about what he doesn't know, as if he did know? ... Have you not noticed that all opinions without knowledge are things of shame? The best of them are blind. Or can you see any difference between blind men who take the right road [surely an allusion to *Meno* 96eff.], and those who have a true belief without *nous*?'

The highest and most metaphysically ambitious doctrine – that of the *Republic* – that the wisest of all men – Socrates – can offer us: even this is not knowledge, but only true belief, an image (*eikona*, 509b1), a comparison or analogy (*apeikasia*, 514a1). It is not the good itself that he offers us but only an *interest payment* on the good. (The Greek word is *tokos*, literally 'child' (507a2); Plato means something derived from the good, by way of the good's own generative powers, which shares its properties and reveals them in small compass. As Plotinians might want to say, an *emanation* of the good; aptly enough, since, as the *Timaeus* tells us (for example, at 47e6–8a6), the only correct way to understand the visible universe is to realize that good order for it means being as much like the rational universe as it can be.) Even at his highest pitch, Socrates is not a knower but a true-believer, with all that that implies. So, in the *Euthyphro,* he possesses, unwillingly, an even scarier skill than Daedalus', destabilizing not only his own products but those of others as well – *eboulomên gar an moi tous logous menein kai akinêtôs hidrusthai* (indeed, I would like my own arguments to stay in place for me, and be fixed and unmoving) (11e2). Again and again in the Platonic corpus, anything like positive doctrine on Socrates' lips is presented as a dream, or a vision, or a mere image, or the report of some inspired prophet or *sophos*. No doubt too, it is Socrates' – or indeed Plato's – lack of knowledge that answers the old question why Plato writes dialogues rather than treatises like, say, Plotinus.

The moral is clear.[24] Since creatures of imperfect knowledge like us cannot hope to attain perfect truth by the rational route of knowledge, we should not

---

[24] Vlastos ('Socratic Piety', p. 66) explicitly opposes this reading. He writes there that, 'however plausible it may seem', the view that Socrates 'would look to the intimations of his *daimonion* as a source of moral knowledge apart from reason and superior to it ... is unsupportable by textual evidence and is in fact inconsistent with it'. However, Vlastos' chief argument against this view is that what Socrates gets from his *daimonion* (and other

neglect the possibility of attaining truth by routes of less rational purity. In fact, if *Phaedrus* 244a8–10 is to be believed, we should actively *court* madness, for 'the greatest of goods come to us through madness, provided it is given by divine gift' (*theiai dosei*; cp. *theia moira* above).[25]

In that famous speech, Socrates goes on to distinguish three kinds of *mania*: *mantikê*, foretelling of the future, a name which he etymologically connects with *mania* (244b); *prophêteia*, divining of *miasma* (244e);[26] and poetry (245a). He then argues (245b8ff.) that love should be distinguished as a fourth kind. This catalogue of kinds of madness is open-ended: there is nothing to stop Socrates from adding the voice of his *daimonion* as a fifth kind, or the positive commands that he hears through dreams as portents as a sixth kind, or indeed more than one kind, of *mania*. Perhaps Socrates also thinks that he already experiences the first three kinds of madness anyway. We have already noted his claim to tell the future at *Apology* 38c (cp. *Phaedrus* 242c) and his practice of poetry in *Phaedo* 603–61b, and maybe finding the hole in a bad argument (or character) is as much like divining a *miasma* as it is like the activity of a midwife (notice too the reference to the *daimonion* at *Theaetetus* 151a3, helping Socrates to decide whom to associate with). In all of these ways and others – Plato is now telling us – we can hope, by the gift of the gods, to attain truth. And how churlish it would be to refuse that gift where we cannot hope to attain perfect knowledge anyway.

VI

Something like this, we might conclude, must be the 'more adequate theology' on the basis of which Euthyphro – and Socrates – might have constructed their divine-command ethics. On the Platonic conception (we might now suggest), Euthyphro's crude exchange-and-mart cultus is replaced by *homoiôsis theôi*, the project of becoming God-like by getting as close as we can to God's or *Nous'* own activity, the philosophical contemplation of the Forms, perhaps even of the Form of the Good itself. We might suggest that one way in which this getting close can happen

---

supernatural sources) is not *knowledge*. First, this is not in dispute here: my claim is only that Socrates gets true beliefs and reliable guidance from such sources. Secondly, Socrates does not get *knowledge* from his reasoning either. That too, as I argue in the main text, gives him no more than true belief.

[25]   The view of *mania* ascribed by Xenophon to Socrates at *Memorabilia* 3.9.6 (madness is pretension to knowledge that you do not have). This is certainly one of the things that Plato's Socrates takes madness to be – but only one.

[26]   Is the diagnosis of *miasma* what is meant? Rather, 265b suggests a sort of religious transport that lifts its subject out of a sense of *miasma* and other kinds of trouble in the soul – perhaps a little like the sense of relief or forgiveness of sin sometimes reported by Christian revivalists, e.g. in Wesley's journals. The lack of match between the two lists may just be an anomaly.

– and always the best way – is through philosophical understanding and reasoning. Where that gives out, however – and it gives out frequently – we are not entirely without resource. Inspiration and revelation are possible too, and this can be a route to the truth, even when it cannot, on its own, be a route to the understanding that goes with knowledge. Such forms of insight may not come rationally, *by way of* reasoning, but that does not make them irrational, contrary to reasoning. *Pace* Vlastos,[27] there is simply no clash between the Socrates who describes himself as a follower of divine commands and the Socrates who describes himself as 'the sort of man who is persuaded by nothing in me but the proposition which appears to me to be the best when I reason about it' (*Crito* 46b). After all, the proposition which 'appears best' to me can easily be 'Obey the god.'

More generally, there can be perception of truths that we cannot arrive at by reasoning.[28] We can have reason, as Socrates has reason, to trust and obey what we take to be a revelation of God's will for us – even where we do not fully understand that revelation. *Timaeus* 70d–72b tells us that alongside the part of the soul that deliberates, and the part that only cares for food and drink and other bodily desires – indeed, physically in between them – there lies the liver, which receives confusedly, a little like a mirror, the clarities of the rational mind and conveys them to the appetites in a vivid form that they will understand. That, Plato tells us, is why the liver is the bodily seat of divination, and a rational man should take its promptings seriously, as the indirect evidence that they are of the dictates of reason (*Timaeus* 71e8–2a2):

> Here is a sufficient sign that God gave [the art of] divination to human madness: no one who is in his right mind (*ennous*) attains true and divinely inspired divination, but only when the power of his understanding is fettered by sleep, or when he is disinhibited through illness or some divine visitation (*dia tina enthousiasmon*). But it is the part of a sane man (*emphronos*) to remember what has been spoken and what has been recollected by divination and the divinely-indwelt nature, either awake or asleep, and whatever phantasms were seen – and to separate them all out by reasoning, seeing what direction they may point in, and for whom they reveal good or bad in the future, the present or the past.

The conception still needs a bit more refining; even though (as this *Timaeus* passage shows) it has some support in Plato's own writings, still, in Plato's own terms, this conclusion has something importantly unsatisfactory about it. At least we have – I hope – shaken off the mere prejudice that anyone who claims to hear

---

[27]   Vlastos, 'Socratic Piety', p. 56.

[28]   See Timothy Chappell, 'Moral Perception', *Philosophy* 83 (2008), 421–38 for an argument that the reasoning and perceiving alternatives may both be available, at least in principle, in ethics.

God speak is 'simply insane or seriously deluded'.[29] Socrates' own case would be excellent evidence against that prejudice, even if it were the only case where an undeniably brilliant person has claimed to hear God's voice (as of course it is not: compare, for a start, Martin Luther King and Blaise Pascal).[30] Still, on this conception, divine commands, inspirations and revelations turn out to be a kind of *pis aller*, a quick and dirty route to truth that is permissible for us only because we cannot manage the longer and purer route of dialectic. Perhaps we should hold such revelations at arm's length if we can; perhaps we should 'investigate the concept of God ... *no further* than is needed to bring it in line with' our ethical views.[31] But here we should heed the final message of Socrates' palinode in the *Phaedrus*, which is surely not merely that inspiration gets you where reasoning would also have got you – less logically and rationally, but faster. Rather, the message is that there are many places that *only* inspiration or ecstatic vision can get you to, places that reason alone will be no more able to arrive at than a frigid speech like Lysias' or Socrates' first will win a lover worth winning.

It may be different for the Demiurge. However, for complex-psyche-d creatures like us, a purely calculative or ratiocinative grasp of the Form of the Good, with no wonder or joy or love or exaltation involved in it, would not be a *grasp* of the Form of the Good at all, no more than Mary the Colour Scientist can know everything that there is to be known about redness merely by fully understanding the physics of redness. The fourth kind of madness is the madness of the lover *and* the philosopher (*Phdr.* 249a1, d5), the man whose vision of beauty 'down here' (*têide*) causes him to recollect the *true* beauty: 'he sprouts wings and longs to take the upward flight, but when he cannot, he gazes upwards like a bird, neglecting things below' (*Phdr.* 249e7–9).

---

[29]   A.A. Long, *From Epicurus to Epictetus: Studies in Hellenistic and Roman Philosophy* (Oxford: Oxford University Press, 2006), p. 65.

[30]   See Martin Luther King, 'Pilgrimage to Nonviolence', in J.M. Washington (ed.), *A Testament of Hope* (San Francisco: HarperCollins, 1986), p. 40: 'God has been profoundly real to me in recent years. In the midst of outer dangers I have felt an inner calm. In the midst of lonely days and dreary nights I have heard an inner voice saying "Lo, I will be with you". When the chains of fear and the manacles of frustration have all but stymied my efforts, I have felt the power of God transforming the fatigue of despair into the buoyancy of hope. I am convinced that the universe is under the control of a loving purpose, and that in the struggle for righteousness man has cosmic companionship. Behind the harsh appearances of the world there is a benign power.' Pascal's 'Memorial' is too long to quote here: it is reproduced in A. Krailsheimer, *Pascal: Selected Works* (London: Penguin, 1966), pp. 309–10. Many further examples of reports of religious experience from people whom there is no question-begging reason to think them either insane or deluded are collected in William James, *The Varieties of Religious Experience* (1899), quoted from Douglas Hedley, *Living Forms of the Imagination* (London: T&T Clark, 2008), p. 103, available online, http://www.psychwww.com/psyrelig/james/toc.htm, accessed 31 July 2011.

[31]   Vlastos, 'Socratic Piety', p. 60.

Having once achieved (some measure of) an experiential grasp of the good, it is not just natural but irresistible to try and rationalize the experience, to try and make sense of it or spin a theory out of it. Of course, this effort can bear fruit, by helping us to understand what has happened to us, and of course experience needs to be subject to the jurisdiction of reason, because experience can, and notoriously often does, lead us astray when we misinterpret its frequently ambiguous oracles. (Remember Euthyphro's own ambiguous oracle that Socrates will surely conduct his defence *kata noun*; and cp. *Timaeus* 72a6–b5 on the need for a *prophêtês* to interpret any *manteia*.)

When experience leads us astray, a dilemma can certainly emerge. This dilemma is a genuine one, but the problem it poses is not (just) theoretical but practical – about whether to follow the experience or the reasoning that suggests that the experience is misleading – and it would be better called Abraham's dilemma than Euthyphro's.

Anyway, in our enthusiasm to register the truth that experience can lead us astray, we should not miss the equal truth that reasoning can lead us astray too – as William James points out in a different context:

> Personal religion will prove itself more fundamental than theology or ecclesiasticism. Churches, when once established, live second-hand upon tradition; but the *founders* of every church owed their power originally to the fact of their direct personal communion with the divine. Not only the superhuman founders, the Christ, the Buddha, Mahomet, but all the originators of Christian sects have been in this case [as too, we can now add, was Socrates]; – so personal religion should still seem to be the primordial thing, even to those who esteem it incomplete.[32]

No doubt, experience without rationality is (that word again) blind. However, it is equally true that rationality without experience – rationality bereft of the kinds of roots in a foundation of experience that Socrates' Dream describes – is empty. What Plato at his best (such as in the *Phaedrus*) points us towards is not merely the slightly condescending moral that revelation or inspiration or divine command has its part to play, given our unavoidable cognitive deficiencies, in getting us towards truths which are, however, *best* grasped by systematic reasoning; rather, the moral is *experience first*, for it is only once you *have* experienced that you can have anything worth systematizing.

How far such systematizing should go, and how much it can in fact add to the cogency of the original vision (whether religious, artistic, intellectual or ethical), is a question for another occasion. My own growing conviction is that most contemporary philosophers, in their understanding of religion, of ethics and indeed of Plato, tend to try and persuade each other and us of the cogency of a

---

[32]   James, *The Varieties of Religious Experience*, www.psychwww.com/psyrelig/james/james4.htm#65, accessed 31 July 2011.

theory or a generalization when what is really cogent – what really persuaded them – is not the theory or the generalization at all but the particular experience from which the theory is an extrapolation, the generalization an *over*-generalization. They tend, in short, to overrate the value of system and to underrate or even ignore the value of epiphany.

To seek our Divinity meerly in Books and Writings, is to *seek the living among the dead*; we do but in vain seek God many times in these, where his Truth too is not so much enshrined, as entomb'd: no; *intra te quaere Deum*, seek for God within thine own soul; he is best discerned... as *Plotinus* phraseth it [*Enneads* 5.3.17], by an *Intellectual touch of him*... the soul itself hath its sense as well as the Body.[33] [34]

————————

[33]   John Smith, *Discourses,* Cambridge 1660, quoted from Hedley, p. 93; cf. Charles Taliaferro and Alison J. Teply (eds), *Cambridge Platonist Spirituality* (Mahwah, NJ: Paulist Press, 2004), p. 158.

[34]   Thanks for comments to Robert Audi, Chris Belshaw, Sarah Broadie, Peter Cave, Nicholas Denyer, John Gingell, Jakub Jirsa, Derek Matravers, Michael Morris, Mark McPherran, Jon Pike, David Sedley, Malcolm Schofield, Nigel Warburton, Robert Wardy, James Warren, and other members of audiences at the B Club in Cambridge, at the Open University Summer School in Bath, August 2009, and at the British Society for Philosophy of Religion in Oxford, Sept 2009.

Chapter 4

Beyond Divine Command Theory:
Moral Realism in the Hebrew Bible

Jaco Gericke

חָלִלָה לְּךָ מֵעֲשֹׂת כַּדָּבָר הַזֶּה לְהָמִית צַדִּיק עִם-רָשָׁע וְהָיָה כַצַּדִּיק כָּרָשָׁע
חָלִלָה לָּךְ הֲשֹׁפֵט כָּל-הָאָרֶץ לֹא יַעֲשֶׂה מִשְׁפָּט

Genesis 18:25

Introduction

The term 'morality' does not appear in the Hebrew Bible (HB). Of course, that does not mean that the concept of morality is missing altogether. Yet, if by the term we understand the coherent and critical philosophical reflection on the nature of right and wrong behaviour, then the HB, with its non-philosophical format, literary variety, historical variability, sociocultural complexity and theological pluralism, can be immensely problematic for any attempt to provide a unified 'biblical' philosophical perspective on the relation between religion and morality. Not surprisingly, in Biblical Ethics, questions of analytical or meta-ethics tend to be bracketed.[1] In fact, Biblical Theology as such tends to be characterized by a pernicious anti-philosophical sentiment, which in turn explains the current lamentable absence of an independent and officially recognized philosophical approach to the study of ancient Israelite religion.[2] Consequently, contemporary biblical scholarship offers little in the way of an indepth descriptive philosophical analysis of the moral assumptions underlying the religious beliefs, concepts and practices encountered in the HB.

---

[1]   John Barton, *Understanding Old Testament Ethics* (Westminster: John Knox Press, 2003), p. 45.

[2]   Rolf P. Knierim, *The Task of Old Testament Theology* (Grand Rapids: Eerdmans, 1995), p. 402; James Barr, *Biblical Theology: An Old Testament Perspective* (Philadelphia: Fortress Press, 1999), pp. 146–71; Jaco Gericke. 'The Quest for a Philosophical Yhwh (Part 3) – Towards a Philosophy of Old Testament Religion', *Old Testament Essays* 20(3) (2007), 669–88.

A Popular Consensus

Despite the fact that no-one has ever written a meta-ethics of ancient Israelite religion, there seems to exist a popular consensus involving the belief that the HB by default presents us with a historical precursor to what nowadays is known in moral philosophy and the philosophy of religion as 'Divine Command Theory' (DCT).[3] Not that biblical scholars classify the divinity–morality relation in the text with the concept of DCT, it is just that, in their theological claims, they seem to imply that in ancient Israelite religion the divine will was assumed to be the ultimate foundation of morality, i.e. that human actions were considered morally good if and only if Yhwh willed or commanded them.[4] As such, one typically encounters prominent biblical theologians over the past 50 years insinuating that Yhwh is the cause and source of the moral order, as seen in the following statements:

> The power of the good rests entirely on the recognition of God as the one who is good. Of moral behaviour for the sake of an abstract good there is none.[5]

> The ancient people, like many today, would not be prone to distinguish sharply between morality and religion. What is morally right to do is so because God wills it or because it is consistent with the divinely ordained structure of the world.[6]

---

[3]   William B. Alston, 'Some Suggestions for Divine Command Theorists', in Norman Beaty (ed.), *Christian Theism and the Problems of Philosophy* (Notre Dame, IN: University of Notre Dame Press, 1990), pp. 303–26; Robert Audi and William J. Wainwright, *Rationality, Religious Belief, and Moral Commitment* (Ithaca, NY: Cornell University Press, 1986); Paul Copan, 'Morality and Meaning Without God: Another Failed Attempt', *Philosophia Christi* Series 2(6) (2003), 295–304; Wes Morriston, 'Must There Be a Standard of Moral Goodness Apart from God?', *Philosophia Christi Series* 2(3) (2001), 127–38; Richard Mouw, 'The Status of God's Moral Judgment', *Canadian Journal of Theology* 16 (1970), 61–6; Richard Mouw, *The God Who Commands* (Notre Dame, IN: University of Notre Dame Press, 1990); Mark Murphy, 'Divine Command, Divine Will, and Moral Obligation', *Faith and Philosophy* 15 (1980), 3–27; Philip Quinn, 'Divine Command Ethics: A Causal Theory', in Janine Idziak (ed.), *Divine Command Morality: Historical and Contemporary Readings* (New York: Edwin Mellen Press, 1979), pp. 305–25; *Divine Commands and Moral Requirements* (Oxford: Clarendon, 1987); Eric Wierenga, 'A Defensible Divine Command Theory', *Nous* 17 (2003), 387–407; and Linda Zagzebski, *Divine Motivation Theory* (New York: Cambridge University Press, 2004).

[4]   Eckhart Otto, *Theologische Ethik des Alten Testaments* (Theologische Wissenschaft 3/2. Stuttgart: Kohlhammer, 1994), p. 94; Rolf Knierim *The Task of Old Testament Theology* (Grand Rapids: Eerdmans, 1995), p. 421.

[5]   Walter Eichrodt, *Theology of the Old Testament*, vol. 2 (Philadelphia: Westminster Press, 1967), p. 316.

[6]   Douglas Knight, 'Old Testament Ethics', *Christian Century* 100 (20 January 1982), 55; http://www.religion-online.org/showarticle.asp?title=1276, accessed 31 July 2011.

Also, the Old Testament is not familiar with the concept of doing good for the sake of the good; rather it is Yhwh's will that lays claim to human lives. Fixed orders are established by Yhwh.[7]

To say that ethical obligation is obedience to the will of the national God is to say that it is not the observation of ... universal human norms.[8]

Interestingly, many philosophers of religion (both theistic and atheistic) have uncritically followed suit and take it for granted that the historical precursor to Judeo-Christian versions of DCT is the HB itself.[9] Many introductory discussions on DCT assume as much and even offer as an illustration references to texts in the HB in which moral norms are apparently acquired solely via divine commands, for example, the giving of the Ten Commandments. Strong arguments for the presence of DCT in the text include the giving of seemingly non-necessary commands (as to Adam and Eve or the rituals of Leviticus) and even seemingly immoral commands (for example, the commanding of Abraham to sacrifice Isaac, that the Israelites plunder the Egyptians, the slaughtering of the Canaanites, Hosea being told to marry a prostitute, etc.). In philosophical terms this would mean that the HB took for granted a subjectivist yet universalist form of cognitivism to be contrasted with other forms of ethical subjectivism (for example, ideal observer theory, moral relativism and individualist ethical subjectivism), moral realism (which claims that moral propositions refer to objective facts independent of anyone's attitudes or opinions), error theory (which denies that any moral propositions are true in any sense) and non-cognitivism (which denies that moral sentences express propositions at all).

That the HB often associates the right actions with what finds favour in the eyes of Yhwh cannot reasonably be denied. However, there is more than one way of interpreting the divinity–morality relation even given DCT (hence strong and weak versions of the theory).[10] This is also readily apparent from any attempt to answer Socrates' question to Euthyphro in Plato's dialogue,[11] which was subsequently adapted to become what is now called the 'Euthyphro dilemma' (ED). In the context of the HB, it involves the following riddle:

---

[7] Horst-Dietrich Preuss, *Theology of the Old Testament*, vol. 2 (Stuttgart: Kohlhammer, 1992), p. 291.

[8] Barton, *Understanding Old Testament Ethics*, p. 46.

[9] John Hare, 'Religion and Morality', in Edward N. Zalta (ed.), *Stanford Encyclopedia of Philosophy* (Winter 2010 edition), forthcoming, http://plato.stanford.edu/archives/win2010/entries/religion-morality, accessed 31 July 2011.

[10] Wierenga, 'A Defensible Divine Command Theory', 387–407.

[11] Plato, *Five Dialogues: Euthyphro, Apology, Crito, Meno, Phaedo*, trans. G.M.A. Grube (Indianapolis, IN: Hackett, 1981).

> Did Yhwh command something because it is moral, or was something moral
> because it was commanded by Yhwh?

Due to problems connected to both possible responses to this question when
stated in the context of DCT (for example, moral relativism vs. redundant divine
revelation), much has been written in an attempt to respond to the dilemma
within the context of both fundamentalist approaches, which interpret biblical
texts factually insofar as they possibly can,[12] and critical Christian philosophy of
religion.[13]

Curiously, however, there is little corresponding concern in Biblical Ethics – to
my knowledge no biblical scholar has tried to establish what a given text in the
HB might imply in response to ED. Consequently, I would like us to consider two
questions:

1. Is DCT the only or default metaethical perspective on the relation between
   divinity and morality in the HB?
2. Do some texts in the HB offer us any hints as to which (if any) of the two
   possible options presented by the ED they imply to be correct?

With these questions in mind, I wish to challenge the popular consensus by
suggesting that the classification of the HB's meta-ethics as *in toto* a form of
DCT is anachronistic and a hasty generalization. I furthermore suspect that the
errant reading resulted from *prima facie* assessments informed by post-biblical
philosophical-theological reinterpretations of the essentially alien historical
metatheistic assumptions of ancient Israelite religion. Moreover, it is possible to
show that many texts in the HB presuppose moral goodness as not in fact something
identical to the property of being contrary to the divine will. Instead, in these texts
both the deity and the divine commands were non-tautologically predicated as
'good' just in case they instantiated goodness as an accidental property ultimately
assumed to be located in an independent and stable transworld moral order.

---

[12]   In order to maintain that the Bible is without error, the fundamentalist interpreter
moves to and fro between literal and non-literal, and factual and non-factual interpretations:
James Barr, *Fundamentalism* (London: SCM, 1977); Harriet A. Harris, *Fundamentalism
and Evangelicals* (Oxford: Clarendon, 1998; 2008). Philosophers of religion who proceed
with factual-where-possible interpretations of scripture include Eleonore Stump, Alvin
Planinga and William Lane Craig, and Richard Swinburne.

[13]   John Frame, *Euthyphro, Hume, and the Biblical God*, http://www.frame-poythress.
org/frame_articles/1993Euthyphro.htm, accessed 31 July 2011; William J. Wainwright,
Religion and Morality (Burlington: Ashgate, 2005).

Arguments for Moral Realism

Given the limitations of time and space in this chapter, I shall be offering only one or two illustrations from the biblical text per argument. The quotations from the HB are not intended as proof-texts used to substantiate that moral realism is the only biblical perspective on the deity–morality relation. Nor am I trying to argue that moral realism has biblical roots and is therefore philosophically credible. Conversely, I am not trying to prove that the basic idea of DCT is absent from the HB altogether or even that it is philosophically outdated. Rather, my aim is purely descriptive and historical, and I make a selective and cursive appeal to particular texts only to verify the presence of moral realist motifs in the biblical discourse in a way suggestive of the possibility that the same motifs might well be more pervasively attested than popular *prima facie* correlations to DCT would seem to imply.

The Argument from the Non-tautological Predication of Goodness

A useful point of departure would be to ask whether there are any examples in the HB of the non-tautological predication of goodness as an extrinsic property of Yhwh based on an alleged synthetic *a posteriori* religious epistemology. If so, it follows that moral goodness was indeed assumed to be something independent from the deity and with reference to which Yhwh could be called 'good' (or not). In this regard cognizance should be taken of the fact that we do indeed encounter such predication, for example, in Psalm 34:9:

> טַעֲמוּ וּרְאוּ כִּי-טוֹב יְהוָה   Taste and see that Yhwh is good;
> אַשְׁרֵי הַגֶּבֶר יֶחֱסֶה-בּוֹ   Happy is the man who takes refuge in him.

The above text assumes that the implied reader already has an idea of what goodness is quite apart from Yhwh and with reference to which it could be determined whether the deity is in fact good or not. This means that the knowledge that Yhwh is good was not assumed to be the result of analytical *a priori* reasoning. To state as the psalmist does that Yhwh is good (and to presuppose that the claim is in theory open to falsification) would not even have been considered meaningful were the goodness of Yhwh believed to be a logically necessary property of absolute divinity. In other words, if Yhwh was assumed to be good by definition – if goodness was assumed to be in the logical constitution of the concept of deity – the stating of the proposition that Yhwh is good is as superfluous as confessing that water (in non-solid states) is wet.

The Argument from Generic Atheodicy by Appeals to the Moral Order

The second argument for moral realism concerns textual examples of instances where God and the gods are charged with moral wrongdoing within a case made by appealing to an objective moral order vis-à-vis deity. For we should remember that, contrary to philosophical theology, the use of the terms for deity in their generic sense with reference also to Yhwh presupposes Yhwh to be part of a genus or natural kind. Crude as it may sound, the extension of the generic concept of godhood did in fact frequently include more than Yhwh alone. Philosophical monotheism is not presupposed in the texts and divinity is predicated in a variety of senses also to the gods of other nations (Judges 11:24), a second generation of divine beings (Genesis 6:1–4); members of the divine council (Psalm 82:1, 6); the king (Psalm 45:7), household spirits (Exodus 20:11), spirits of the dead (1 Samuel 28:13) and demons (Deuteronomy 32:8). When we consider the relation between divinity and morality in the HB, we should take account of the fact that the nature of divinity was often assumed to be instantiated in, but not only in, the nature of Yhwh. Of course, many Bible translations are seriously ideological in agenda, in that they render the generic term for divinity with a capital G when used of Yhwh, even when it is clearly not a proper name (the god of Israel). Translations also substitute the generic term when applied to praeternatural or human entities with euphemisms, such as 'judges', 'angels', 'mighty ones' or 'heavenly beings'. This obscures the divinity–morality relation, for example, in Psalm 58:2:

הַאֻמְנָם אֵלֶם צֶדֶק תְּדַבֵּרוּן	Do you gods really speak just?
מֵישָׁרִים תִּשְׁפְּטוּ בְּנֵי אָדָם	With uprightness judge humans?

Many translations here have 'judges' of 'rulers', yet in this text (as in many others in the HB) the existence of divine beings other than Yhwh is taken for granted. It is also taken for granted that the gods are not by definition moral, which in turn presupposes the existence of a moral order vis-à-vis divinity and with reference to which divine acts could be judged. The gods may be able to do what they like because they have the power to do so, but that still does not mean that whatever they do is by definition good. Might was not assumed to make right and the appeal to the moral order in the charges against the gods suggests a form of moral realism where right and wrong are what they are, irrespective of divine whim. A similar scenario is found in Psalm 82:

אֱלֹהִים נִצָּב בַּעֲדַת-אֵל	God stands in the divine assembly;
בְּקֶרֶב אֱלֹהִים יִשְׁפֹּט	in the midst of the gods he judges:
עַד-מָתַי תִּשְׁפְּטוּ-עָוֶל	How long will you judge unjustly,
וּפְנֵי רְשָׁעִים תִּשְׂאוּ	and lift the faces of the wicked?

Again, many translations try to evade the 'theodiversity' of the 'divine condition' implicit by rendering 'gods' with a host of more 'orthodox' substitutes. The

Hebrew, however, is clear, for it presupposes the entities to be immortal prior to the divine judgment (Psalm 82:6). Moreover, that gods could be caught behaving badly suggests moral realism. And lest someone objects by pointing out that in neither of the above instances is Yhwh himself being accused of doing wrong, the fact is that there are such texts, for example, Psalms 44 and 89, in which the psalmists blatantly accuse the god of Israel of betraying the covenant. In both Psalms 44 and 89, Yhwh is at the receiving end of the critique, again presupposing the justification of the charges as coming from the appeal to what is given in the moral order. So it would seem that there are texts in the HB where even divinity could be judged with reference to a supposedly universal moral norm.

The Argument from Divine Mutability

The third argument for moral realism takes its cue from the second, taking seriously the meta-ethical presuppositions underlying the HB's mythological motif of divinity as 'judge'. Consider the role of a judge vis-à-vis the law – a judge does not make the law, nor does a judge determine good or bad absolutely, nor can morality be defined with reference to the person of the judge. Rather, a judge acknowledges the law as it exists independent of him or her, without him or her being above the law. This was also often considered to be the case with the divine judge in the HB. A classic example comes from Genesis 18:25, where Abraham appeals to the moral order to prevent Yhwh from what is understood to be an act of immoral retribution:

חָלִלָה לְּךָ	Far be it from you
מֵעֲשֹׂת כַּדָּבָר הַזֶּה	To act in this way
לְהָמִית צַדִּיק עִם-רָשָׁע	to slay the righteous with the wicked,
וְהָיָה כַצַּדִּיק כָּרָשָׁע;	so that the righteous should be as the wicked;
חָלִלָה לָּךְ—	Far be it from you
הֲשֹׁפֵט כָּל-הָאָרֶץ לֹא יַעֲשֶׂה מִשְׁפָּט.	Shall not the Judge of all the earth do justly?

Presupposing DCT, how could Abraham make a case? Can DCT explain why the divine judge can be 'morally' taken to task through disobedience? Why did Abraham not modify his view of what is just? Surely it is because the text assumes that justice is a good thing and that its goodness is determined by the moral order independent of Yhwh. A similar scenario of corrective chutzpah is shown between Yhwh and Moses deliberating on an appropriate punishment for the 'Golden Calf' incident. First, there is the divine command in Exodus 33:10:

וְעַתָּה הַנִּיחָה לִי	Now leave me alone,
וְיִחַר-אַפִּי בָהֶם וַאֲכַלֵּם;	So that my anger may burn against them and consume them
וְאֶעֱשֶׂה אוֹתְךָ לְגוֹי גָּדוֹל	And I will make of you a great nation.

Now, on DCT the 'moral' thing to do would have been for Moses to drop it. However, Moses, like Abraham, frustrates the divine will and convinces Yhwh *qua* divine judge what the moral (and shrewd) thing to do actually is. Thus we read in Exodus 33:11:

וַיְחַל מֹשֶׁה אֶת-פְּנֵי יְהוָה אֱלֹהָיו	And Moses calmed the face of Yhwh his god and said:
וַיֹּאמֶר לָמָה יְהוָה יֶחֱרֶה אַפְּךָ בְּעַמֶּךָ	Yhwh, why does your anger burn against your people
אֲשֶׁר הוֹצֵאתָ מֵאֶרֶץ מִצְרַיִם	who you took out of the land of Egypt
בְּכֹחַ גָּדוֹל וּבְיָד חֲזָקָה	with great power and a strong hand?

After reminding Yhwh how his reputation would suffer in the face of the foreign peoples had he now wasted the Israelites and broken the promise to Abraham, Moses' disobedience to the divine command to be left alone has the following result (Exodus 33:14):

וַיִּנָּחֶם יְהוָה עַל-הָרָעָה	And Yhwh repented of the evil
אֲשֶׁר דִּבֶּר לַעֲשׂוֹת לְעַמּוֹ	which he said he would do to his people.

A scenario like this may be crude to the modern philosophical theologian and indeed apologists since the times of the HB itself have sought to reinterpret the idea of Yhwh changing his mind. My concern here is not divine immutability or its opposite, but rather the implication of the text that disobedience to the divine command can be a good thing for both the deity and humans in the vicinity. On DCT, Moses acted immorally. However, if we presuppose that the meta-ethical assumptions of this text operated with a version of moral realism and a belief in a moral order independent of the deity, then the allowance for disobedience and debate with an implicit appeal to what is the right thing makes perfect sense. Another good example of similar pious 'backchatting' with fortuitous consequences can be found in Amos 7:1–3.

The Argument from Goodness as a Stable Accidental Transworld Property

A fourth argument for moral realism concerns the stable actual worlds-in-the-text identity of the extension of the concept of goodness. Consider the moral status of the virtues vis-à-vis the deity as mentioned in Psalm 15:1–3, where we read:

יְהוָה מִי יָגוּר בְּאָהֳלֶךָ	Yhwh, who shall dwell in your tent?
מִי יִשְׁכֹּן בְּהַר קָדְשֶׁךָ	Who shall live in your holy mountain?
הוֹלֵךְ תָּמִים וּפֹעֵל צֶדֶק	He that walks uprightly, and does
וְדֹבֵר אֱמֶת בִּלְבָבוֹ	righteousness, and speaks truth in his heart;
לֹא רָגַל עַל לְשֹׁנוֹ	He does not slander with his tongue
לֹא עָשָׂה לְרֵעֵהוּ רָעָה	He does not do evil to his friend
וְחֶרְפָּה לֹא נָשָׂא עַל קְרֹבוֹ	And he does not heap insults on his neighbour

In this text it seems that Yhwh was assumed to command these acts because they are moral and because Yhwh was assumed to be a moral god. To be sure, the psalm first intends to demonstrate Yhwh's moral requirements, but it does not seem to imply that had Yhwh willed the opposite, the divine will could change the moral status of the particular acts. Rather, what would change is the view of the deity as (only) moral, as we saw the case to be in Psalms 44 and 89. Aside from Psalm 15 (cf. Psalm 24), the stableness of the moral order vis-à-vis the possible vicissitudes of accidental divine moral properties are clearly assumed in the text, which reads:

הֲשָׁכַח חַנּוֹת אֵל	Has God forgotten to be gracious?
אִם-קָפַץ בְּאַף רַחֲמָיו	Did he shut up in anger his compassions?'
וָאֹמַר חַלּוֹתִי הִיא	And I say, 'This is my illness,
שְׁנוֹת יְמִין עֶלְיוֹן	The changing of the right had of the most high.'

In this text the imaginary scenario of God ceasing to be 'good' is assumed to occur in at least one possible world, such as in Psalm 77:9–10. Yet, across all possible worlds, compassion and mercy are considered to be virtues. Thus, the entire psalm presupposes and depends on the idea of an objective moral order in relation to which Yhwh appears to have changed and with reference to which his nature may be described. It also assumes that 'maximal greatness' does not exclude the possibility of evil as a great-making property, which it was in ancient Near Eastern conceptions of deity with worshippers not imagining a god had to be only good to be worthy of worship. What made a god was power (hardly omnipotence though) and not simply congeniality and user-friendliness. Without this assumption, there would be no reason for the consternation the psalmist believed himself to be in (see also Psalm 44).[14]

The Argument from 'Bad' Divine Commands

In non-fundamentalist biblical theology it is taken for granted that some texts in the HB did not assume Yhwh to be perfect in goodness, in that he was at times held responsible for the actualization of not only natural but also moral evil.[15] In the context of ancient Israelite religion, both philosophical theology's 'perfect-being theology' and the problem of evil in its classical formulation are anachronistic, as the HB often assumed good and evil to be complementary rather than incompatible properties of the divine nature (see Isaiah 45:7). In this regard, particularly relevant

---

[14]   James Crenshaw, The Divine Helmsman: Studies on God's Control of Human Events (New York: KTAV Publishing House Inc, 1980); Theodicy in the Old Testament (IRT4. Philadelphia: Fortress Press, 1983); A Whirlpool of Torment: Israelite Traditions of God as an Oppressive Presence (Minneapolis, MN: Fortress Press, 1984).

[15]   Jaco Gericke, 'Beyond Reconciliation – Monistic Yahwism and the Problem of Evil in Philosophy of Religion', *Verbum et Ecclesiae* 26(1) (2005), 64–92.

to our discussion are those texts depicting Yhwh as issuing 'bad' commands. On the one hand, this sometimes involved Yhwh's commands to spiritual entities to commit immoral acts, for example, in texts like Job 1–2 and 1 Kings 22:19–22. On the other hand, on occasion it also involved the divine commands to humans being considered as immoral, for example, in Ezekiel 20:25:

וְגַם-אֲנִי נָתַתִּי לָהֶם חֻקִּים לֹא טוֹבִים	Wherefore I gave them also statutes that were not
וּמִשְׁפָּטִים לֹא יִחְיוּ בָּהֶם	good, and ordinances whereby they should not live;

To be sure, in the context of Ezekiel 20, these 'bad' divine commandments are previously said to have been issued because of sin (Ezekiel 20:24). However, the very possibility of divine commands being not good (irrespective of the motive for issuing them) certainly complicates DCT's equation of the good with whatever the deity commands. Even if Yhwh's act is assumed to be fair and just, this changes nothing about the fact that the divine command itself could not be looked to in order to determine what is moral. So, whatever we think about the nature of the deity himself implicit in Ezekiel 20:25, the divine commands themselves were not assumed to instantiate the property of goodness just in case they were issued by Yhwh. The good was therefore assumed to exist vis-à-vis the commands with reference to which they themselves could be judged as being either good or not.

The Argument from Relative Mediatory Functionality in Moral Epistemology

The final argument pertains to the way in which the concept of goodness is predicated of the divine commands themselves. Good illustrations in this regard come from the so-called 'Torah Psalms', especially Psalms 19 and 119. In Psalm 19:9 we read:

פִּקּוּדֵי יְהוָה יְשָׁרִים מְשַׂמְּחֵי-לֵב	The precepts of Yhwh are right, rejoicing the heart;
מִצְוַת יְהוָה בָּרָה מְאִירַת עֵינָיִם	the commandment of Yhwh is pure, lighting the eyes.

On what grounds and with what criteria are the above claims made? Do they not presuppose that the concept of what is right and pure is already possessed and that the nature of the divine law fulfils all the necessary conditions for its application? If the divine ordinances determined what is right and pure, how does it make sense to add the superfluous detail predicating these qualities of the commands themselves? Surely there must have been sufficient reason to assess the commands as such, other than this again being an allegedly tautological predication?

The same trend continues in Psalm 119 where the divine commands are in the centre of the psalmist's meditations. The ascription of the property of good to the commands and laws of Yhwh also presupposes that these were judged to be good with reference to the moral order itself and not because it went without saying (Psalm 119:39):

הַעֲבֵר חֶרְפָּתִי אֲשֶׁר יָגֹרְתִּי   Turn away my reproach which I dread;
כִּי מִשְׁפָּטֶיךָ טוֹבִים   for your ordinances are good.

How could the psalmist need to imply that the reproaches are not good if whatever the deity did was good by definition? Why did he have to state that the divine ordinances instantiate the property of goodness if it was an essential and necessary property, and goodness was in the logical constitution of the concept of divine commands? To be sure, morality in the Psalms is often equated with and discerned with reference to the divine commands. Yet we often find the foundations for the good being deferred:

1. The divine commands are good because they reveal the divine will.
2. The divine will is good because it reveals the divine nature.
3. The divine nature is good because x.

On DCT assumptions, the buck stops here and there is no sufficient reason as to why the divine nature is to be called good: it is good by definition, whatever it may happen to be in all possible worlds. However, on a moral realist sequence, the equation of the good with the divine commands looks a little different and x is the moral order itself. Not surprisingly, a closer inspection of the biblical data reveals the following subtle distinctions to be presupposed in many texts:

4. The divine commands mediate (rather than create) moral norms.
5. The divine will corresponds to (rather than causes) what is good.
6. The divine nature instantiates (rather than defines) the property of goodness.

On this reading, it would mean that it is not the deity or the divine commands that ultimately create the moral order; rather, it is humans who, from their point of view, could determine what is good by referring to the divine commands, which were called good because they corresponded to the moral order.

Conclusion

Together, these arguments cumulatively demonstrate the presence of marked traces of moral-realist assumptions in the HB, showing that DCT was not the only meta-ethical trajectory operative in the history of ancient Israelite religion. The particular kind of moral realism involved had little in common even with a weak DCT in which the deity has a mediatory function, as should be readily apparent from the alien metatheistic assumptions in ancient Israelite religion on which its moral-realist meta-ethical assumptions are based. Yet, because DCT is anachronistic in the context of the HB, the upside is that the ED *qua* dilemma is also not as problematic as it might otherwise be. For while the HB often implies that Yhwh commanded something because it is good, the deity was not thereby made redundant, as is the case with DCT when this divinity–morality relation is chosen. The reason for this is that, unlike what is assumed in the ED, the ancient Israelites were not optimists in their religious epistemology. Even though the moral order was believed to have existed independently of the divine, the divine will – if the deity was of the moral type – was still believed to be humanity's only access to that order. The deity was thus assumed to function in relation to the moral order as an instructor, a mediator, a judge and an authority on right and wrong – not its creator. From this it follows that at least in the context of those texts in the HB where moral realism is presupposed, the ED indeed represents a false dilemma. This is not because goodness is an essential part of the divine nature, as Aquinas suggested, but because the underlying moral epistemology assumed that humans needed good gods to tell them what the good life is all about.

Chapter 5

Does Divine Simplicity Solve the Euthyphro Dilemma?

Anders Kraal

The main purpose of this chapter is to support the claim that the doctrine of divine simplicity – according to which God and God's intrinsic properties are identical – provides a logically possible solution to the Euthyphro dilemma. By a 'logically possible solution' I mean a solution that has not been shown to be false by means of the rules of standard logic.

I will argue for this claim in four steps. First, I will give a statement of the Euthyphro dilemma as presently understood. Secondly, I will explain how the doctrine of divine simplicity provides a logically possible solution to the Euthyphro dilemma. Thirdly, I will present some major objections to the doctrine of divine simplicity, raised by Alvin Plantinga, which, if sound, will invalidate the divine simplicity solution to the Euthyphro dilemma. In a fourth and final step I will argue that these objections are fallacious, at least insofar as the validity of an argument is understood in terms of the capacity to be expressed in and inferred within standard first-order logic, and hence that 'standard logic', if taken to mean 'standard first-order logic', allows the divine simplicity solution to the Euthyphro Dilemma as a logical possibility.

The Euthyphro Dilemma

The Euthyphro dilemma can be spelt out in various ways and can be posed from within different religious contexts. When the dilemma was originally posed by Socrates in Plato's *Euthyphro*, the religious context was that of Greek polytheism. There the question was:

- Is what is pious loved by the gods because it is pious or is it pious because it is loved?[1]

---

[1] Plato, 'Euthyphro', in *Plato: The Last Days of Socrates*, trans. H. Tredennick (New York: Penguin Books, 1980), p. 31 (9A–10B).

For a Christian, this is obviously not a pressing or even relevant question, since he or she will not believe that there are any such things as 'the gods' in the sense spoken of by Plato's Socrates; there is only the one true God.

However, the above question easily translates into a question also of interest to a Christian, which is as follows:

- Is what is pious loved by God because it is pious or is it pious because it is loved by God?

Replacing talk of piety with talk of goodness, we arrive at the more general question:

- Is what is good good because God wills it or does God will it because it is good?

For the Christian, or at any rate the Christian who adheres to classical Christian doctrine (which we may here take to comprise the intersection of the major Roman Catholic and Protestant creedal documents), this generalized question gives rise to an interesting dilemma – the Euthyphro dilemma. One way of fleshing out this dilemma is as follows: if what is good is good independently of whether God wills it, then what is good is good independently of God's essence inasmuch as God's will is included in or is identical to God's essence, and this seems incompatible with classical Christian doctrine. But if the good is good because God wills it, then the good is not intrinsically good but good only relative to God's will; this seems equally incompatible with classical Christian doctrine. In either case, then, we will end up with an answer that fits ill with classical Christian doctrine.

This dilemma gives rise to two immediate questions:

1. Why should it be thought incompatible with classical Christian doctrine to think that what is good is good independently of God's will?; and
2. Why should it be thought incompatible with classical Christian doctrine to think that what is good is not good intrinsically but only relative to God's will?

The answer to both of these questions is that in classical Christian doctrine, God and the good are held to be inseparable in a very deep sense. Thus, already in the New Testament we find Jesus being reported as teaching that 'There is only One who is good, that is, God' (οὐδεις αγαθός ει μη εις ὁ Θεός).[2] In line with this, traditional Roman Catholic dogmatics textbooks, such as Ludwig Ott's *The Fundamentals of Catholic Dogma*, assert that 'God is absolute ontological

---

[2]   Matthew 19:17 (my translation, following the *Textus Receptus*).

goodness'.[3] Protestant confessional documents affirm basically the same thing. The Lutheran *Large Catechism*, for example, asserts that '[God] is the only eternal good'[4] and the Reformed *Belgic Confession* says that God is '[t]he overflowing fountain of all good'.[5] Clearly, if God is goodness itself, the only eternal good or the fountain of all goodness, then it is wrong to say that what is good is good independently of God's will or essence, but it is also equally wrong to say that what is good is not intrinsically good but good only in a relative sense – hence the Euthyphro dilemma.

The Divine Simplicity Solution

One way of responding to the Euthyphro dilemma consists in appealing to the doctrine of divine simplicity. In modern times this response has been suggested by the philosophers Eleonore Stump and Norman Kretzmann, who in turn trace it back to Thomas Aquinas.[6]

The doctrine of divine simplicity says, in its classical Augustinian explication found in *The City of God*, that God's simplicity means that the being or substance of God and the attributes or intrinsic properties of God are identical.[7] In the classic Augustinian phrase: God is what he has (*quod habet, hoc est*). God is his goodness, his love, his power and so on.

If this doctrine is accepted, then the Euthyphro dilemma can be diagnosed as *a false dilemma*. It is a false dilemma because there is a further alternative: that the good is neither good independently of God's will, nor because God wills it, for God and goodness are identical.

This is the first step of the divine simplicity solution to the Euthyphro dilemma.

The second step consists in explaining how the goodness of various objects other than God can be accounted for, given that God and goodness are taken to be identical. Aquinas' account is as follows: objects other than God are good in the

---

[3]   Ludwig Ott, *The Fundamentals of Catholic Dogma*, trans. P. Lynch (Rockford, IL: TAN Books and Publishers, 1974), p. 34.

[4]   Martin Luther, 'Large Catechism', in F. Bente (ed. and trans.), *Triglot Concordia: The Symbolical Books of the Evangelical Lutheran Church: German-Latin-English* (St Louis, MO: Concordia Publishing House, 1921), http://bookofconcord.org/lc-3-ten commandments.php#para15, accessed 1 August 2011.

[5]   Guy de Brés, 'The Belgic Confession' in P. Schaff (ed. and trans.), *The Creeds of Christendom*, vol. 3 (New York: Harper & Brothers Publishers, 1877), p. 384.

[6]   See, e.g., Norman Kretzmann, 'Abraham, Isaac and Euthyphro', in Eleanore Stump (ed.), *Hamartia* (Toronto: Mellan, 1983), pp. 27–50; and Eleanore Stump, *Aquinas* (London and New York: Routledge, 2003), pp. 27–8.

[7]   See St Augustine, *The City of God*, trans. D. Wiesen (Cambridge, MA: Harvard University Press, 1968), pp. 462–70.

sense that God's goodness 'flows'[8] to them or, alternatively, that they 'participate in'[9] God's goodness. It might be thought that this account, contrary to Aquinas' intention, entails that objects other than God that have the property of being good are in fact somehow divine, such that, say, the creation's property of being good – according to the famous statement of Genesis 1:31, God's creation is 'very good' – is the same thing as God. This would seem to create problems for an adherent of classical Christian doctrine, who would typically want to uphold an ontological distinction between God and creation.

An alternative account, which fits better with the ontological distinction between God and creation, would be to say that objects other than God can be said to be good inasmuch as they 'reflect' God's goodness, just as the moon can be said to be bright inasmuch as it reflects the brightness of the sun. A consequence of this account will be that it is not strictly true that objects other than God have the property of being good, for what they have is rather a reflection of God's property of being good. Strictly speaking, nothing will be good save God, which, as we have seen, is what Jesus is reported as saying in Matthew 19:17.

If one concedes the above diagnosis of the Euthyphro dilemma as a false dilemma and also accepts the above account of what it means to say that objects other than God are good, one will in effect have arrived at a coherent solution – or rather *dis*solution – of the Euthyphro dilemma.

Plantinga's Objections

A major criticism to the doctrine of divine simplicity, and therewith to the divine simplicity solution to the Euthyphro dilemma, was raised by Alvin Plantinga.

In *Does God have a Nature?*, Plantinga launches two objections to the doctrine of divine simplicity. The objections have been widely discussed for almost three decades and it might well be that they are *the* most debated objections to a theological doctrine in modern philosophical theology.

The first objection is as follows:[10]

- If God is identical with each of his properties, then each of his properties is identical with each of his properties, so that God has but one property.

---

[8]   Aquinas, *Summa Theologica* (I, q13, a6), trans. the Fathers of the English Dominican Province (London: Sheed & Ward, 1948), http://dhspriory.org/thomas/summa/FP/FP013.html#FPQ13OUTP1, accessed 1 August 2011: 'perfections flow from God to creatures'.

[9]   Aquinas, *Summa Theologica* (I, q6, a4), http://dhspriory.org/thomas/summa/FP/FP006.html#FPQ6OUTP1, accessed 1 August 2011: 'all things are called good by way of participation [in God's goodness]'.

[10]   All of the objections can be found in Alvin Plantinga, *Does God Have a Nature?* (Milwaukee, WI: Marquette University Press, 1980), p. 47.

The second objection goes like this:

- If God is identical with each of his properties, then, since each of his properties is a property, he is a property – a self-exemplifying property.

That God has only one property, or that God is a property, is taken by Plantinga to be incompatible with classical Christian doctrine, according to which God, *qua* personal, cannot be a property.[11]

Plantinga claims that the inferential steps used in the above arguments accord with 'our usual styles of inference' or 'our usual modes of inference'.[12] What exactly does he mean by 'our usual modes of inference'? An answer to this is suggested towards the end of *Does God Have a Nature?*, where he explicitly takes logic in the sense of 'first-order logic with identity'.[13] Taking this into consideration, we could perhaps condense Plantinga's two foregoing objections into the following unified objection to the doctrine of divine simplicity:

- If God is identical to God's properties, then we can by means of first-order logic with identity argue our way to the conclusions that i) God has but one property, and that ii) God indeed is a property, both of which conclusions are incompatible with classical Christian doctrine.

In speaking of 'Plantinga's objection to divine simplicity' in the following discussion, I will be referring to the above-stated objection.

A Counter-objection

I will now proceed to argue that Plantinga's objection to divine simplicity is fallacious. This claim, if correct, will undermine the presently considered Plantingian objection to the divine simplicity solution to the Euthyphro dilemma.

The gist of my counter-objection consists of the following claim:

- Plantinga's arguments for the claim that divine simplicity entails that God has but one property or is a property cannot, contrary to what Plantinga assumes, be expressed or obtained by means of standard first-order logic, and so his objection to divine simplicity turns out to be fallacious.

My argument for this claim is as follows. Plantinga's arguments against divine simplicity involve the premise that God is identical to His properties. But standard first-order logic does not allow for the expression or formalization of any such

---

11   Ibid., p. 47.

12   Ibid., p. 58.

13   Ibid., p. 144.

premise, and so the conclusions of the arguments cannot be obtained by means of standard first-order logic.

That standard first-order logic does not allow for the expression or formalization of the premise that God is identical to His properties can be inferred from the fact that standard first-order logic does not allow for the identification of a property-bearer and its property.

To show that this is so, let us turn to a consideration of standard first-order logic with identity, i.e. 'FOL='. In FOL=, the identity relation obeys the four laws of reflexivity, symmetry, transitivity and Leibniz's law; in symbols:

$$\forall(x)(x=x)$$
$$\forall(x)\forall(y)((x=y) \rightarrow (y=x))$$
$$\forall(x)\forall(y)\forall(z)((x=y) \land (y=z) \rightarrow (x=z))$$
$$\forall(x)\forall(y)((x=y) \rightarrow (\Psi(x) \leftrightarrow \Psi(y)))$$

The variables in the above formulae range over individuals – their so-called 'values' – in a specified domain of discourse, and the 1-place predicates in the above formulae – '$\Psi(x)$', for example – express either properties (if they are interpreted intentionally) or determine sets (if they are interpreted extensionally). The values of the variables in the formulae will be bearers of properties or members of sets, depending on whether one takes an intentional or extensional approach to the interpretation of the 1-place predicates.

Now, in FOL=, it will not be possible to express or formalize an identity relation between a property-bearer and a property or between a set and its member, for '$\Psi=x$' is not a well-formed formula in FOL=. An identity relation can hold between whatever is the value of the variables x, y or z (if 'α' and 'β' denote the values of 'x' and 'y', for example, then '$\exists(x)(x=\alpha)$' and '$\alpha=\beta$' will be well-formed formulae), but not between these values and the properties expressible by 1-place predicates.

Since Plantinga's objection requires that the conclusions of his arguments against divine simplicity can be obtained by means of first-order logic and, as we have seen, the premises of these arguments cannot be expressed in standard first-order logic, it follows that Plantinga's objection is fallacious, at least if by 'first-order logic' we mean *standard* first-order logic.

A Quinean Way Out?

But *must* we understand 'first-order logic' in the above standard sense? Are there not any alternative systems of first-order logic with different identity theories that could be used to express or formalize the arguments appealed to in Plantinga's objection?

The most natural suggestion in this direction would probably be W.V.O. Quine's well-known identity theory for first-order logic found in his *Mathematical Logic* and *Set Theory and its Logic.*

An original idea in these two books is that singleton sets (i.e. sets consisting of just one member) are identifiable with their members. Let us call this idea the Singleton Set Assimilation Thesis. Given the Singleton Set Assimilation Thesis, the claim that God is identical to one of his properties, say divine goodness, could be formalized. We need then only take 'divine goodness' as determining a singleton set – for example, the set of objects satisfying the 1-place predicate 'x has divine goodness' (or 'x is Ψ'), i.e. ' $\{x \mid x$ is $\Psi\}$ ' – and then take 'God' (or 'α') to denote the sole member of that set, i.e. God. It would then follow in Quine's system that God's goodness and God are identical, i.e. that '$\alpha = \{x \mid x$ is $\Psi\}$ '.

Quine argues for the Singleton Set Assimilation Thesis from two assumptions. The first assumption consists of an interpretation of the membership relation '$\hat{I}$' of elementary set theory and the second assumption consists of a definition of the identity relation '='. According to the membership-relation assumption:

- 'x ∈ y' abbreviates 'x is a member of y or is the same as y according to whether y is or is not a class'.[14]

According to the identity-relation assumption:

- 'x = y' abbreviates '$(z)(z \in x \equiv z \in y)$'.[15]

The above two assumptions entail that with regard to any singleton set $\{x\}$, ' $\{x\} = x$' follows. This is because if x is an individual and y is $\{x\}$, then 'z $\hat{I}$ y' will be true if and only if z is the individual x, and 'z $\hat{I}$ x' will be true if and only if z is the individual x; thus, by transitivity, x will be identical to y.[16]

What are we to make of this? My view is that in assuming that an identity between $\{x\}$ and x entails an 'assimilation' of $\{x\}$ to x, Quine goes wrong. My reason for thinking this is as follows. If x and y are identical, then there can be no sense in talk of x being assimilated to y, for x and y are the very same thing. For x to be assimilated to y, x and y must be different things; that is, they must be non-identical.

The above point can be made clearer by noting that assimilation is an *asymmetrical* relation: x can be assimilated to y without y being assimilated to x. The identity relation, however, is *symmetrical*, as Quine also concedes,[17] so the

---

[14]   W.V.O. Quine, *Mathematical Logic* (Cambridge, MA: Harvard University Press, 1951), p. 122.

[15]   Quine, *Mathematical Logic*, p. 134.

[16]   Quine, *Mathematical Logic*, p. 135. for a similar explanation, see §4 of *Set Theory and Its Logic* (Cambridge, MA: Belknap Press, 1963).

[17]   Quine, *Mathematical Logic*, pp. 137–8

relation of assimilation is not entailed by or equivalent to the identity relation; they are different things.

If what I have just said is correct, then to think that Quine's above-cited membership and identity assumptions allow us to identify God and God's properties is wrong. What Quine must say given these assumptions is that singleton sets are *both* sets and individuals. And this result is indeed, as Quine himself concedes, '*prima facie* unacceptable'.[18] This is because sets are sets and individuals are individuals; things are not both. However, Quine views this problem as 'harmless', for:

> ... none of the *utility* of class theory is impaired by counting an individual, its unit class, the unit class of that unit class, and so on, as one thing.[19]

From a practical point of view, the problem might indeed be harmless, but it seems nevertheless to be mistaken.

I do not want to deny that pragmatic concerns have a role to play in logical theory; certainly they do. But to appeal to pragmatic concerns in order to paper over an obvious contradiction is another thing. Accordingly, the Singleton Set Assimilation Thesis is, in my view, flawed.

My conclusion, then, is that Quine's alternative theory of identify for first-order logic does not provide us with a means for overcoming my above-presented counter-objection to Plantinga's objection against divine simplicity.

What About Some Other Formal Logic?

I have argued above that first-order logic – taken either as standard FOL= or as Quinean first-order logic with the Singleton Set Assimilation Thesis – does not provide us with a way of expressing or formalizing the arguments appealed to in Plantinga's objection to divine simplicity. Suppose we grant this. Could we not then simply say that Plantinga just over-estimated the expressive resources of *first-order* logic, and conjecture that his arguments could be successfully run through some alternative system of formal logic?

Perhaps this would be the best course for Plantinga to take. However, the sort of alternative formal logic that is needed must meet two criteria. First, it must allow for the expression or formalization of an identity relation between properties and property-bearers or sets and members of those sets. Secondly, it must be possible to show, within this alternative system of formal logic, that the conclusions of the arguments appealed to in Plantinga's objection to divine simplicity do indeed follow in this alternative system. If a formal logic that meets these criteria can

---

[18]   Quine, *Set Theory and Its Logic*, p. 31.

[19]   Quine, *Set Theory and Its Logic*, p. 31 (my emphasis).

be developed, then we will have reason to believe that Plantinga's objections are successful, but if not, then not.

In my book *First-Order Logic and Classical Theism: Toward Logical Reorientation*,[20] I develop a non-standard system of formal logic – called 'CT-Logic', since its aim is to be useful for the analysis of *c*lassical *t*heistic doctrines about the nature and intrinsic properties of God – that fulfils the first above-mentioned criterion, but not the second one. Whether there is some other non-standard formal logic that fulfils *both* of the above criteria remains to be seen. But until such a formal logic is developed, it cannot be said that Plantinga's objection appeals to arguments that are formally valid within some existing system of formal logic.

Conclusion

Pending the development of an alternative formal logic of the above-envisioned sort, I take it to be reasonable to think that the doctrine of divine simplicity cannot properly be taken to be undermined by Plantinga's objection to it. If this is right, then one of the main objections to the divine simplicity solution to the Euthyphro dilemma in the contemporary philosophical literature will be overcome. Accordingly, the divine simplicity solution to the Euthyphro dilemma remains a live option.

---

[20]   Kraal, *First-Order Logic and Classical Theism: Toward Logical Reorientation* (Uppsala: Universitetstryckeriet, 2010); see esp. §10.4. For CT-Logic's underlying rationale, see Kraal, 'Logic and Divine Simplicity', *Philosophy Compass* 6/4, 282–94.

Evolution and the
Grounds of Morality

Chapter 6
Piety, Purity and the Sacred

Roger Scruton

I want to consider some concepts and conceptions which have been important in mediating between the belief in God and the exercise of moral judgment. The concepts I have in mind are those of piety and impiety, the sacred and the sacrilegious, the pure and the impure. And the associated conceptions are those of obedience, right feeling and purity of heart – conceptions which belong to the God-fearing life, as our ancestors would have described it. These concepts and conceptions constitute the primary input of religion into the moral life of human beings. Moreover, they establish firm contours in the moral landscape. Without them, and without the experiences and beliefs that they designate, we are apt to err and stray like lost sheep, as the Prayer Book puts it. However, if these concepts and conceptions are ignored today, it is not only because they suggest an underpinning of religious belief but it is also for ideological reasons. This is because they present obstacles to the propagation of orthodoxies that are rooted in the academic way of life.

As such, the ideas I shall be discussing do not receive much attention in the literature of moral and political philosophy. They have little or nothing to do with equality, justice or rights; they touch on the theory of the virtues, but only in ways that are apt to raise eyebrows among its usual proponents; and they speak of regions of the human psyche which, to the academic philosopher, seem to belong more to pre-history than to the modern world. True, anthropologists make use of these conceptions in describing the behaviour and belief systems of the people they study, but they use them to describe the minds of the people observed, without suggesting that they correspond to any beliefs in the minds of their observers.

There is a kind of moral philosophy, widely taught in the academy today, which represents morality as a system of interpersonal coordination among people with potentially competing 'conceptions of the good'. This system safeguards the individual from harm by inculcating virtuous habits in his or her neighbours – habits of respect and benevolence which guarantee the general safety. Fashionable political philosophy begins from a similar picture, but goes one stage further by exploring the virtues of a benevolent state, thus making social justice into the over-arching aim of government. For both moral and political philosophy, as these are taught in the modern academy, the critical instruments of social coordination are the moral law, the virtues that motivate us to obey it, and the political system which makes obedience possible and which coordinates the projects of free moral agents. The moral law is conceived largely in Kantian terms – as the system of duties which safeguards human rights and the system of rights which justifies these duties. The political order supplements the moral law with a positive law designed to guarantee our freedom and to rectify the systemic injustices that arise through its exercise. The moral law and the positive law are in turn justified by abstract theories which make no reference to the spooky motivations of primitive and religiously minded people, and which are understood entirely in terms of individual autonomy and the freedoms and rights implied by it.

OK, this is something of a caricature, but it is not far from the truth. It corresponds to the agenda set out in Rawls' *A Theory of Justice* and Nozick's *Anarchy, State and Utopia*, to the vision of human beings assumed in the legal philosophy of Ronald Dworkin and Joseph Raz and in the moral philosophy of Tim Scanlon. From David Gauthier's *Morals by Agreement* (1986) and Loren Lomasky's *Persons, Rights and the Moral Community* (1987) to Stephen Darwall's *The Second-Person Standpoint* (2006) and Martha Nussbaum's *Frontiers of Justice* (2009), we find near-universal agreement among American moral philosophers that individual autonomy and respect for rights are the root conceptions of moral order, with the state conceived either as an instrument for safeguarding autonomy or – if given a larger role – as an instrument for rectifying disadvantage in the name of 'social justice'. The arguments given for these positions are invariably secular, egalitarian and founded in an abstract idea of rational choice. And they are attractive arguments, since they seem to justify both a public morality and a shared political order in ways that allow for the peaceful coexistence of people with different faiths, different commitments and deep metaphysical disagreements.

However, there is a cost. Areas of moral thinking that have been, and still are, of enormous importance to ordinary people get dropped from the agenda. Sex is the most obvious instance. In his pioneering study *Sexual Ethics*, first published in 1930, Aurel Kolnai argued that the root of sexual morality lies not in cost and benefit but in cleanliness and dirt. The core concept in any sexual ethic worth the name is that of defilement (*das Schmutzig*). Of course, anthropologists had pointed this out before and Freud had made quite a fuss about it. But Freud was a debunker and in his wake the orthodox opinion had arisen that the basis of traditional sexual morality is *irrational* – primitive fears and superstitions that should have no place in the life of a modern person. Kolnai's phenomenological method did not enable him to mount an effective reply to that. Nevertheless, he remained convinced that this feeling of defilement is an objective indicator of what is wrong with the experiences that produce it.

Therefore, insofar as sexual morality is discussed by modern moral philosophers, it is almost always in terms of the autonomy of the individual. The task of philosophy is seen as one of 'freeing up' the sexual impulse for guilt-free enjoyment by debunking the superstitions that have been heaped across the path of pleasure.[1] The crucial matter is that of consent – informed consent between the partners being regarded as the necessary (and for many thinkers the sufficient) condition for legitimate sexual relations. The suggestions that certain partners are ontologically forbidden (because they are of the wrong sex), that sex within marriage is morally of a different kind from what used to be called fornication or that there are real temptations which should be resisted, even when the temptation is mutual – all such suggestions seem groundless, mere superstitions hanging over from an unenlightened age. I was interested recently to read, in a textbook devoted to the philosophy of psychiatry, an article praising masturbation, unaccountably and harmfully forbidden in previous times, as a consoling and relieving practice.[2] It is not that the conclusion is absurd – rather, that it was reached without any awareness *whatsoever* of the reasons that had led our ancestors to disagree with it. Lacking the concept of pollution, a whole area of moral thinking and feeling had been obliterated in the author's mind.

Why is rape so much worse a crime than spitting on someone? In what does the harm consist? Is it just that something is done to someone without her consent? If so, does this not happen all the time, without provoking the severe punishments inflicted on the rapist? Nobody who denies himself concepts of defilement and desecration can even begin to encompass the feelings of the rape-victim. Forced against her will to experience her sex as a bodily function rather than an intimate gift, she feels assaulted and polluted in her very being. And how the victim *perceives* the act is internally connected to what the act *is*. The sense of pollution and desecration is not an *illusion* on the victim's part; it is an accurate perception of what has been done to her. However, if we re to follow the account of sexual interest and sexual pleasure purveyed by the standard liberal literature, this perception must appear entirely irrational, and rape victims who make a fuss must be compared to people who try to sue those who bump into them in the street. (By standard liberal literature I mean the well-known current of thinking

---

[1]   Examples include the following works: Igor Primoratz, *Ethics and Sex* (London: Routledge, 1999); Richard Posner, *Sex and Reason* (Cambridge, MA: Harvard University Press, 1992); and Alan Soble, *Sex from Plato to Paglia: A Philosophical Encyclopedia* (two volumes) (Westport, CT: Greenwood Press, 2005).

[2]   Nancy Potter, 'Gender', in Jennifer Radden (ed.), *The Philosophy of Psychiatry: A Companion* (Oxford: Oxford University Press, 2004), p. 240: 'masturbation is a way towards autonomy through self-soothing and through an increased understanding of one's body and how it meet its needs. Masturbation … is an important activity that promotes healthy development'. Note that the goal is autonomy, but the means is the body and its needs. This is the old Platonic fallacy of placing sexual pleasure in the domain of the body, and sexual satisfaction in the realm of the soul, though the author's style betrays that such thoughts would never have occurred to her.

that received such a sudden inflation with the Kinsey Report[3] and the philosophy behind which is epitomized in the encylopaedia by Alan Soble entitled *Sex, from Plato to Paglia.*)

It is much the same with incest. You can feel sympathy towards Siegmund and Sieglinde in *Die Walküre*[4] because they recognize their consanguinity only when it is too late – in a state of mutual arousal. They had not shared a home and their siblinghood only dawns on them in the course of their desire. Such exceptional cases apart, incest gives rise to profound feelings of revulsion in almost all of us. Freud gave an explanation of this – the revulsion against incest is a defence against a deep desire to do it. Evolutionary psychology gives another and conflicting explanation – namely that this revulsion is an adaptation. Genes that do not produce it in their human avatars have all died out. But neither Freud nor evolutionary psychology puts us in touch with the moral heart of the matter, which is the experience of revulsion itself, the experience that we conceptualize in the way I have suggested, through notions of pollution and desecration. These conceptions explain why Jocasta hanged herself and why Oedipus stabbed out his eyes. In comparison, neither Freud nor evolutionary psychology make sense of what is – from their rival points of view – highly eccentric behaviour.

Modern moral philosophy recognizes that personhood is a central moral category – maybe the qualification for entry into the realm of moral subjects. And many philosophers acknowledge that personhood is a relational idea: you are a person to the extent that you can participate in a network of interpersonal relationships.[5] To be a person, therefore, you must have the capacities that make those relationships possible. These include self-awareness, accountability and practical reason. Persons fall under the scope of Kant's moral law: they must respect each other as persons. In other words, they should grant to each other a sphere of sovereignty. Within your sphere of sovereignty, what is done, and what happens to you, insofar as it depends on human choices, depends on your choices. This can be guaranteed only if people are shielded from each other by a wall of rights. Without rights, individuals are not sovereigns but subjects, and these rights

---

[3]   Alfred C. Kinsey, Wardell B. Pomeroy and Clyde E. Martin, *Sexual Behaviour in the Human Male* (Philadelphia, PA: W.B Saunders Company, 1948; renewed Bloomington, IN: Indiana University Press, 1975); and Alfred C. Kinsey, Wardell B. Pomeroy, Clyde E. Martin and Paul H. Gebhard,, *Sexual Behaviour in the Human Female* (Philadelphia, PA: W.B Saunders Company, 1953; renewed Bloomington, IN: Indiana University Press, 1981).

[4]   *The Valkyrie*, Richard Wagner, WWV 86B.

[5]   This position is implicit in Kant's original account of persons in the Second *Critique* and the lectures on anthropology. It was taken up by Fichte and elaborated upon in a moving and subtle way by Hegel in *The Phenomenology of Spirit*. And it informs such modern restatements as Stephen Darwall's *The Second-Person Standpoint: Morality, Respect and Accountability* (Cambridge, MA: Harvard University Press, 2006), in which Darwall explicitly draws on Fichte.

are 'natural' in that they are inherent in the condition of personhood and are not derived from any convention or agreement.

Does that explain the revulsion against rape? I think not. The concept of a natural right is too formal a notion: it tells us that a person has a right not to be raped, since rape casts aside her consent, rides over her will and treats her as a means to pleasure. All of this is bad, of course. But the same offence is committed by the one who hugs a woman against her will or who, unknown to her and in a state of excitement, watches her undress. Without the element of pollution, we have not identified the real measure of the crime. (Come to think of it, why is voyeurism so sinful? Surely, again, it is because it imports an element of pollution. The woman who discovers that, while undressing, she has been excitedly watched by a lustful stranger feels defiled by this and wants to wash herself clean of those eyes, which have left their slimy tracks on her body.)

This does not mean that the Kantian morality of interpersonal respect is irrelevant. On the contrary, it accounts for many of our moral intuitions. But my argument suggests that the abstract liberal concept of the person as a centre of free choice, whose will is sovereign and whose rights determine our duties towards him delivers at best only a part of moral thinking. Persons can be harmed in ways which are not adequately summarized in the idea of a violation of rights. Persons can be polluted, desecrated, defiled – and in many cases this disaster takes a bodily form. If we do not see this, then not only will traditional sexual morality appear opaque and inexplicable to us, but we will also be unable to develop any alternative sexual morality more suitable (as we might suppose) to the age in which we live.

Many features of our present situation provide incidental confirmation of the point. For instance, there is the profound feeling of disgust that people feel towards paedophilia. What explains this? Just that the child has not yet reached the 'age of consent'? Is child abuse like serving alcohol to a minor? And is that the only reason why we loathe child pornography or wish to keep pornography out of the reach of children (not to speak, though it is now pointless to speak, of everyone else)? Alternatively, consider the new sexual crimes, often committed on the campus, where young people are taught, by their courses in sex education, that consent is what it is all about, the necessary and sufficient condition for 'good sex'. Sometimes the result is 'bad sex' – that sudden sense of violation which ensues when the girl recognizes, too late, that consent is after all *not* what it is all about. The result is a charge of 'date rape', in itself an unjust assault on the girl's seducer, but a last-ditch attempt to make sense of her own moral feelings. The mess in which many young women find themselves today is sufficient proof, it seems to me, that the desacralized morality of the liberal consensus is inadequate to deal with our sexual emotions and with the hair-raising tactics that they require of us if we are to live together in charity.

Unless we put ideas of 'pollution and taboo' back into the discussion of sexual morality, there is no way, it seems to me, in which we will generate a viable sexual morality. What might then emerge is a question that lies outside the scope of the present discussion. However, I am willing to bet that the old rules against masturbation, homosexuality and pre-marital sex – not to speak of paedophilia, sado-masochism, necrophilia and bestiality – will not look as absurd at the end of the attempt as they do to most liberals at the beginning, even if we find no compelling reason to accept them.

My concern in this chapter, however, is not sex but the wider sphere of 'unchosen' moral requirements. The all-important concept in articulating these requirements is that of piety – the ancient *pietas* which, for many Roman thinkers, identified the true core of religious practice and of the religious frame of mind and which, in the easygoing temper of the Augustan age, seemed scarcely to require a belief in the gods or in anything beyond the natural order.

Piety is a posture of submission and obedience towards authorities that you have never chosen.[6] The obligations of piety, unlike the obligations of contract, do not arise from the consent to be bound by them; they arise from the ontological predicament of the individual. Filial obligations provide a clear example. I did not consent to be born from and raised by this woman. I have not bound myself to her by a contract and there is no knowing in advance what my obligation to her at any point might be or what might fulfil it. The Confucian philosophy places enormous weight on obligations of this kind – obligations of 'Li' – and regards a person's virtue as measured almost entirely on the scale of piety. The ability to recognize and act upon unchosen obligations indicates a character more deeply imbued with generous and trustworthy feeling than would issue from the ability to make deals and abide by them – such is the thought. As Cordelia puts it, when unjustly asked to rewrite a bond of piety as a contractual deal: 'According to my bond, no more, no less.'

Our academic political philosophy has its roots in the Enlightenment, in the conception of citizenship that emerged with the social contract and in the desire to replace inherited authority with popular choice as the principle of political legitimacy. Not surprisingly, it has had little time for piety, which – if acknowledged at all – is confined to the private sphere or to those 'conceptions of the good' which Rawls puts to one side in his version of the social contract, since they are the proof that, in their hearts, ordinary people are nothing like the fictions he imagines. It would be fair to say, I think, that the main task of political conservatism, as represented by Burke, de Maistre and Hegel, was to put obligations of piety back where they belong, at the centre of the picture. And they were right to undertake this task. One thing that is unacceptable in the bloodless political philosophies that compete for our endorsement today is their failure to recognize that most of what we are and owe has been acquired without our own consent to it.

In Hegel's *Philosophy of Right* the family is defined as a sphere of pious obligations, while civil society is defined as a sphere of free choice and contract. And there is a dialectical opposition between them – young people naturally struggling against the ties of family in order to launch themselves into the sphere of choice, only to be ensnared by love and the new unchosen bond that comes

---

[6]   In my view, it would be a great advance if people were to recommend that *this* is the way to translate that awkward word *Islâm*.

from love. This dialectical conflict reaches equilibrium for Hegel only because it is *aufgehoben* (transcended and preserved) in a higher form of unchosen obligation – that towards the state, which surrounds and protects all our arrangements, by offering the security and the permanence of law. The bond of allegiance which ties us to the state is again a bond of piety that is not dissimilar to that quasi-contract between the living, the unborn and the dead of which Burke writes so movingly in his devastating answer to Rousseau.

Working out those suggestive ideas in a language that would suit them to the time and place in which we live is not easy: it is what I have tried to do in my political writings. But if it is not done, we will never arrive at a cogent notion of political obligation or at a view of political order that grants to it any status more secure that that of a temporary, provisional and undefended agreement. To work it out fully, we must, I believe, accept the deep insight that Burke, Maistre and Hegel all share, which is that the destiny of the political order and the destiny of the family are indissolubly connected. Families, and the relationships embraced by them, are non-accidental features of interpersonal life, just like the experiences of pollution and violation which I described above. As such, we should not be surprised by the findings of modern psychotherapy that disorders of the family show themselves in disorders of the personality – radical distortions in self-awareness, accountability and the ability to adopt the 'second-person standpoint', as Stephen Darwall has described it.

But this brings me to another deficiency in the liberal individualist world-view, which is the cavalier attitude to the family. The emphasis on autonomy and the expropriation of justice by the impartial state mean that families are considered only as defeasible ties, which originate in a contract between two individuals to get together and produce, or at any rate raise, children. Marriage and the family are matters to be regulated privately and according to the fundamental principle of liberal morality, which is that all arrangements should be consented to by those involved. Children, of course, are only *on the way* to consenting to the arrangement that includes them. However, the arrangement is legitimate provided that they can reasonably be expected, on reaching the age of consent, to endorse it.

Here we come to another set of concepts which push us towards a richer, and darker, description of human ties – the concepts of the sacred and the sacramental. Marriages belong with Christenings, Bar Mitzvahs and funerals to the ceremonies which anthropologists, following Van Gennep, have grouped together as 'rites of passage'. Their near-universality suggests that they provide an answer to a deep need in human nature, and once again it is not a need that can be easily embraced by the standard liberal view of the human condition. In all societies rites of passage have a sacramental character. They are episodes in which the dead and the unborn are present, and in which the gods take a consuming interest, sometimes attending in person. In these moments time stands still, or rather they are peculiarly timeless. The passage from one condition to another occurs outside time – as though the participants bathe themselves for a moment in eternity. Almost all religions treat rites of passage in such a way, as 'points of intersection of the timeless with time'.

Rituals of birth, marriage and death exemplify the wider concept of the sacred. This too has received little recognition from modern analytical philosophy. Some anthropologists and sociologists have ventured to give genealogical explanations of the experience of sacred things, the most famous being René Girard, who traces the experience to the sacrificial scapegoating whereby communities rid themselves of the poison of 'mimetic desire'.[7] Girard's theory is problematic for many reasons, not least because it seems to assume what it is trying to explain – to assume, that is, that the original scapegoat already possesses, in his or her sacrificial state, the aura of sanctity. And maybe this is a difficulty for all genealogical accounts – that they either begin from a state in which the concept is already applied or they do not succeed in showing how we can come to apply it. Still, in the course of his highly suggestive theory, Girard argues for connections which clearly belong to the concept of the sacred and which must be borne in mind if we are to understand the place of that concept in practical reasoning. Sacred things are both forbidden (to the uninitiated) and commanded (to those who would live in the true path). They are revealed in 'sacraments' – that is, actions which lift their participants out of the run of day-to-day events and raise them to a higher sphere, setting them down among the immortals. Furthermore, they can be desecrated and polluted – and this is the most remarkable feature of them. The one who touches the sacred objects without due reverence, or in an 'uninitiated' state, or who mocks them or spits on them commits a kind of metaphysical crime. He or she brings what is sacred into the world of everyday things and wipes away its aura. For this people have traditionally suffered the most dreadful of punishments, and the desire to punish remains to this day. One reason why liberal morality is such a slender resource in the dangerous times we are now entering is that it routinely ignores the concepts of the sacred and the sacrilegious, and the experiences that feed into them. The Western way of life, in which contractual relations and autonomous choices have become the norm, stands firmly accused of sacrilege by the Islamists. And it is unable to answer the charge, since it is unable to understand it.

In a celebrated study, the nineteenth-century jurist and historian Sir Henry Maine argued that modern societies were uniformly experiencing a change from relations of status to relations of contract.[8] This was perhaps the first of many attempts to look with a sociologist's eye at the liberal world order and to recognize the deep changes in institutions which are the inevitable result of the emphasis on individual choice as the basis of legitimacy. And the most important institution to be affected by these deep changes is that of marriage, an example which shows that

---

[7]   See especially René Girard, *Violence and the Sacred*, trans. Patrick Gregory (Baltimore, MD: Johns Hopkins University Press, 1977); *The Scapegoat* (Baltimore, MD: Johns Hopkins University Press, 1989); and *Things Hidden Since the Foundation of the World: Research Undertaken in Collaboration with Jean-Michel Oughourlian and G. Lefort* (Stanford, CA: Stanford University Press, 1987).

[8]   Sir Henry Maine, *Ancient Law: Its Connection with the Early History of Society, and its Relation to Modern Ideas* (London: John Murray, 1861).

Maine's analysis does not go far enough. It is not merely that marriage was once regarded as effecting a radical change of status. Like all rites of passage, it was imbued with an air of sanctity. The marriage ceremony was, if not a sacrament, at least something that involved sacred things and sacred obligations. Marriage was regarded as a vow, and a vow is not the same thing as a contract: it does not have terms, there is no action or event that fulfils it and there is no action or event that voids or defeats it. It is an existential tie, from which obligations flow inexhaustibly. And it is only as so conceived that a marriage can serve as the way into that sphere of unchosen obligations – the sphere of *pietas* – on which children depend for their protection.

Now, Roman law regarded marriage as a civil institution, even if it involved a ceremony to which the gods were invited and at which sacred vows were taken. It was only in the Middle Ages that the Church decided that it must officially recognize the sacred nature of the marriage bond by explicitly defining marriage as a sacrament. Nevertheless, I think we can see that the history of this institution is not – and has never been until recently – the history of a contractual tie and that marriage has become redefined as a contractual tie only to lose its essential nature. This redefinition is the direct result of two factors: the liberal view of institutions, as validated by the consent of their members, and the liberal view of the state, as providing the only objective form of social authority – all other forms of authority being merely 'private', reflections of a particular 'conception of the good' that has no part in the public sphere. Since marriages are founded in consent, they must be contracts, and since they are a bid for recognition by society, that recognition must be conferred by the state. As such, marriage becomes a purely civil institution – the recognition by the state of a contractual tie. And the contract can be dissolved, amended or voided by the thing that originally endorsed it, namely the state. Furthermore, there is no reason in principle why marriage should be a relation between a man and a woman. The same contract could be made between a man and a man, a man and two women, a woman and three men, and so on, and so long as the state upholds the contract, there will be a valid marriage. This of course is what we are seeing, and it is surely proof of the fact that civil marriage and the old sacramental marriage are not instances of the same kind of thing. Sacramental marriage is not simply one case among many of 'civil union' since, unlike a civil union, it is not a contract. The new forms of civil union have the fluctuating and unstable nature of personal agreements, and neither provide special protection for children nor impose special obligations on adults. They simply add the rubber stamp of state approval to whatever arrangements people should choose for the time being to make.

To see marriage as a 'civil union' is therefore to consign it to oblivion. Why bother to solicit that rubber stamp when it merely endorses an agreement and adds nothing of its own? The loss of the sacramental view of marriage is the loss of marriage, and with the loss of marriage comes the fragmentation of the family. Families become provisional, fissiparous and deeply insecure. They occur without foundations, and children raised in such foundationless arrangements often fail to acquire the full repertoire of social emotions. Sociological studies have offered overwhelming proof of this, but the observation is not only an empirical one. As with the concepts of purity and desecration, as with the obligations of piety, so too with the idea of the sacramental tie and the vow of marriage – we are identifying not arbitrary or parochial additions to the thinking of the human person, but fundamental components of a fully personal approach to life. The abstract chooser, bearer of rights and duties, who is the subject of moral and political order on the liberal view, must see the world in ways that are not fully recorded in the language of rights and duties if he or she is to have a full conception of his or her predicament. His or her moral situation as a free being cannot be fully specified without describing the forbidden ways of pollution and sacrilege, the fulfilling ways of piety and sacrament, and the sense of a higher order in things, which can be entered through creating substantial and sacramental ties. Only if individuals see themselves in this way, it seems to me, is their own happiness and the future of society in any way secured. It is not an accident that our own societies are becoming increasingly childless and that children are growing up without the basic forms of accountability to others and capacity for attachment and love. These developments are an inevitable consequence, as soon as people acquire the habit of thinking of themselves in the ways assumed by the official liberal position – as freely choosing individuals whose obligations are founded in the deals they have made and who are not hampered at any point by the threat of pollution or sacrilege, by respect for sacred ties and unchosen obligations or by the belief that vows are eternal and made outside time.

An orthodox Christian or Muslim would agree with all that I have said, but would go on to add that, without the belief in God, the concepts of the sacred and the sacramental, the pure and the impure have no foundation or are merely elaborate metaphors, and that obligations of piety would have no force, since they are obligations to God. For such a person, these concepts are part of the *a priori* endowment of the human being. They are contours of our thinking which prepare us for a life in the service of God. Indeed, for believers, there is no clearer proof of God than the fact that we can make sense of our moral experience only by employing concepts like those of the pious, the sacrilegious and the sacred, which point beyond this world to its transcendental ground.

Of course, evolutionary psychology will take a more empirical approach, and it will find nothing strange in a view that gives a central place to concepts of pollution, piety and the sacred in the life of the moral agent. These concepts, and the conceptions that expound them, are easily seen as 'adaptations' belonging to 'evolutionarily stable strategies' of the genes that propel them. And, indeed, when it comes to sex and sexual morality, it is remarkable to see how wide is the gulf between what evolutionary psychology would lead us to expect and what liberal theory might acknowledge as legitimate. But I hesitate to rely on evolutionary psychology for the reason that its findings are, if valid at all, entirely negative. A trait is shown to be an 'adaptation' just as soon as we can show that its absence will be a genetic disadvantage. In this sense the revulsion against incest is clearly an adaptation. But that does not distinguish the revulsion against incest that comes from a blind instinct from the revulsion founded in a sense of pollution or the revulsion based on a reasoned morality of the home. In other words, it says nothing about the *thoughts* on which the revulsion is founded, nothing about the *deep intentionality* of the feelings that it purports to explain. It is therefore entirely neutral concerning their real justification and the ontological ground of the concepts used to express them. An evolutionary psychology of religion will almost certainly show religious belief to be a reproductive advantage in just the same way that mathematical competence is a reproductive advantage (the others have all died out). But it will leave questions of religious epistemology where they were, just as it leaves the standard of mathematical proof unaltered.

As such, we cannot rely on evolutionary psychology to underpin the concepts and conceptions that I have been considering. That is why we find, in the emerging atheist culture, the otherwise rather surprising combination of two views – first, that the human condition is to be understood in evolutionary terms and, secondly, that ideas of the sacred, the pure and the pious are merely 'residues' of early adaptations and have no objective basis. This is because orthodox opinion holds that the only objective basis for anything lies in the world as science describes it. The reasons for our beliefs must be rooted in the causal order, otherwise the beliefs themselves are unreasonable.

It is no answer to this sceptical position to give a genealogy of our spiritual concepts. Even if we accept the elaborate story told by Girard concerning the origin of the notion of the sacred in scapegoating and ritual violence, this does not *entitle* us to that concept and the remarkable conceptions that go with it. For sacred things are seen as belonging to *another order* than the order of the empirical world. They are visitors from another sphere: they mark the places in the empirical world from which we look out towards the transcendental. We could *justify* describing them in this way only negatively, by showing the inadequacy of any purely empirical analysis to capture their content, while insisting that it is a *genuine* content and one that we clearly understand. This is, in my view, one of the primary tasks of a philosophy of religion – namely to take the concepts that I have touched on in this chapter, and the beliefs and conceptions that seem naturally to flow from them, and to give a transcendental deduction of their validity. It is not an easy task and I am not at all clear how to proceed with it. Nevertheless, I am fairly clear about the first step, which is to show that the moral life – the life of freedom, self-awareness and accountability – commits us to thinking in the way that these concepts require. We cannot encompass our experience of good and evil, of duty and fulfilment, if we do not describe our world as one in which the distinctions between the pure and the impure, the sacred and the profane, the pious and the impious are real and motivating. And maybe it is enough to show that that is so.

Chapter 7

Evolution and Agapeistic Ethics

Robin Attfield

Introduction

The ethic of love of the New Testament clearly presupposes that people have the capacity to behave with love or not, and to show more love or less love in their actions. In other words, it presupposes that they could act otherwise than the way in which they do act, not just occasionally, but frequently. Otherwise they could either not be more or less loving than they are, or they could manage this, but only on rare occasions; but if so, there would be no point in advocating acting lovingly in the first place. New Testament ethics are not alone in making these presuppositions; thus, Old Testament ethics make them too, as plausibly do most forms of humanistic ethics, and, to the extent that they diverge from humanism, the ethics of the animal welfare movement and the deeper varieties of environmental ethics. Admittedly, there are problems for New Testament ethicists in upholding all this consistently, in view of the claims in works like Romans about human actions being uniformly foreknown,[1] for these claims supply problems both for human freedom and for the capacity ever to act otherwise. But this is not the occasion to discuss those problems; maybe passages about foreknowledge can be so interpreted as to overcome the problems, possibly in the way in which Boethius attempted to interpret them.[2] Or maybe they should simply be regarded as rhetorical exaggerations. For present purposes, I will assume that the problems have some kind of solution that leaves the capacity to act otherwise intact.

Evolutionary theory, however, generates some new problems for these presuppositions. For if our actions are moulded either entirely or in large measure by selfish genes,[3] then we seldom if ever have options to act except in ways that maximize the survival prospects and/or the advantage of our kin group, and genuinely altruistic action is either impossible or is confined, at best, to a marginal

---

[1] Romans 8:29.

[2] For Boethius, see H. Liebeschutz, 'Boethius and the Legacy of Antiquity', in A.H. Armstrong (ed.), *The Cambridge History of Later Greek and Early Medieval History* (Cambridge: Cambridge University Press, 1970), pp. 538–64, at pp. 549–50. In this connection, J.R. Lucas cites Boethius, *De Consolatione Philosophiae*, V, iv, ll. 13ff. and 63ff.; see J.R. Lucas, *The Freedom of the Will* (Oxford: Clarendon, 1970) p.72, n. 1 and p. 73, n.3.

[3] Richard Dawkins, *The Selfish Gene*, 2nd edn (Oxford: Oxford University Press, 1989).

role. Either we never have options about how to behave at all, or our repertoire of behaviour is so constrained by our genes that the only kind of altruism that is within our powers is reciprocal altruism, behaviour that benefits others in circumstances where there is a strong prospect of a payback, or of reciprocation from the benefited party either to ourselves or to our kin.[4] However, this is not quite accurate, as some socio-biologists and evolutionary psychologists believe that our behaviour is moulded not entirely by our genes alone but also by cultural ideas or memes that colonize our heads and join with our genes in controlling our actions.[5] More accurately, then, our repertoire of behaviour is supposedly so constrained by our genes and by our memes that little or no altruism, other than reciprocal altruism, is within our powers. But if so, then our capacity for agapeistic action that does not coincide with reciprocal altruism is vanishingly slender. Much the same verdict follows by parity about our capacity for the kinds of actions advocated by humanistic ethics and, come to that, about our capacity for the actions advocated by the deeper kinds of environmentalism, such as those that advocate putting the interests of members of other species on occasion before both our own, those of our families, however extended, and indeed those of fellow humans too.[6]

This chapter discusses these problems, generated as they are by the application of evolutionary theory to human psychology. I shall argue that, properly understood, evolutionary theory does not preclude the possibility of altruistic behaviour, even where altruistic behaviour is not confined to reciprocal altruism, but includes what Kate Adie has called 'the kindness of strangers',[7] such as the behaviour of the Good Samaritan in Jesus' parable. Certainly, if genetic determinism were true and unlimited in scope, and agents were constrained by their genes to promote, in their behaviour, the welfare of themselves and their kindred alone, except where opportunities for 'reciprocal altruism' arose, things would be otherwise. But evolutionary theory need not be understood as having these implications, as I will now argue.

---

[4]   See George C. Williams, 'Huxley's Evolution and Ethics in Sociobiological Perspective', *Zygon* 23(4) (1988), 383–407; *Plan and Purpose in Nature* (London: Weidenfeld & Nicolson, 1996).

[5]   Dawkins, *Selfish Gene*; Daniel Dennett, *Darwin's Dangerous Idea: Evolution and the Meanings of Life* (London: Penguin, 1995).

[6]   For a clear presentation of the contradictions between moral obligations and a deterministic view of evolutionary psychology, see Keith Ward, *God, Chance and Necessity* (Oxford: Oneworld, 1996), p. 183.

[7]   Kate Adie, *The Kindness of Strangers: The Autobiography* (London: Headline, 2002).

Why Evolutionary Theory Does Not Preclude Altruism

First, not all behaviours, and certainly not all human behaviours, are the results of adaptation, contrary to the claims of adaptationist evolutionists. Darwin recognized that factors other than natural selection can figure in biological explanations; for him, adaptation was an important cause but was far from a complete or sufficient one.[8] For example, factors other than competition for food, mates or survival are often held by biologists to be significant, such as intra-species cooperation (as attested by Frans de Waal),[9] and even if some such cooperation could be held to have an advantage in terms of survival – and thus to be a further instance of adaptation rather than a supplementary factor – it is far from clear that this interpretation needs to be put on all such intra-specific cooperation (much of which is cultural and non-Darwinian rather than genetic, Darwinian adaptation). To take another example, the late Stephen Jay Gould wrote, together with Elizabeth S. Vrba, of exaptation, a phenomenon in which traits developed for one function receive another, as when bones, originally a store, come to supply anchorages and rigidity, when mother's milk, originally a source of antibodies, comes to supply nutrition,[10] and when wings, once probably a device for either warmth or gliding, come to facilitate free flight. While adaptationists can adapt their adaptationism to accommodate these phenomena, the resulting theory already modifies the kind of adaptationism that explains all traits as first-order adaptations and allows in numerous further possibilities. Another example could be found in the phenomena that Gould and Lewontin labelled 'spandrels',[11] which are effectively evolutionary byproducts, but the previous examples are already enough to illustrate the point without the need to go into their concept of a building plan and its role. Nevertheless, the further possibility is worth mentioning that human language should be regarded as, in part, a fruit not of natural selection but of cultural selection, grounded in myriads of human choices, and thus comprises behaviour not to be construed simply as adaptation through natural selection, as has been argued by Stephen Clark.[12] If so, many of the speech acts that we use language to perform are not

---

[8]   Charles Darwin, *The Origin of Species* (Darwin's last edition) (London: John Murray, 1872), p. 395.

[9]   Frans de Vaal, *Good Natured: The Origins of Right and Wrong in Humans and Other Animals* (Cambridge, MA and London: Harvard University Press, 1996).

[10]   Stephen Jay Gould and Elizabeth S. Vrba, 'Exaptation: A Missing Term in the Science of Form', in David L. Hull and Michael Ruse (eds), *The Philosophy of Biology* (Oxford: Oxford University Press, 1998), pp. 52–71.

[11]   Stephen Jay Gould and Richard Lewontin, 'The Spandrels of San Marco and the Panglossian Paradigm: A Critique of the Adaptationist Programme', in Elliott Sober (ed.), *Conceptual Issues in Evolutionary Biology*, 2nd edn (Cambridge, MA: MIT Press, 1998), pp. 73–90.

[12]   Stephen R.L. Clark, 'The Evolution of Language: Truth and Lies', *Philosophy* 75 (2000), 401–21.

to be explained as adaptations, let alone as genetically determined, but as acts of improvisation, wit and ingenuity that exploit and develop the range of options and the resources for choice that human language embodies.

Secondly, since genes seem not to explain everything, Richard Dawkins and Daniel Dennett introduce into their theories supplementary determinants by way of self-replicating memes (of thoughts, tunes or images), which invade our minds and hold us in bondage to related ideas.[13] Worship of God or the gods is explained in this way, as would also be people's adherence to principles of religious ethics. (Matters of behaviour and practice, by contrast, would largely be controlled by genes and make agapeistic religious ethics inoperable.) Our thoughts and behaviour are thus held to be governed by genes and memes together. But this is to suggest that there is no role for rationality in our reflections and deliberations, for our conclusions, both theoretical and practical, are the inevitable resultants of those hidden controllers, our genes and memes. Even the reasoning that generates belief in memes would, it seems, have to be controlled in this way, which raises a question mark over the entire theory; theorists of memes might be wiser to exempt reasoning about memes from the scope of their theory. But in any case the theory is at odds with the pervasive belief (which also leads people into scientific investigation) that it is possible for human beings to reflect rationally about the world around them and to embody this reflection in their behaviour. Thus, the theory of memes should be regarded as implausible, and the thoughts and behaviours supposedly explained by memes are not to be regarded as explicable in this way.[14] The theory seems to make the true agents of history not human beings but the theoretical micro-agents that control them. But this is to depersonalize humanity, deny human autonomy and transfer it to newly personalized forces, at least some of which seem to be imaginary. Evolutionary theory can only gain from discarding the epicycle of memes.

Thirdly, evolutionary theory may well supply causes for human behaviour without supplying determinants. Let us assume that adaptation is agreed to be a cause of many biological phenomena. Would it follow that the theory governing its causality need be a deterministic one or that such causes should be construed as determinants? If accounts of causes were complete accounts of the sufficient conditions of the phenomena that the causes generated, then this might be so, but in fact causes are often just necessary conditions, or part of necessary conditions; there again, significantly, they are often parts or elements of what would be sufficient conditions but not sufficient themselves alone. To cite one

---

[13]   Dawkins, *Selfish Gene*; Dennett, *Darwin's Dangerous Idea*.

[14]   Mary Midgley, 'Gene-Juggling', *Philosophy* 54 (1979), 438–58, at 456–8; Mary Midgley, 'Why Genes?', in Hilary Rose and Steven Rose (eds), *Alas, Poor Darwin* (London: Jonathan Cape, 2000), pp. 67–84; David Holdcroft and Harry Lewis, 'Consciousness, Design and Social Practice', *Journal of Consciousness Studies* 8 (2001), 43–58.

recently revived theory of causation,[15] causes may be construed as tendencies or powers, powers which make things happen unless something intervenes; thus, they are not sufficient conditions when considered alone. (As such, they are more than mere capacities, but less than necessitating factors or determinants.) This is admittedly a very un-Humean and un-Kantian account of causation, but, as argued by Peter Geach and Elizabeth Anscombe, it emerges as (to say the least) a cogent account, based on the teachings of Aquinas, which avoids all kinds of pitfalls and inconsistencies.[16] An example of the bearing that all this has on the behaviour of animals or of humans is the likelihood that even if genetic factors are causes of altruistic behaviour being restricted to kin altruism and reciprocal altruism, this restriction will only be embodied in behaviour if nothing intervenes; however, if sympathy, friendship or (say) the milk of human kindness intervenes, then the behaviour will not be restricted in this way. These further motives have not been made inoperative in elephants by elephant genes or by bonobo genes among bonobos, and there is no reason to suppose that human beings are any different in this respect. (How to reconcile the survival of such motivations with genetic theory is not a matter that needs to be resolved in the current connection.)

Some neo-Darwinians believe that their Darwinism commits them to a deterministic account of human behaviour. But if, as I have argued, causal explanations are not to be regarded as intrinsically deterministic, then it is difficult to see what such deterministic theories can appeal to. Here it is worth remarking that proponents of the cognitive science of religion sometimes disavow deterministic interpretations of their claims. Thus, Theodore Brelsford notes that:

> the claim that religious beliefs derive from basic human intuitions and that these intuitions derive from basic evolved structures of mind does not imply necessary *determinism* of beliefs by evolutionarily determined intuitions ... Further, intuitions are not to be viewed as fixed outcomes of structures of mind but may be honed, ignored, reformed and so on.[17]

---

[15]   Stephen Mumford, 'Modelling Powers as Vectors', unpublished paper, presented to the Cardiff Branch of the Royal Institute of Philosophy, 2008

[16]   See P.T. Geach, 'Aquinas', in G.E.M. Anscombe and P.T. Geach, *Three Philosophers* (Oxford: Blackwell, 1961), pp. 61–125, at pp. 99–109; G.E.M. Anscombe, 'Causality and Determination', in *Metaphysics and the Philosophy of Mind* (Oxford: Blackwell, 1981), pp. 133–47.

[17]   Theodore Brelsford, 'Lessons for Religious Education from Cognitive Science of Religion', *Religious Education* 100(2) (2005), 174–91, at 175–6. The possibility of a non-deterministic understanding of Darwinism is discussed in Robin Attfield, *Creation, Evolution and Meaning* (Aldershot and Burlington, VT: Ashgate, 2006), pp. 118–19, and in Robin Attfield, 'Darwin's Doubt, Non-deterministic Darwinism and the Cognitive Science of Religion', *Philosophy* 85 (2010), 465–83.

Not even our unreflective assumptions, then, need be regarded as determined by mental structures resulting from evolutionary processes, and the same would go for the behaviour that they largely shape. But if deterministic explications of causation are in any case dispensable and at worst misguided, then the spectre of determinism need not haunt our beliefs about the limits of altruism.

Fourthly, in any case, how do our genes make us do things? The genes of heterosexuals have a tendency to steer them towards bonding and mating with a member of the opposite sex, but do not seem to make them do this all the time or uncontrollably, or in some cases at all. Maternal and parental genes tend to get us to protect our young, but do not prevent us from interfering to stop our young behaving aggressively or unfairly to the young of others. Indeed, whatever natural selection may be thought to programme us to do, we ourselves seem free to select otherwise. (Not all selection could be natural selection, or there would be no artificial or cultural selection for natural selection to be contrasted with.) What I suggest we should say is a variation on a remark of Leibniz about motives: genes may incline without necessitating.[18] Without them, we would, perhaps, lack for a nature. But we are not obliged to follow or conform with nature (or with our nature), as those who urge us to conform to nature implicitly recognize by making this a matter not of reportage but of advocacy, for you cannot advocate people doing what they are bound to do in any case. The metaphor of inclination is quite an apt one; we are, perhaps, placed on a sloping playing-field, but there is nothing to prevent us from running along contours or even uphill if we so choose, or from doing so for most of our waking hours. We may even become fitter through doing so, and such 'sprightly running' can become second nature, genetic predispositions notwithstanding.

The Possibility of Non-familial, Non-reciprocal Altruism

In any case, the possibility of altruistic behaviour cannot be precluded because it actually happens, such as in the behaviour of donors whenever there is a disaster emergency appeal. Human altruistic behaviour, like its counterpart, apparently altruistic behaviour in other primates, cannot be confined to 'reciprocal altruism'. Indeed, in order to be plausible, evolutionary theory needs not to deny this possibility but to accommodate it. In this closing section, I discuss three possible ways of doing so.

Non-reciprocal altruism could be reconciled with evolutionary theory because it has some kind of unnoticed survival advantage and is thus a further instance of adaptation. As such, maybe altruistic agents become through their altruism better motivated towards reciprocal altruism, little as this coheres with tales of people who campaign for the victims of distant disasters and ignore their own

---

[18]   Gottfried Wilhelm Leibniz, 'Fifth Paper to Clarke', paragraph 9, in G.H.R. Parkinson (ed.), *Leibniz, Philosophical Writings* (London: J.M. Dent & Sons, 1973), p. 222.

families. For there could still be an overall tendency of the kind suggested. If so, then adaptationism could be largely right after all, at least if adopted on a non-deterministic basis.

A second possibility concerns the human need for self-transcendence, and has been suggested by Ernest Partridge. Some (and possibly most) human beings, he suggests, need to identify with a cause or movement that is greater than themselves.[19] Such causes and movements, we might add, frequently involve altruistic ideals, and commitment to them often induces altruism in practice. Maybe the vigour and the psychological health of either individuals or communities (or of both) depend on such commitment. If so, then evolutionary theory would need to be modified to incorporate provision for this need. Modified in this way, it would probably not be a variety of adaptationism.

My third route to reconciliation is more formal. Maybe evolutionary theory cannot supply sufficient conditions of human behaviour, or of a good deal of it, at all. This would be unsurprising if some such behaviour reflects not natural selection but cultural or even individual selection, however this might come to be motivated. Maybe evolutionary theory sometimes furnishes the necessary conditions for forms of behaviour or (more cogently) elements of such necessary conditions, and sometimes components of sufficient conditions, without supplying complete sufficient conditions without qualification. (As we have seen, all this is compatible with its ability to supply causes.) If so, then it could not expect to be able to predict behaviour in advance as if it had to be thus and could not be otherwise, for something or other (a choice, maybe) could intervene and change the character of actions for which the conditions might otherwise have been sufficient.

There again, evolutionary theory could not normally expect to demonstrate that certain forms of behaviour are impossible, except where it can specify sets of complete necessary conditions that are fully sufficient in this role. Sometimes, admittedly, this could probably be brought off; however, this too would be unsurprising, since we already know that human beings lack what they would need to jump a mile or achieve unassisted flight. But no-one would need to be troubled if the possibility of finding the necessary conditions for action precluded behaviour such as this. Nothing would follow about the impossibility of our harbouring the kind of assumptions, intuitions or beliefs capable of shaping behaviour hospitable to strangers. Thus, it would remain unsurprising if evolutionary theory were unable on most occasions to preclude non-reciprocal altruism. As far as I can see, Darwin himself could have gone along with this non-deterministic and probably non-adaptationist view.[20]

---

[19] Ernest Partridge, 'Why Care about the Future?', in Ernest Partridge (ed.), *Responsibilities to Future Generations: Environmental Ethics* (Buffalo: Prometheus, 1981), pp. 195–202.

[20] I am grateful to the Oxford University Cognition, Religion and Theology project for making possible the presentation of an earlier draft of this chapter at the biennial conference

Chapter 8
God, Ethics and Evolution

Herman Philipse

In his popular book *The Language of God. A Scientist Presents Evidence for Belief,* the eminent geneticist Francis Collins argues that human awareness of what he calls 'the Moral Law' should be explained by the God-hypothesis of theism.[1] More specifically, he holds that the occurrence of genuinely unselfish altruism in humans cannot be accounted for by evolutionary models, such as kin-selection or tit-for-tat.[2] He also rejects the Darwinian conjecture of group-selection as an ultimate explanation of selfless human altruism, because allegedly most evolutionary theorists agree today with regard to complex populations that natural selection operates not at the group level but at the individual level.[3] In line with traditional Christianity, Collins holds that Christian theism yields both an *explanation* of our moral sense and a *justification* of our moral obligations. The voice of our moral conscience is said to be a 'special glimpse' of God Himself.[4] Many religious believers will feel strongly encouraged by this expert opinion on God, ethics and evolution.

However, those who have studied the recent literature on psychological and evolutionary altruism will reject Collins' contention that evolutionary models or other secular hypotheses cannot explain in principle the occurrence of phenomena such as the altruistic behaviour of Oskar Schindler and Mother Teresa. In the first two sections below, which are introductory, a brief survey of this literature will

---

[1] Francis S. Collins, *The Language of God. A Scientist Presents Evidence for Belief* (New York: Free Press, 2006), Chapter 1 and *passim*. Collins was Director of the National Center for Human Genome research or NHGRI (1993–2008) and was leader of the Human Genome Project. In 2009 President Obama nominated him to the position of Director of the National Institutes of Health. Collins' book spent many weeks on the *New York Times* bestseller list.

[2] W.D. Hamilton, 'The Genetical Evolution of Social Behaviour I and II', *Journal of Theoretical Biology* 7 (1964), 17–52; and R. Trivers, 'The Evolution of Reciprocal Altruism', *Quarterly Review of Biology* 46 (1971), 35–57. I call acts of altruism 'unselfish' if they are not intended at all as instrumental to one's own well-being. I apologize for the apparent pleonasm of this expression. Collins speaks of 'selfless' altruism (p. 27).

[3] Collins, *The Language of God*, p. 28; cf. Charles Darwin, *The Descent of Man and Selection in Relation to Sex* (1871), with an introduction by James Moore and Adrian Desmond (London, Penguin, 2004), pp. 130, 153, 155–8, 211ff.

[4] Collins, *The Language of God*, p. 29.

show that Collins' case for God as the best explanation of our moral sense is based upon an *argumentum ad ignorantiam*. Undoubtedly, the existence of a moral conscience in humans can be explained much better by purely secular factors, and evolutionary models may account for some of its fundamental features.

In the three central sections of this chapter that follow, I shall endorse specific answers to the following two questions, which have preoccupied philosophers (and many others) for the last 150 years.[5] If the existence of our conscience and some of its contents can be explained ultimately by evolutionary models, at least in part, what are the implications for normative ethics, if any? And how should we adjust our meta-ethical views to these results of explanatory ethics? With regard to this latter question, I shall focus on what may be called a disputational model of ethical justification and on the issue of meta-ethical realism or objectivism. Finally, I argue in the final section that the God-hypothesis cannot have any predictive power, even given the best defensible version of realism, which takes evolutionary explanatory ethics into account. My aim in this chapter is not to propose radically new answers to the questions raised but rather to explore the interconnections between the various issues discussed. Inevitably, my choice of interlocutors is somewhat arbitrary.

Collins' Contention Criticized

How does Francis Collins argue that instances of altruistic behaviour, such as Oskar Schindler's rescue of more than 1,000 Jewish people from Nazi extermination camps or Mother Teresa's dedication to helping the poor of Calcutta, should be explained by postulating God? We would expect that Collins carefully compares his God-hypothesis with specific rival secular explanations and concludes that the former is superior to the latter in terms of the usual theoretical virtues, such as a large likelihood ratio, empirical adequacy, the avoidance of ad hoc explanations, the capacity to predict new data, the coherence with background knowledge and so on. But that is not at all how he proceeds.

Rather, Collins seems to argue that *no* secular or natural explanation of such phenomena is *possible*, so that we cannot but take refuge in a supernatural hypothesis.[6] As we saw, he explicitly excludes the possibility of evolutionary ultimate explanations of Schindler's and Teresa's altruistic behaviour, such as kin-selection, reciprocal altruism or group selection. But the thesis that no secular

---

[5]   Cf. Paul Lawrence Farber, *The Temptations of Evolutionary Ethics* (Berkeley, CA: University of California Press, 1994) for an historical overview of evolutionary ethics in the Anglo-American world.

[6]   Cf. Collins, *The Language of God*, pp. 28–9: 'If the Law of Human Nature cannot be explained away as cultural artifact or evolutionary by-product, then how can we account for its presence?' Collins says that when he first discovered this argument from the Moral Law to the existence of God in the writings of C.S. Lewis, he was 'stunned by its logic' (p. 29).

explanation will be possible in principle is an extravagantly strong one, and Collins' arguments to this effect are clearly insufficient.

First of all, it may be doubted whether the cases of *psychological* altruism he mentions really are instances of (genuine or apparent) *evolutionary* altruism.[7] This is because it might be the case that at the time in which the proximate causal mechanisms underlying unselfish altruistic behaviour (in the psychological sense) evolved, these mechanisms did not dispose our ancestors to behaviour that diminished the relative reproductive fitness of the agent while raising it for the recipient.[8] It was evolutionary altruism that seemed to resist evolutionary explanations. But it is psychological altruism that matters to morality. Collins does not even mention this crucial distinction in his argument to the effect that evolutionary scenarios cannot explain altruism.

Admittedly, if evolutionary altruism were defined as a disposition to behave in such a way that, statistically speaking, the *inclusive* relative fitness of the agents is diminished while the inclusive relative fitness of the recipients is enhanced, it would be impossible to explain its long-term continuing presence in a population by evolutionary models.[9] If such dispositions and the underlying causal mechanisms arose by random mutation in some of a population's individuals, the genes that account for them would disappear in later generations. Evolutionary models can ultimately explain apparent, but not real evolutionary altruism in this inclusive

---

[7] On the difference between psychological or commonplace altruism on the one hand and evolutionary altruism on the other hand, cf., for example, David Sloan Wilson, 'On the Relationship Between Evolutionary and Psychological Definitions of Altruism and Selfishness', *Biology and Philosophy*, 7 (1992), 61–8; and Philip Kitcher, 'Psychological Altruism, Evolutionary Origins, and Moral Rules', *Philosophical Studies*, 89 (1998), 283–316. Whereas the biologist takes items of behaviour to be (evolutionarily) altruistic if and only if they diminish the expected reproductive success of the actor while raising the expected reproductive success of the recipient(s), behaviour is (genuinely) altruistic in the psychological or commonplace sense if and only if actors consciously adjust their preferences to the perceived wants or needs of the recipients. In other words, acts are psychologically altruistic if and only if actors: (a) positively value things they pass on to the recipient; (b) do so because they emphatically think that the recipient needs or values these things; and (c) the satisfaction of the recipient is considered to be an end in itself.

[8] Behaviour is explained *proximately* by the causal mechanisms and motives or reasons that induce the actor to behave in this manner. An *ultimate* explanation will have to account for the fact that these causal mechanisms are present in the actor, and that the actor is able to have such motives and reasons. An explanation by an evolutionary model is an ultimate explanation of types of behaviour.

[9] There are a number of different definitions of evolutionary altruism. I argue here that evolutionary altruism cannot be explained ultimately by evolutionary models if it is defined in terms of inclusive fitness, which is the sum of an organism's classical fitness (the probability that it produces and supports its own offspring) and the probability that it adds genetic equivalents of its own offspring to the population by supporting others.

sense. However, if evolutionary altruism is defined in terms of classical fitness, as it usually is, this *aporia* does not arise.

Let us suppose for the sake of argument that the altruistic acts of Oskar Schindler and Mother Teresa are instances of evolutionary altruism as traditionally defined. Then we should raise a second objection against Collins: that present-day evolutionary game theorists endorse further, alternative models of an ultimate evolutionary explanation of selfless altruism than kin-selection and tit-for-tat. Various models of group-selection are proposed and seriously considered, whereas prominent biologists such as Edward O. Wilson now endorse multilevel selection theory as an elegant theoretical foundation for future socio-biology.[10]

Even if we reject evolutionary game-theoretical models of group-selection as possible ultimate explanations of selfless psychological altruism in humans, we should raise a third objection against Collins: that other explanations partly in evolutionary terms are not at all excluded.[11] For example, the following scenario offers a plausible draft of an explanation based upon kin-selection. During the long pre-history of humanity, our ancestors lived in small bands of relatives. During these many millions of years, the proximate mental mechanisms that induce humans to be (sometimes) selflessly altruistic evolved and the model of kin-selection can explain this evolution.[12] In very recent times (on the evolutionary timescale), however, most humans stopped living in extended kin-groups. Because the altruistic mechanism is still part of our mental makeup, we often use other markers than consanguinity or family resemblance in order to select possible recipients of our altruistic actions, such as skin colour, language, religion or, after some reflection, any group of humans in great need. Because of genetic variation and upbringing, the altruistic urge will be much stronger in one human being than in another. Oskar Schindler and Mother Teresa apparently had potent altruistic mechanisms.

Furthermore, if evolutionary models and genetic inheritability cannot account completely for the proximate mechanisms or motives that induce us to behave altruistically, it does not follow that the God-hypothesis is the only alternative and, indeed, is the best explanation of our altruistic urges and moral considerations. There may be many other explanations that refer to purely secular factors, such as the subconscious impact of the social prestige that psychological altruists earn in

---

[10]   David Sloan Wilson and E.O. Wilson, 'Rethinking the Theoretical Foundation of Sociobiology', *Quarterly Review of Biology* 82 (2007), 327–48. Cf. Elliott Sober and David Sloan Wilson, *Unto Others: The Evolution and Psychology of Unselfish Behavior* (Cambridge, MA: Harvard University Press, 1998); and Alan Carter, 'Evolution and the Problem of Altruism', *Philosophical Studies* 123 (2005), 213–30.

[11]   Cf. Frans de Waal et al., *Primates and Philosophers. How Morality Evolved* (Princeton, NJ and Oxford: Princeton University Press, 2006), p. 16: 'Personally, I remain unconvinced that we need group selection to explain the origin of these tendencies – we seem to get quite far with the theories of kin selection and reciprocal altruism.'

[12]   Hamilton, 'The Genetical Evolution of Social Behaviour I and II'.

specific cultural contexts or the presence of religious beliefs, which may motivate people to act altruistically, although they are in fact false.[13]

We have ample reasons for concluding, then, that Collins' explanation of our moral awareness by the hypothesis of theism merely postulates a god-of-the-gaps. His argument that the human moral sense cannot be explained in principle by secular scientific disciplines is nothing but an *argumentum ad ignorantiam*. As the Princeton ethicist Peter Singer says: 'Morality is a natural phenomenon. No myths are required to explain its existence.'[14] In the next section, I shall dwell somewhat longer on what I call 'explanatory ethics', that is, the endeavour to explain the human moral sense and its many cultural manifestations.

Explanatory Ethics

An objection often raised to evolutionary explanations of our moral capabilities is that they can perhaps account for human *inclinations* to behave altruistically or courageously, for example, but not for the fact that we feel the *obligation* to do so.[15] Formulated in Kantian terms, we might say that evolutionary explanations can merely account for our *Neigung* (propensity) to altruism and other praiseworthy behaviour, but not for our awareness of a *Pflicht* (duty)[16] The brief answer to this objection is that we would never feel obliged in the moral sense (that is, by moral norms) if we did not have any natural moral inclinations, whereas categorical 'oughts' are needed if our moral inclinations are insufficiently strong for the occasion. In other words, the 'Kantian' view of ethics has to be combined with a 'Humean' one, and both aspects of morality can be explained to some extent by evolutionary models.[17] Let me elaborate by sketching very briefly the research programme of explanatory ethics.

---

[13]   Of course, the presence and persistence of these religious beliefs should be explained by secular mechanisms. Cf., for example, David Sloan Wilson, *Darwin's Cathedral. Evolution, Religion, and the Nature of Society* (Chicago and London: University of Chicago Press, 2002). Incidentally, if religious believers think that they will enter heaven because of their altruistic actions, these actions are not selflessly altruistic in the psychological sense.

[14]   Peter Singer, 'Ethics and Intuitions', *Journal of Ethics* 9 (2005), 331–52, at p. 337.

[15]   Cf. David C. Lathi, 'Parting with Illusions in Evolutionary Ethics', *Biology and Philosophy* 18 (2003), 639–51, at p. 643: 'We don't just feel like doing altruistic behavior *x*; we feel, or think, that we *ought* to do *x*, and that others in present circumstances should do it too, and that we have no choice about this obligation, and so on. No explanation has been provided for why [we] tend to think some options are *right* and others *wrong*.'

[16]   Cf. Christine M. Korsgaard, 'Morality and the Distinctiveness of Human Action', in de Waal et al., *Primates and Philosophers*, p. 113: 'The morality of your action is not a function of the content of your intentions. It is a function of the exercise of normative self-government.'

[17]   This is also argued by Kitcher, 'Psychological Altruism', §§ vi–vii.

Of course, explanatory ethics can never *justify* moral obligations. Its task is to *explain* why humans feel or think that they have them and why human beings living in a specific culture, and fulfilling specific social roles, consider themselves to be under particular moral obligations. In other words, the business of explanatory ethics is to account for 'descriptive oughts', that is, the fact that specific people feel morally obliged in certain ways. Its explanations will never yield 'normative oughts', which I shall discuss in the next section.[18]

Roughly speaking, the research programme of explanatory ethics consists of three stages. In a first, explorative stage, anthropologists, psychologists, sociologists and historians describe and systematize as precisely as possible the moral norms endorsed explicitly or implicitly by the many different groups of humans on earth at present and in the past. This research in descriptive ethics has revealed great moral variety, but also moral universals, which we find in all cultures.

The second stage is concerned with proximal explanations. We should attempt to identify the proximate mechanisms that induce humans to display moral behaviour and to form specific moral judgments. These mechanisms may belong to individual human beings and consist of emotional dispositions, intellectual capacities, virtuous or vicious habits, willpower and the human sensitivity for the opinions of others. But social structures such as cultural institutions, group habits of gossip, criminal law and other sociological factors also contribute to the propensity of people to behave morally and to pass particular moral judgments.

Finally, in a third stage, we should attempt to construct convincing ultimate explanations of these proximate mechanisms. How can we explain that we humans have them? It is here that evolutionary scenarios have their proper place, and other types of historical explanation will play a role as well.

In order to rule out simplistic accounts of explanatory ethics, I would like to stress two things. First of all, its *explananda* are extraordinarily complex.[19] Charles Darwin realized this clearly when in *The Descent of Man* he purported to explain ultimately what he called the human 'moral sense'. According to Darwin, this 'most noble of all the attributes of man' consists of at least four different types of ingredients in each human individual: 1) social instincts such as empathy and sympathy; 2) highly developed mental faculties; 3) the power of language, which enables us to express 'the common opinion how each member ought to act for the public good'; and 4) habits, which strengthen dispositions to behave in certain ways.[20]

---

[18]   For this distinction, cf. Peter G. Woolcock, 'The Case Against Evolutionary Ethics Today', in Jane Maienschein and Michael Ruse (eds), *Biology and the Foundation of Ethics, Cambridge Studies in Philosophy and Biology* (Cambridge: Cambridge University Press, 1999), pp. 284–5.

[19]   Cf. John Rawls, *A Theory of Justice* (Cambridge, MA: Harvard University Press, 1971), p. 46: 'Clearly, this moral capacity is extraordinarily complex.'

[20]   Darwin, *The Descent of Man*, Chapter 4, pp. 121–2.

Darwin mentioned in particular the mental faculty of recollecting our past actions and motives, which produces a feeling of misery or guilt when we notice that our enduring social instincts have yielded to some intermittent rival urge. Other writers, such as Philip Kitcher, have focused on our mental capacity for forming 'higher-order volitions' or a 'system of normative control', which enables us to achieve consistency in behaviour when various instinctive drives or emotional impulses are in mutual conflict.[21]

Kitcher proposes the following hypothesis concerning the adaptive function of this higher-order capacity. If our nature was to be completely selfish, we would not live in social groups and would not need morality. There would be no need for morality either if we were perfectly social and altruistic. But since the social instincts of humans and closely related species are fragile, and can easily be overruled by other impulses, social bonds are often disrupted. This is why chimpanzees have to spend many hours a day on peacemaking by grooming each other.[22] Compared to this time-consuming practice of grooming, a capacity of forming higher-order volitions or rules, which resolve social conflicts mostly by pre-emption rather than by reaction, has a clear adaptive advantage.[23] In other words, the 'Kantian' system of morality evolved because the 'Humean' system is insufficiently strong, and evolutionary models can explain the existence of both types of mental mechanism in humans.[24]

The next point that I would like to stress is that explanatory ethics is a multidisciplinary endeavour. One of its tasks is to elaborate a coherent overall view of our moral capacities, the elements of which can often be disclosed by a consilience of inductions taken from many different disciplines. Let me mention by way of example dispositions in humans to have specific emotions, such as sympathy, a feeling of fairness, revenge, forgiveness, gratitude and guilt, which are relevant to morality. Research in behavioural biology concerning species closely related to humans by Frans de Waal and others reveals that many instances of animal behaviour may be explained proximally by assuming that they are triggered by emotional mechanisms closely akin to those that we humans have. This type of explanation is not necessarily an anthropomorphic over-interpretation of animal behaviour, as behaviourists and many behavioural biologists used to

---

[21]   Kitcher, 'Psychological Altruism', pp. 303–4; cf. Alan Gibbard, *Wise Choices, Apt Feelings* (Cambridge, MA: Harvard University Press, 1990).

[22]   Cf. Frans de Waal, *Peacemaking Among Primates* (Cambridge, MA: Harvard University Press, 1989).

[23]   Kitcher, 'Psychological Altruism', p. 304.

[24]   Cf. ibid., p. 308: 'Moral agency depends fundamentally on both the natural dispositions to sympathy and on the normative guidance that makes up for their shortcomings.'

aver; rather, it may be in line with the theory of evolution because it exemplifies evolutionary parsimony.[25]

De Waal describes these emotional capacities as elementary 'building blocks' or important 'prerequisites' of human morality.[26] This claim can be justified by psychological research, which reveals that many instances of typically moral human behaviour or moral judgment are triggered by emotional reactions and do not result from the slower processes of rational deliberation.[27] The crucial importance of our emotional capacities for morality is further confirmed by research on patients with brain damage to the medial frontal gyrus or the ventromedial portion of the frontal lobes, who show the surprising combination of intact reasoning abilities and insensitivity to moral and social standards.[28] Clearly, reason alone cannot sustain human morality, at least not *de facto*, and our emotional capacities are essential as well.

Confirmation of the thesis that emotional dispositions are important building blocks of morality has equally been provided by brain-imagining studies, which reveal a correlation between anti-social behaviour and deficiencies in the size of, or the amount of metabolic activity in, the prefrontal cortex.[29] Yet another type of

---

[25]   Cf. de Waal et al., *Primates and Philosophers, passim* and Appendix A. As de Waal says, evolutionary parsimony posits 'that if closely related species act the same, the underlying mental processes are probably the same too' (p. 62). Of course there may be scientific disputes concerning the adequacy of de Waal's explanations of specific instances of animal behaviour. Cf. Johan J. Bolhuis and D.D.L. Wynne, 'Can Evolution Explain How minds Work?', *Nature* 458 (2009), 832–3.

[26]   De Waal et al., *Primates and Philosophers*, pp. 20–21; Cf. J.C. Flack and F.B.M. de Waal, 'Any Animal Whatever: Darwinian Building Blocks of Morality in Monkeys and Apes', *Journal of Consciousness Studies* 7 (2000), 1–29; Frans de Waal, *Good Natured: The Origins of Right and Wrong in Humans and Other Animals* (Cambridge, MA: Harvard University Press, 1996).

[27]   Cf. Jesse J. Prinz, *The Emotional Construction of Morals* (Oxford: Oxford University Press, 2007), pp. 21–49 for an overview of the literature. Prinz defends what he calls 'strong emotionism'. For the thesis that moral judgments are often triggered by emotional responses, cf.: Jonathan Haidt, 'The Emotional Dog and its Rational Tail: A Social Intuitionist Approach to Moral Judgment', *Psychological Review* 108 (2001), 814–34; Joshua D Greene and Jonathan Haidt, 'How (and Where) Does Moral Judgment Work?', *Trends in Cognitive Sciences* 6 (2002), 517–23.

[28]   Cf. Singer, 'Ethics and Intuitions', pp. 338–9, referring to Antonio R. Damasio, *Descartes' Error: Emotion, Reason, and the Human Brain* (New York: Grosset/Putnam, 1994), pp. 3–9 and 34–51 (discussion of the case of Phineas Gage); Steven W Anderson, Antoine Bechara, Antonio R. Damasio et al., 'Impairment of Social and Moral Behavior Related to Early Damage in Human Prefrontal Cortex', *Nature Neuroscience* 2 (1999), 1032–7; and Greene and Haidt, 'How (and Where) Does Moral Judgment Work?'.

[29]   Singer, 'Ethics and Intuitions', p. 339, referring to Adrian Raine, Todd Lencz, Susan Bihrle et al., 'Reduced Prefrontal Gray Matter Volume and Reduced Autonomic Activity in Antisocial Personality Disorder', *Archives of General Psychiatry* 57 (2000), 119–27.

confirmation stems from functional magnetic resonance imaging (fMRI), which also reveals the role of emotions when people make moral judgments.[30] Clearly, even the investigation of one type of ingredient of our moral sense, its emotional building blocks, is already a multidisciplinary endeavour, and there is a consilience of inductions obtained in many fields of empirical research supporting the crucial role of emotional capacities in our moral awareness.[31]

In order to reconstruct on an empirical basis the development of human morality from the proto-moral stage of our early ancestors, which we have in common with chimpanzees and bonobos, to the stage of the human hunter-gatherer bands from which we descend, some speculative assumptions have to be made and other disciplines must be involved. We might presuppose, for example, that the social structure of groups of our early common ancestors resembled the social structure of chimpanzees living in the wild today, in which we usually find a dominant alpha male, and that the social structure of the hunter-gatherer bands from which we have descended more recently resembled the more egalitarian organization of hunter-gatherer societies studied by anthropologists during the last 100 years. On these assumptions, anthropologists and sociologists may develop hypotheses concerning the pre-history of human morality.[32] More recent stages of the development of human morality in different cultures may be explained by cultural historians. I shall leave open here the contentious issue as to what extent evolutionary models of group selection or models of meme-selection can be used as ultimate explanations of recent stages of moral development in human cultural history.[33]

Ethicists who focus on our capacity to form second-order volitions or on our capacity for autonomy in the Kantian sense will tend to think that what makes an action 'moral' in the ordinary sense of the term is not the content of our intentions but rather the fact that we have exercised autonomous normative self-governance.[34] Accordingly, they might say that evolutionary explanations of our

---

[30]   Singer, 'Ethics and Intuitions', pp. 339–42, referring to Joshua D. Greene, R. Brian Sommerville, Leigh E. Nystrom et al., 'An fMRI Investigation of Emotional Engagement in Moral Judgment', *Science* 293 (2001), 2105–8; Greene and Haidt, 'How (and Where) Does Moral Judgment Work?'; and H.R. Heekeren, I. Wartenburger, H. Schmidt et al., 'An fMRI Study of Simple Ethical Decision-Making', *Neuroreport* 14 (2003), 1215–19.

[31]   Of course, how this role should be specified more precisely is an issue for further debate. Cf. Prinz, *The Emotional Construction of Morals*, pp. 13–21 for various types of 'emotionism'.

[32]   For a discussion of this issue, cf.: Boehm and critics, in Leonard D. Katz, *Evolutionary Origins of Morality. Cross-Disciplinary Perspectives* (Thorverton: Imprint Academic, 2000), pp. 79–183.

[33]   Cf. Wilson, *Darwin's Cathedral* for a defence of such an approach to the ultimate explanation of religions in particular.

[34]   Cf., for example, Korsgaard, in de Waal et al., *Primates and Philosophers*, p. 112. Of course, Korsgaard might respond that the Kantian concept of morality is meant to be an explication, and not a lexical definition, of our ordinary sense of the word 'moral'. However, the explication should be largely adequate with respect to our ordinary concept.

moral capacities can never explain the *content* of human morality. However, this would be a serious mistake. The everyday meaning of the adjective 'moral' is determined, at least in part, by paradigmatic examples of moral behaviour, such as telling the truth when this harms one's interests or educating one's children well. Such actions are called 'moral' irrespective of the question to what extent they resulted from an application of the categorical imperative test.

In fact, a strong case can be made for an evolutionarily ultimate explanation of the content of quite some fundamental moral beliefs, which we find in all human cultures. Let us suppose that moral convictions such as that we should put the interests of our children before those of complete strangers or that we should reciprocate favours are based upon deep instinctive or emotional evaluative attitudes, as the empirical research recapitulated above suggests. Then it is the case that the forces of natural selection will have favoured the evolution of these evaluative attitudes in humans and related species rather than the evolution of the opposite ones, assuming that they are genetically heritable. When humans developed languages, they became able to express such evaluative attitudes in normative moral judgments. As Sharon Street and others have argued quite convincingly, it follows that 'the forces of natural selection have had a tremendous influence on the content of human evaluative judgements'.[35] Let me call this the Thesis of Evolutionary Content (TEC).

We now have to raise two pressing questions. First of all, what are the implications for normative ethics, if any, of the thesis that the forces of natural selection were important causal factors shaping the content of at least some of our fundamental moral beliefs? Secondly, which meta-ethical views are most plausible, given the background knowledge of an evolutionary origin of the content of fundamental moral convictions, which we find in all human cultures? I discuss the first question briefly in the next section, whereas the two subsequent sections will be devoted to meta-ethics. Let me stress again that I am interested here in the interconnections between these various issues. The reader should not expect a profound analysis of any of them.

Normative Ethics

If evolutionary theory provides a scientific explanation, at least in part, of the human moral sense and of some of its central contents, can it also contribute to the justification or refutation of (specific) moral norms? Does evolutionary explanatory ethics have any (positive or negative) implications for normative ethics?

---

[35]   Cf. Sharon Street, 'A Darwinian Dilemma for Realist Theories of Value', *Philosophical Studies* 127 (2006), 109–66, at pp. 113ff.; Richard Joyce, *The Evolution of Morality* (Cambridge, MA: MIT Press, 2006), *passim*; Michael Ruse, 'Evolutionary Ethics: A Phoenix Arisen', *Zygon* 21 (1986), 95–112; Sober and Wilson, *Unto Others*; and many others.

From a perspective of cultural history, it is easy to understand why between 1859 and 1945 many authors answered this question in the affirmative. Christian metaphysics had had a double function with regard to human morality. It (allegedly) explained why humans have a sense of right and wrong and it justified moral obligations by interpreting them as God's commands. If the theological explanation of our moral awareness has been superseded by an evolutionary explanation, might we not expect that evolutionary theory can inherit Christianity's foundational function for ethics as well? Could evolutionary theory not finally provide us with a *scientific* justification of normative ethics? And might the content of this new normative ethics not be different in some respects from traditional morality, so that evolutionary explanatory ethics opens up possibilities for moral innovation and progress?[36] No wonder that many scientists placed their hopes on evolutionary ethics or Social Darwinism.[37]

As is well known, however, in around 1900 philosophers such as Henry Sidgwick and G.E. Moore argued convincingly that this approach to the foundations of ethics is logically flawed. Hume had already pointed out that we cannot validly deduce an 'ought' from an 'is'.[38] Sidgwick agreed and Moore showed by a perceptive analysis of Herbert Spencer's writings that evolutionary ethicists surreptitiously identify descriptive concepts such as 'more evolved' or 'more fit' with the notion of morally better.[39] As Moore stressed, 'this forms no part of Darwin's scientific theory'.[40] Using his 'open question argument', Moore attempted to establish the thesis that all naturalistic (and all metaphysical) systems of ethics commit the so-called naturalistic fallacy, because normative terms such as 'good' cannot be defined purely in descriptive terms.[41]

---

[36] For a contemporary scientist who endorses this view, cf.: Edward Osborne Wilson, *Sociobiology. The Abridged Edition* (Cambridge, MA: Harvard University Press, 1980), p. 287: 'Scientists and humanists should consider together the possibility that the time has come for ethics to be removed temporarily from the hands of the philosophers and biologized.' In line with his empirical research, Wilson proposed some new moral norms. For a review, cf. Philip Kitcher, 'Four Ways of Biologicizing Ethics', in Elliott Sober (ed.), *Conceptual Issues in Evolutionary Biology. An Anthology*, 2nd edn (Cambridge, MA: Bradford/MIT Press, 1993).

[37] Cf. Farber, *The Temptations of Evolutionary Ethics* for an overview.

[38] David Hume, *A Treatise of Human Nature* (1739/40), ed. P.H. Nidditch (Oxford: Clarendon, 1978), p. 469.

[39] Henry Sidgwick, *The Methods of Ethics*, 7th edn (London: Macmillan, 1907, first edn 1874), p. 81: 'every attempt thus to derive "what ought to be" from "what is" palpably fails, the moment it is freed from fundamental confusions of thought'; and G.E. Moore, *Principia Ethica* (1903), revised edn, edited with an introduction by Thomas Baldwin (Cambridge: Cambridge University Press, 1993), §§ 30–35.

[40] Moore, *Principia Ethica*, p. 99. Cf. Hume, *A Treatise of Human Nature*, p. 469.

[41] Moore, *Principia Ethica*, Chapter I B. In what follows, I shall use the label 'naturalistic fallacy' not only for the definitional move criticized by Moore but also for violations of Hume's law.

Although the limitations of Moore's open question argument are generally recognized, he was right in pointing out that purely factual premises, such as those of evolutionary science, will never suffice for justifying normative conclusions.[42] All recent attempts to refute this elementary logical insight, which is sometimes called 'Hume's law', turn out to involve subtle conceptual confusions, such as mistaking a descriptive 'ought' (the fact that specific people feel a specific obligation) for a normative 'ought' (which says that we should behave in a specific way). If we account for the former by a deductive-nomological explanation, we have deduced a descriptive 'ought' from an 'is' without committing any fallacy. But such an explanation does not amount to justifying the corresponding normative 'ought'.[43]

Should we conclude, then, that 'Evolution has very little indeed to say to Ethics', as G.E. Moore inferred, and that evolutionary explanatory ethics is simply irrelevant to normative moral theory?[44] There is no doubt that evolutionary theory 'cannot serve the moral-reassurance role previously filled by religion' in the sense that the theory of evolution cannot be a normative foundation for ethics, as monotheist religions typically purport to be.[45] Yet it is precisely by reflecting on this difference between religious moral doctrines such as those of Christianity or Islam on the one hand and evolutionary theory on the other that we might perhaps discover indirect implications of the latter for normative ethics.

As already stated, the religious theories of monotheism both explain our human moral sense and justify moral imperatives. Because God is thought to be eternal, believers often conclude that the moral convictions which we find in alleged revelations must be *eternally* valid as well and that these moral beliefs could not have been otherwise. However, if the TEC is correct, there is an evolutionary explanation of the content of many fundamental moral beliefs or evaluative attitudes. This implies that these contents are radically contingent in the sense that other contents would have evolved if the conditions of our evolution had been different. Let me call this implication of the TEC the Radical Contingency Thesis (RCT).

---

[42] For a critical analysis of Moore's open question argument, cf., e.g. Alexander Miller, *An Introduction to Contemporary Metaethics* (Cambridge: Polity Press, 2003), Chapter 2.

[43] Cf. Woolcock, 'The Case Against Evolutionary Ethics Today' for a critical analysis of attempts to derive 'ought' from 'is'. Similar criticisms also apply to more recent attempts to derive an 'ought' from an 'is', such as Prinz, *The Emotional Construction of Morals*, p. 5. Prinz admits on pp. 6–7 that he has not shown how to derive an ought from an is if 'oughts' are prescriptions.

[44] Moore, *Principia Ethica*, p. 109. Of course, *given* specific normative premises, many scientific theories will be highly relevant to ethics, because they enable us to derive new normative results, which are based in part on scientific facts. But this is not what Moore meant.

[45] Woolcock, 'The Case Against Evolutionary Ethics Today', p. 303.

That the RCT is implied, or at least made plausible, by the TEC has been acknowledged by many authors.[46] For example, Charles Darwin wrote in *The Descent of Man*:

> I do not wish to maintain that any strictly social animal, if its intellectual faculties were to become as active and as highly developed as in man, would acquire exactly the same moral sense as ours. If, for instance, to take an extreme case, men were reared under precisely the same condition as hive-bees, there can hardly be a doubt that our unmarried females would, like the worker-bees, think it a sacred duty to kill their brothers, and mothers would strive to kill their fertile daughters; and no one would think of interfering. Nevertheless, the bee, or any other social animal, would gain in our supposed case, as it appears to me, some feeling of right or wrong, or a conscience.[47]

In itself, the thesis of radical contingency is not a normative one. Furthermore, the discovery that some of our moral attitudes are not adaptive in the present stage of human evolution would not be a normative discovery either, because the evolutionary concept of adaptation is not a normative concept. Yet we might think that the RCT nevertheless has normative implications. Let me discuss one author who draws this conclusion.

Recently, Peter Singer has attempted to refute objections to his utilitarian ethics by using the following argument.[48] Critics sometimes claim that Singer's normative ethical theory must be incorrect, because in many circumstances it leads to moral judgments that are in conflict with our common moral 'intuitions'.[49] For example, Singer's preference for utilitarianism implies that the interests of one's children ought not to have a greater importance for the parents than the interests of strangers, because ethical conduct essentially is conduct that can be justified from the point of view of an impartial spectator. Surely, this theorem of preference utilitarianism contradicts the moral intuitions of most human beings. However, Singer argues that if these intuitions are residues of the contingent evolutionary history of humanity, we should not attribute any normative authority to them. In other words, because the TEC implies the RCT, explanatory research on the origins of our moral sense is allegedly 'highly significant for normative ethics, but in an indirect way'.[50] According to Singer, evolutionary research suggests 'that normative ethics should disregard our common moral intuitions'.[51]

---

[46] Cf., for example, Ruse, 'Evolutionary Ethics', pp. 108–10.

[47] Darwin, *The Descent of Man*, pp. 122–3.

[48] Singer, 'Ethics and Intuitions'.

[49] By 'intuitions' one means in this context the spontaneous moral judgments pronounced on being presented with a moral problem.

[50] Singer, 'Ethics and Intuitions', pp. 343 and *passim*.

[51] Ibid., p. 349.

Singer illustrates this argument by psychological tests concerning a familiar (all too familiar) 'trolley problem'. Test subjects are asked to imagine that they are standing alone by a railroad track, noticing that a trolley without anyone aboard is racing down towards a group of five people. Because these people do not notice the trolley, they will be killed if nothing interferes. The test subjects are presented with two scenarios. In the first, the only thing you can do is to throw a switch that will divert the trolley onto a sidetrack, where it will crush one other person. In the second scenario, you are standing on a footbridge without railings next to a stranger, who is so large that if you push him off the bridge onto the track, the trolley will be stopped and the stranger will be squashed. Suppose that you can push him onto the track without any effort. In both scenarios you sacrifice one person in order to save five. When asked what action ought to be taken in these circumstances, however, most test subjects respond that we should throw the switch in the first scenario, but that we should not push the stranger in the second.[52]

Philosophers may take the moral intuitions elicited by these two scenarios as authoritative and attempt to legitimize them by deriving them from normative ethical theories. For example, by pushing the stranger off the footbridge, we would use another person merely as a means, which is forbidden by Kantian ethics. But, unfortunately, such attempts can be refuted easily by other scenarios and by the corresponding responses of test subjects. For example, we might imagine that by throwing the switch, the trolley is diverted on a loop before it arrives at the five people imperilled by it. On this loop, the large stranger is lying and will be killed by the trolley, which will be blocked by his body. In this scenario, the stranger is also used merely as a means, whereas most respondents say that we ought to throw the switch.[53]

Singer concludes that we should not attempt to *justify* such moral intuitions by an ethical theory. Instead, we should merely *explain* them. In the present case, empirical research reveals that people have a strong negative emotional response to the proposed push in the second scenario, whereas this emotional response is lacking with regard to throwing the switch in the first.[54] The activation of the emotive proximate mechanism by the second scenario, and its inertness concerning the first, can be accounted for by an evolutionary ultimate explanation. Since human beings lived in small kin-groups for most of their evolutionary history, where primitive technology did not allow killing at a distance, other human beings could be killed only in a close-up and personal way. Evolutionary hypotheses can explain why we developed instant emotional responses that prohibit these killings. Such a response is triggered by the second scenario, but not, or not as strongly, by the first. Singer concludes as follows:

---

[52]   Ibid., pp. 339-340, referring to Judith Jarvis Thomson, 'Killing, Letting Die, and the Trolley Problem', *The Monist* 59 (1976), 204–17.

[53]   Singer, 'Ethics and Intuitions', p. 340.

[54]   Ibid., p. 341, referring to Greene et al., 'An fMRI Investigation of Emotional Engagement in Moral Judgment'.

So the salient feature that explains our different intuitive judgments concerning the two cases is that the footbridge case is the kind of situation that was likely to arise during the eons of time over which we were evolving; whereas the standard trolley case [= scenario one] describes a way of bringing about someone's death that has only been possible in the past century or two, a time far too short to have any impact on our inherited patterns of emotional response. But what is the moral salience of the fact that I have killed someone in a way that was possible a million years ago, rather than in a way that became possible only two hundred years ago? I would answer: none.[55]

According to Singer, advances in our scientific understanding have some normative significance not only at the particular level of a moral problem such as the trolley case, but also at the more general level of methodology in ethics. Let us briefly consider these two levels.

In the particular trolley case discussed, one of our moral intuitions is in conflict with the rational insight that if in general it is bad when people are killed, five people being killed is worse than one person being killed. An evolutionary explanation of the moral intuition that we ought not to push the stranger onto the track might convince us that the repugnance we would feel in doing so should be overcome. Instead of trying to find moral principles that justify this intuition, we might conclude that there is no morally relevant difference between the two scenarios. In this case, the evolutionary explanation of our moral repugnance to pushing the stranger is considered to be a *debunking* explanation of the difference between the moral judgments concerning the two scenarios. After some reflection, we conclude that there is no valid moral difference between them.

Singer boldly generalizes from this particular case of a (supposedly) debunking evolutionary explanation. Concerning the more general level of methodology, he argues that the evolutionary understanding of how we make moral judgments also 'casts serious doubt on the method of reflective equilibrium' proposed by John Rawls as the proper method of ethical justification:[56]

There is little point in constructing a moral theory designed to match considered moral judgments that themselves stem from our evolved responses to the situations in which we and our ancestors lived during the period of our evolution as social mammals, primates, and finally, human beings. We should, with our current powers of reasoning and our rapidly changing circumstances, be able to do better than that.[57]

In other words, Singer not only concludes from the evolutionary origin of our emotionally based moral intuitions (the TEC) that these intuitions are radically

---

[55] Singer, 'Ethics and Intuitions', p. 348.

[56] Singer, 'Ethics and Intuitions', p. 348; Rawls, *A Theory of Justice*, § 9.

[57] Singer, 'Ethics and Intuitions', p. 348.

contingent (the RCT), but also that we should not attribute any moral authority to them.

To this conclusion we might raise two objections, of which Singer discusses the second only. First, if we infer from the evolutionary contingency of our moral intuitions that they should not have normative authority, we commit a naturalistic fallacy in the broad sense that we derive a normative 'ought' or 'should' from an 'is'. Concerning the normative impact of evolutionary explanations of our moral intuitions, we should pay close attention to the scope of the negation. If we explain our immediate moral intuitions by interpreting them as the 'voice of our conscience', whereas this voice is attributed to God, these intuitions will have moral authority for us, if at least we attribute a moral authority to God. But if these intuitions are explained as contingent products of our evolutionary history, this explanation in itself yields *no reason to attribute* moral authority to them, because an 'is' does not entail an 'ought'. However, it does not follow that there are *good reasons not to attribute* moral authority to these intuitions. When he draws this latter conclusion, Singer commits the naturalistic fallacy by illegitimately shifting the scope of the negation.

Some readers will find it shocking to accuse an accomplished ethicist such as Peter Singer of committing a naturalistic fallacy. But I am not deeply committed to this particular diagnosis of his argument. Perhaps we should diagnose Singer's fallacy as that of a hasty generalization. From the particular case in which an evolutionary explanation of an evaluative attitude (allegedly) is also a debunking explanation, he draws without further argument the universal conclusion that all evolutionary explanations of our normative attitudes are debunking. Or perhaps Singer's fallacy is a version of the genetic fallacy, because he concludes from a specific causal history of moral intuitions without further argument that these beliefs are not justified. Or, finally, Singer's reasoning might rely on a hidden premise of meta-ethical realism or objectivism. If this premise were correct, an evolutionary explanation of moral beliefs might imply that these beliefs probably do not track the objective moral truth, so that evolutionary explanatory ethics implies moral scepticism, or a so-called 'error theory', concerning our ethical intuitions. This is one reason why I investigate the assumption of meta-ethical realism in the section entitled 'Evolution and Meta-ethical Realism', below.

The second objection will be raised by those, among others, who endorse the method of reflective equilibrium in ethics.[58] Against Singer's thesis that we should disregard our common moral intuitions in normative ethics, they will protest that without any moral intuitions, no moral judgment whatsoever can be justified. Philosophers who wanted to derive all moral judgments from rational

---

[58]   Cf. Joakim Sandberg and Niklas Juth, 'Ethics and Intuitions: A Reply to Singer', *Journal of Ethics*, published online 29 July 2010, for a well-developed version of this objection.

first principles have failed to find self-evident ones, whereas even utilitarianism rests on a fundamental intuition about what is good.[59]

Singer answers this second objection by making a distinction between two types of moral intuitions. On the one hand, there are emotionally triggered moral intuitions, such as our repulsion to pushing the stranger, which are the product of our evolutionary past. On the other hand, there are insights that we might call 'rational intuitions', such as the '"intuition" that tells us that the death of one person is a lesser tragedy than the death of five'.[60] According to Singer, we face a choice in the light of the best scientific understanding of ethics. Either we accept that ultimately our moral judgments will always be based upon emotionally triggered intuitions and use our rational faculties to reach the best possible decision in each particular case, for example, by the method of reflective equilibrium, or we set ourselves the 'large and difficult task' of 'separating those moral judgments that we owe to our evolutionary and cultural history, from those that have a rational basis'. Singer opts for this second alternative, claiming that the first 'leads to a form of moral scepticism'.[61]

But are there any substantial moral judgments that have a purely rational basis and which we do not owe somehow to our evolutionary and cultural history? Surely Singer's example is not a case in point, and I do not think that there are any. The statement that the death of one person is a lesser tragedy than the death of five is based upon two premises. The first, that one is less than five, may be called a purely rational or conceptual insight, but it is not a moral intuition. The second, that death is a tragedy or that it is a bad thing if people are killed without justification, is indeed a substantial moral intuition, but it is not a 'rational' premise or insight in the sense in which it is rational to believe that $5 > 1$. Our deep conviction that it is bad when people are killed without good reason may very well be a result of our evolutionary and cultural past. It belongs to our moral bedrock, which cannot be justified any further by deriving it from more fundamental and purely 'rational' premises.

Singer denies that the second premise may be due to our evolutionary past by arguing that 'there is no evolutionary advantage in concern for others simply because they are members of our species'. Selection between different species happens too slowly and rarely compared to the selection of individual organisms within the species to play a role in evolution.[62] Yet our evolved capacity of empathy, originally limited to members of our own group, may come to encompass more and more people in the course of time as we learn about other cultures. The intuition that any undeserved human death is bad undoubtedly has an emotional basis, the

---

[59]   Singer, 'Ethics and Intuitions', p. 349.

[60]   Singer, 'Ethics and Intuitions', pp. 350–351.

[61]   Ibid., p. 351. This claim by Singer may be thought to confirm the fourth diagnosis of his global argument against attributing any authority to our moral intuitions hinted at above.

[62]   Ibid., p. 350, and pp. 334–5.

presence of which can be explained by our evolutionary and cultural history. The same holds for many of our beliefs about well-being, without which utilitarianism is empty of any content.

We come to the conclusion that although the thesis of evolutionary content (the TEC) implies the RCT, this does not mean that explanatory ethics by itself has any normative impact. Even if our most fundamental moral judgments have no other psychological basis than contingently evolved emotions or evaluative attitudes, it does not follow that these judgments should not have any moral authority for us. On the contrary, it may very well be that there is no other or better basis for moral authority, as I shall argue in the following section.

Models of Ethical Justification

Let us now inquire whether evolutionary explanations of our evaluative attitudes have any implications for meta-ethics.[63] In fact, the RCT already belongs to meta-ethics and not to normative ethical theory. It does not state a moral norm, but is concerned with the status of our evaluative attitudes and normative judgments. In this section, I try to determine which model of ethical justification is the most promising, given the background knowledge of evolutionary explanatory ethics. In the next section, I shall investigate the implications of the TEC for the issue of meta-ethical realism.

Secular ethicists such as Immanuel Kant and John Stuart Mill modelled their theory of justification in ethics on the axiomatic-deductive method in mathematics as it was often understood before the rise of non-Euclidean geometry and David Hilbert's *Grundlagen*.[64] As Mill said in *Utilitarianism*, 'there ought either to be some one fundamental principle or law, at the root of all morality, or if there be several, there should be a determinate order of precedence among them; and the one principle, or the rule for deciding between the various principles when they conflict, ought to be self-evident'.[65] But, as many philosophers have argued, this 'Cartesian' model of justification, according to which all our moral judgments should be derivable ultimately from a few self-evident ethical axioms in combination with factual premises, fails for two reasons. Either the derivations do not succeed or the axioms are not self-evident, and usually both.

---

[63]   Meta-ethics raises questions about ethics in general, such as whether moral judgments state facts, how they can be justified, whether they are about moral properties that exist independently of human evaluative attitudes and so on. Cf. Miller, *An Introduction to Contemporary Metaethics*, pp. 1–3.

[64]   In D. Hilbert, *Grundlagen der Geometrie* (Leipzig: Teubner, 1899); *Foundations of Geometry*, translated by E. Townsend (La Salle, IL: Open Court, 1959), axioms of geometry are not taken as self-evident truths but as a formal set.

[65]   John Stuart Mill, *Utilitarianism* (1861), in John Stuart Mill and Jeremy Bentham, *Utilitarianism and Other Essays*, ed. Alan Ryan (London: Penguin, 2004), p. 274.

According to Kant's Categorical Imperative, for example, we ought to act in such a way that the maxim on which we act can be endorsed without contradiction as a universal law by all rational beings. However, as Mill rightly objected, Kant fails 'almost grotesquely, to show that there would be any contradiction … in the adoption by all rational beings of the most outrageously immoral rules of conduct'.[66] Furthermore, Kant also failed to show that the Categorical Imperative is self-evident. In his *Groundwork of the Metaphysics of Morals* of 1785, he attempted to establish this axiom of his moral theory by arguing that it is implied by the nature of pure reason alone, or, more precisely, that it follows from the nature of morality.[67] But other philosophers, such as Peter Singer, claim to derive different moral axioms from the very nature of morality, which are incompatible with the Categorical Imperative, such as the principles of preference utilitarianism.[68] However, if various incompatible axioms of ethics are said to be implied by the nature of morality and there is no method accepted by most experts to sort out who is right at this point, we cannot claim with confidence that such axioms are more robust and reliable than our emotionally based moral intuitions, as Singer seems to argue.[69]

Mill's own axiom, the Greatest Happiness Principle, according to which actions are right in proportion as they tend to promote the happiness of all concerned, does not perform any better than Kant's Categorical Imperative, for it also fails to be self-evident.[70] Mill attempted to argue for its self-evidence or rational acceptability as follows:

> The only proof capable of being given that an object is visible is that people actually see it. The only proof that a sound is audible, is that people hear it: and so of the other sources of our experience. In like manner, I apprehend, the sole evidence it is possible to produce that anything is desirable, is that people do actually desire it. If the end which the utilitarian doctrine proposes to itself were not, in theory and in practice, acknowledged to be an end, nothing could ever convince any person that it was so. No reason can be given why the general happiness is desirable, except that each person, so far as he believes it to be attainable, desires his own happiness. This, however, being a fact, we have not only all the proof which the case admits of, but all which it is possible to require.[71]

---

[66]   Ibid., p. 275.

[67]   Immanuel Kant, *Groundwork of the Metaphysics of Morals* (1785), trans. Mary Gregor (Cambridge: Cambridge University Press, 1997), pp. 23–31.

[68]   Peter Singer, *Practical Ethics*, 2nd edn (Cambridge: Cambridge University Press, 1993), pp. 8–15. The incompatibility is due to the fact that Kant's Categorical Imperative presupposes that derived moral maxims are categorical, whereas utilitarianism implies that all derived moral rules are teleological.

[69]   Cf. Sandberg and Juth, 'Ethics and Intuitions', § 4.

[70]   Mill, *Utilitarianism*, pp. 278, 288.

[71]   Ibid., pp. 307–8.

In this passage, however, Mill clearly commits a naturalistic fallacy, because the analogy between being visible and being desirable does not obtain. That people actually see an object proves that it is visible because 'visible' means '*can* be seen'. However, that people actually desire a thing does not prove that it is desirable, because 'desirable' is a normative adjective, meaning what is *worth* desiring, what *ought* to be desired or what is good, and not what *can* be desired. As G.E. Moore observed with biting irony, 'Mill has made as naïve and artless a use of the naturalistic fallacy as anybody could desire'.[72]

Peter Singer also seems to be tempted by what he calls '"foundationalist" attempts to build an ethical system outward from some indubitable starting point', and he contrasts such attempts with the method of reflective equilibrium as developed by Rawls for the public justification of principles of justice.[73] Which of these models of justification is the more promising one for ethics, we may wonder, if we consider them against the background of evolutionary explanations of our moral sense? Or should we perhaps prefer yet another model of ethical justification, given this background knowledge?

Behavioural biologists and evolutionary ethicists will stress the great diversity of emotional building blocks of our moral sense. Apart from empathy and sympathy, there are retributive emotions such as feelings of revenge, resentment or anger, and more positive prosocial feelings such as forgiveness, compassion and gratitude. Furthermore, there are the feelings evoked by the immorality of our own actions, like shame and guilt. Most moral virtues, such as courage or fairness, also have an emotional basis. All these emotions will qualify as 'moral' ones as soon as they are more or less disinterested and impartial.[74]

Given this great diversity of emotional building blocks of human morality, it is very unlikely that we will be able to justify the resulting moral norms by deriving them from a small number of self-evident ethical axioms. In other words, the axiomatic model of ethical justification not only fails for the two reasons illustrated above; it is also not a promising model to start with, given the evolutionary background knowledge concerning our human moral sense. Admittedly, it could be argued that there is a unified *explanation* of all these building blocks, to the extent to which we can account for them by the mechanism of natural selection. But this explanation is not a *justification*, since the evolutionary notions of fitness and adaptation are not normative concepts.

In view of the diversity of emotions that typically trigger our intuitive moral judgments, the model of reflective equilibrium is a much more promising model of

---

[72] Moore, *Principia Ethica*, p. 118. There are other fallacies involved in Mill's attempt to ground the utility principle, for example, in his argument to the effect that happiness is the *only* ultimate objective of all our desires (cf. Moore, §§ 41ff.). Also, from the fact that each of us desires his or her own happiness, it does not follow that each of us desires the happiness of all living beings concerned, which is what utilitarianism says we should do.

[73] Cf. Singer, 'Ethics and Intuitions', p. 347.

[74] Cf. de Waal et al., *Primates and Philosophers*, pp. 19–20.

ethical justification. According to this model, we just start with the moral intuitions that we happen to have. From these, we select what Rawls calls our 'considered convictions', that is, those moral judgments that are formed under conditions in which our capacity for judgment is likely to have been fully exercised and not to have been hampered by distorting influences.[75] All these considered moral judgments have a *prima facie* intrinsic ethical authority for us, and we try to formulate them as general rules.

However, soon we will discover that with regard to concrete situations, these *prima facie* rules will often be in conflict with each other. In order to deal with such conflicts of *prima facie* rules, we might attempt to formulate an overall view or particular ethical theory concerning situations of this type and we will endorse the theory that makes the fewest revisions to our initial considered judgments, or the theory that will not compel us to revise considered judgments to which we attach great weight. For example, the second trolley scenario implies a conflict between, on the one hand, our moral judgment that the undeserved death of five is worse than that of one and, on the other hand, our intuitive moral revulsion against killing the stranger by pushing him over the bridge.

Finally, we might attempt to unify all particular situational theories within one over-arching moral doctrine. In *A Theory of Justice*, Rawls interprets such an ethical theory as an attempt to *describe* our moral capacity by formulating a set of principles which, when conjoined to our beliefs and knowledge of the circumstances, would lead us to make our considered judgments with their supporting reasons, were we to apply these principles conscientiously and intelligently.[76] He compares the task of the moral theorist with that of the grammarian, who attempts to formulate a set of grammatical principles that characterize the linguistic competence of native speakers, because it implies the same discriminations between well-formed and grammatically incorrect sentences that the native speakers make.[77]

However, the task of the normative ethicist is not to *describe* in an integrating manner; rather, that task belongs to the first, descriptive stage of explanatory ethics, as specified above (in the section entitled 'Explanatory Ethics'). What the normative ethicist does is *to propose moral norms*, which 'can serve as part of the premises of an argument which arrives at the matching judgments'.[78] In

---

[75]   Rawls, *A Theory of Justice*, § 9, pp. 47–8; and John Rawls, *Justice as Fairness. A Restatement*, ed. Erin Kelly (Cambridge, MA: Harvard University Press, 2001), § 10, p. 29. Cf. also John Rawls, 'Outline of a Decision Procedure for Ethics', *Philosophical Review* 60 (1951), 177–97.

[76]   Rawls, *A Theory of Justice*, p. 46.

[77]   Ibid., p. 47. We should distinguish between, on the one hand, the traditional axiomatic-deductive method of ethical justification as practised by Kant and Mill and, on the other hand, the justification by means of reflective equilibrium of axiomatic-deductive ethical theories. I reject the first, whereas I would accept the second, if there are such theories in ethics at all.

[78]   Cf. Rawls, *A Theory of Justice*, p. 46.

other words, the integrating ethical theory put forward by the moral philosopher is prescriptive. Its general principles are proposed as having normative force, and in some cases they may overrule some of our intuitive judgments.[79]

This is exactly what a reflective equilibrium means: it is an equilibrium between our initial considered normative judgments and a holistic normative theory. The theory is better to the extent that more of our initial considered judgments can be derived from it, and such a judgment may acquire more moral authority when it can be derived from the best overall theory. Sometimes we will revise an initial particular judgment because it is in conflict with the moral theory we endorse after having compared the theories known to us and after having studied the relevant facts. Clearly, then, the methodology of 'considered judgments in reflective equilibrium' has a strong coherentist flavour.[80] We start with the intrinsic normative force of our considered normative judgments. With respect to a particular judgment, this force may be enhanced or diminished, respectively, if the judgment coheres with or is in conflict with our overall view. According to a coherentist theory of ethical justification, nothing more can be done in order to justify normative 'oughts'.

However, as far as I have characterized the method of reflective equilibrium, it is not yet a model of ethical justification in the full sense of the term. As Rawls says in *A Theory of Justice*, the method may be used 'to characterize one (educated) person's sense of justice'.[81] In this case, 'justification is a matter of the mutual support of many considerations, of everything fitting together into one coherent view'.[82] Let me call this a soliloquious model of justification. But, as Rawls observes, 'justification is argument addressed to those who disagree with us, or to ourselves when we are of two minds. It presumes a clash of views between persons or within one person, and seeks to convince others, or ourselves, of the reasonableness of the principles upon which our claims and judgments are founded'.[83] Apart from the soliloquious method of reflexive equilibrium, then, we

---

[79]   Traditionally, grammarians also conceived of their task as a prescriptive one, but today many grammarians interpret their discipline as a purely empirical one.

[80]   Cf. Rawls, *Justice as Fairness. A Restatement*, pp. 31–2. According to Rawls, the reflective equilibrium obtained after selecting the best ethical theory might motivate 'a radical shift' in one's moral sense, that is, in the set of one's *prima facie* considered judgments (*A Theory of Justice*, p. 49). But, surely, such a shift cannot be so radical that one gives up *all* one's initial moral intuitions, as Singer requires. For a different interpretation of Rawls, cf. Sandberg and Juth, 'Ethics and Intuitions', § 5.

[81]   Rawls, *A Theory of Justice*, p. 50.

[82]   Ibid., p. 579. In his *Justice as Fairness. A Restatement*, Rawls distinguishes between 'wide' reflective equilibrium, which requires that we have selected the best global moral theory from the set of theories prominent in our cultural tradition, and 'narrow' reflective equilibrium, in which the subject merely endorses the moral conception that calls for the fewest revisions to achieve consistency. As he says, wide reflective equilibrium is 'plainly the important concept' (pp. 30–31).

[83]   Rawls, *A Theory of Justice*, p. 580.

should also develop a method of justification that is explicitly 'disputational', as I shall call it, because it applies to disagreements with others.

Rawls seems to think that the method of reflective equilibrium can also be used for resolving interpersonal controversies. But this view presupposes that in a moral disputation with another party, equal weight is attributed by all involved to the corresponding sets of considered judgments of each side. In our globalized world, in which citizens 'have conflicting religious, philosophical, and moral views', this will often not be the case.[84] Although parties may succeed in reaching an overlapping consensus concerning the best *political* system for a pluralist society, they often will not be able to agree on specific *moral* matters by the method of reflective equilibrium. For example, a believing Christian might reject the considered moral judgments of an unbelieving opponent simply because they are not based upon an alleged divine revelation.

In such cases of moral conflict, the parties have to adopt a far less sophisticated and more pragmatic model of moral justification. They will have to look for considered moral judgments on which they happen to agree and attempt to build a consensus concerning the controversy at issue from this starting point, given all the relevant factual information. What can be justified in this manner is the derived moral judgment concerning the controversy at issue. But the considered moral judgments on which the parties happen to agree, and which they use as starting points, often cannot be justified any further. Justification simply stops at the basic moral intuitions we happen to have.

With regard to this disputational model of moral justification, background knowledge concerning the evolution of our moral sense is of importance in the following way. If the existentialism of Jean-Paul Sartre were correct, according to which our deepest moral convictions are the product of absolutely free decisions, it would not be very probable that the parties in a moral dispute can find deeper moral principles on which they happen to agree. But, given the evolutionary explanations of our moral sense, we expect to find moral agreement on many intuitive judgments. In light of this evolutionary background knowledge, the disputational model can be seen as a promising one, even though success will never be guaranteed.

How promising the model is for resolving specific ethical controversies will depend on many factors. Subjects raised within the same cultural tradition will probably agree on more considered judgments than subjects raised within different traditions. If the moral dispute involves normative judgments that are deeply rooted in diverging comprehensive views of the world, such as religions or totalitarian political ideologies, it will be less probable that parties will reach agreement. But, ultimately, there are quite some moral universals, which we find in all human cultures, so that even in our globalized multicultural societies, moral disputes can often be resolved, if at least the disputants aim at being reasonable. The evolutionary explanation of our human moral sense accounts for this important

---

84   Cf. Rawls, *Justice as Fairness. A Restatement*, p. 32.

fact. Hence, evolutionary theory can to some extent serve 'the moral-reassurance role previously filled by religion', after all.

Evolution and Meta-ethical Realism

In the section on 'Normative Ethics' above, I contrasted evolutionary explanations of important ingredients of our moral sense, such as emotional evaluative attitudes having a specific content, with monotheistic explanations. According to the latter, God revealed to us some fundamental moral truths that hold independently of all human evaluative attitudes. This independence thesis (IT) – that fundamental moral truths hold independently of all human evaluative attitudes – is generally regarded as the defining clause of 'strong meta-ethical realism'.[85] According to the former (evolutionary) explanations, the contents of many of our moral convictions are radically contingent (the RCT), because they are due, indirectly, to the influence of Darwinian forces (the TEC). What is the relation between, on the one hand, the claim that the contents of quite some central moral beliefs which we endorse are due, ultimately, to evolutionary processes (the TEC) and, on the other hand, the thesis of strong meta-ethical realism that at least some fundamental moral truths hold independently of all human evaluative attitudes (the IT)? How is evolutionary explanatory ethics related to strong meta-ethical realism?

Clearly, these two doctrines are not mutually contradictory. It is logically possible that both the TEC and the IT are true, and their conjunction may describe a number of different possible states of affairs. For example, it may be that the evolution of our moral convictions did not track the truth, so that most of our evolved moral beliefs are in fact false. Perhaps we do not know any of the moral truths that according to the IT hold independently of our evaluative attitudes. But it may also be that the evolution of our moral convictions did in fact track the truth. In that case, many of our moral beliefs will both be true in the sense of the IT and also have an evolutionary origin. Something like this has occurred, for example, with regard to our perceptual faculties and beliefs. A more adequate capacity to discover relevant features of the environment by sense perception will have enhanced the fitness of our individual ancestors. Accordingly, an evolutionary explanation of our capacity to form perceptual judgments will make it probable that most of our perceptual judgments are true of an independent reality.

However, the reason why specific moral evaluative attitudes and beliefs have been fitness enhancing seems to be a very different one. Evaluative attitudes and moral beliefs are generally thought to be intrinsically action motivating, regardless of their truth. If the behaviour motivated by specific moral emotions and beliefs enhanced reproductive success in the ancestral environment, most human beings

---

[85]   There are many weaker versions of meta-ethical realism, such as Simon Blackburn's quasi-realism.

living at the present time will exhibit the corresponding emotive and doxastic tendencies. This 'adaptive link account' is endorsed by many authors.[86]

It will now become clear that there may be a tension between evolutionary explanatory ethics and strong meta-ethical realism. It seems that the adaptive link account of the evolution of our moral sense is vastly superior to the truth-tracking account. If the former can explain many of our emotionally based moral beliefs, the latter becomes superfluous as an explanation. Yet the tension between evolutionary explanatory ethics and (strong) moral realism is not due merely to an argument from explanatory parsimony.[87] If the RCT and the TEC are correct, there is a somewhat stronger argument against meta-ethical realism, which has been suggested by Michael Ruse, for example, and has been developed in detail by Sharon Street.

As Ruse wrote, if the evolution of our moral sense is contingent and if strong meta-ethical realism is true, the following scenario would be a real possibility: 'whatever objective morality may truly dictate, we might have evolved in such a way as to miss completely its real essence'.[88] Since this scenario is considered to be counter-intuitive or even absurd, evolutionary explanatory ethics allegedly yields a convincing argument against strong meta-ethical realism. Assuming that evolutionary forces 'have played a tremendous role in shaping the content of human evaluative attitudes' in ethics, Sharon Street has formulated this argument as a destructive 'Darwinian Dilemma' for the realist:

1. The realist has to hold either a) that there is *no* relation between evolutionary influences on the contents of our moral beliefs and the independent moral truths that strong meta-ethical realism posits, or b) that there *is* a relation, because natural selection favoured ancestors who were able to grasp those truths.

2. But a) implies either the sceptical conclusion that most of our moral judgments probably are off-track due to the distorting pressure of Darwinian forces, which seems to be absurd, or that a detailed coincidence took place, which is very implausible.

---

[86] For example, Joyce, *The Evolution of Morality,* Chapters 1–4; Kitcher, 'Psychological Altruism', p. 305; Ruse, 'Evolutionary Ethics'; and Street, 'A Darwinian Dilemma'.

[87] As David Copp, 'Darwinian Skepticism about Moral Realism', *Philosophical Issues* 18 (2008), 186–206, argues, such an argument from explanatory parsimony in itself would not be conclusive (pp. 190–191).

[88] Ruse, 'Evolutionary Ethics', p. 108. Cf. Joyce, *The Evolution of Morality*, pp. 130–131. Of course, this claim does not depend on the particular evolutionary scenario that we consider. If a scenario of adaptation is not truth-tracking concerning moral beliefs, a scenario of genetic drift might be even less so.

3. Meanwhile, b) assumes a truth-tracking account of the evolution of our moral sense, which seems to be incompatible with, and is scientifically inferior to, the adaptive link account.
4. Thus, strong meta-ethical realism cannot accommodate the fact that Darwinian forces have deeply influenced the content of our moral convictions. Accordingly, the TEC yields a convincing argument against strong meta-ethical realism.[89]

Does this argument, which I shall not analyse in detail here, really yield the conclusion that strong meta-ethical realism is incompatible with evolutionary science, as Street concludes?

Michael Dummett once wrote that '[a]t one time it was usual to say that we do not call ethical statements "true" or "false", and from this many consequences for ethics were meant to flow'.[90] But fashions have changed. In our days, meta-ethical realists or objectivists affirm that we *do* call ethical statements true or false, although the relevant empirical linguistic research is usually lacking. However, which consequences follow from this alleged linguistic habit depends on how meta-ethical realists construe the 'truth' of moral judgments, which is said to hold independently of all our human evaluative attitudes. David Copp, among others, has argued that there is a plausible construal of the truth of normative moral statements such that it satisfies the conditions of strong meta-ethical realism *and* that the adaptive link account makes truth-tracking very likely. If this argument is correct, the third premise is false and Street's destructive dilemma against strong meta-ethical realism collapses.[91]

Copp construes his analysis of the truth of moral judgments within the framework of what he calls a 'society-centred theory' of meta-ethical realism.[92] According to such a theory, a stable society needs to be governed by shared norms or standards, which, when internalized widely enough, will induce its members to behave in a cooperative and peaceful manner, so that social order is sustained. A collection of such norms or standards may be called a moral code. Copp now states

---

[89]   Street, 'A Darwinian Dilemma for Realist Theories of Value', p. 109 and *passim*. Of course, if strong meta-ethical realism is false, cognitivism in meta-ethics becomes very implausible, so that so-called 'error theories' of ethics will be false as well, unless it can be shown by empirical research that in fact most human beings are meta-ethical cognitivists. Error theorists stick to their cognitivism and bite the bullet. They accept point 2, but argue that it is less absurd than it seems, because illusions and fictions may be useful. Cf., for example, Joyce, *The Evolution of Morality*.

[90]   Michael Dummett, 'Truth' (1959), in his *Truth and Other Enigmas* (Cambridge, MA: Harvard University Press, 1978), p. 3.

[91]   Copp, 'Darwinian Skepticism about Moral Realism', p. 192: 'Given an appropriate account of the truth-conditions of moral beliefs, a realist theory can accept the adaptive link account and use it to underwrite the tracking thesis.'

[92]   Ibid., pp. 198ff.

the truth-condition of moral propositions as follows: a basic moral proposition is true if and only if the moral code that would best serve the function of enabling society to meet its needs included or entailed the corresponding norm or standard.[93]

As Copp explains, this account of what makes moral judgments true has two aspects. On the one hand, there is the condition that the moral code to which the corresponding standard belongs *best serves* the function of enabling a society *S* to meet its needs. This he calls the relevant 'truth-grounding status' of a standard. On the other hand, there is the 'standard-based account' of moral propositions' truth-conditions, according to which a moral proposition is true if and only if the corresponding moral standard has the relevant truth-grounding status.

This society-centred and standard-based view of the truth-conditions of moral propositions will enable us to show that the adaptive link account of the evolution of our moral beliefs makes truth-tracking likely, so that the third premise is mistaken.[94] According to the current evolutionary scenarios, our remote ancestors will have developed altruistic evaluative attitudes and a capacity for normative governance because these were adaptive in the ancestral environment. In subsequent stages of cultural development, including the evolution of language, our ancestors will have come to share a system of moral beliefs that reinforces these prosocial dispositions. Such systems of moral beliefs were also adaptive because they enhanced in-group cooperation, peacefulness and social stability. Up to this point, there is no suggestion whatsoever that these moral beliefs have to be 'true'. The adaptive link account does not require this at all.

However, if we endorse the society-centred and standard-based account of what makes moral beliefs true proposed by Copp, we will have to conclude that sets of moral beliefs that were *adaptive* according to the adaptive link account will also *tend to approximate the truth* according to the standard-based account. According to this latter account, a moral belief is true if and only if the corresponding standard belongs to the moral code that best serves the function of enabling a society *S* to meet its needs. It is plausible to assume that the sets of moral beliefs accounted for by evolutionary explanations were adaptive because they served the function of enabling society *S* to meet its needs to quite a considerable extent. In short, the standard-based account of moral truth refutes the third premise of Street's destructive dilemma.

We might raise many questions concerning this defence of meta-ethical realism. Copp's standard-based account of moral truth is a version of strong meta-ethical realism only if the needs of society *S* can be established independently of all evaluative attitudes of its members and, indeed, independently of *our* evaluative attitudes. As Copp says, '[t]he society-centred theory is a realist theory according to which the moral facts are identical to certain ordinary natural facts having to do with the needs of society'.[95] What are these basic needs of a society? According

---

93   Ibid., pp. 198–9. I have simplified Copp's formulation somewhat.
94   Cf. ibid., pp. 200–202.
95   Ibid., p. 203.

to Copp, this is a difficult question, but he thinks that at least the following things are obvious. 'A society needs to ensure that its population continues to exist. It needs to ensure that there is and continues to be a system of cooperation among its members. It needs to ensure internal social harmony. It needs peaceful and cooperative relationships with neighbouring societies.'[96]

When reading this list, however, we will wonder whether it merely describes 'natural' needs the existence of which can be established empirically, independently of human evaluative attitudes. Do Copp's own evaluative attitudes not implicitly play a role here? For example, from an evolutionary point of view, a belligerent society might be much more successful than a peaceful neighbour, in the sense that more offspring are produced by its members, if its warriors kill the males of neighbouring tribes and appropriate the females. Copp's claim that each society 'needs peaceful and cooperative relationships with neighbouring societies' seems to reflect his own (laudable) moral preferences rather than being a purely descriptive analysis of the 'needs' of a society in terms of the evolutionary fitness of its members. If this criticism is correct, Copp's meta-ethics is not 'realist' in the required sense, which is targeted by Street's Darwinian Dilemma.[97]

Furthermore, issues of relativism are relevant here. Does Copp's meta-ethical realism not imply that a moral proposition may be true in relation to society S but false in relation to society S^*? For example, the proposition that the emancipation of women is good might be false for societies in which the rate of infant mortality is very high, but true for our own medically sophisticated society. Or are moral truths limited to propositions that correspond to standards which are best for *all* human societies?[98] In any case, Copp's society-based realism implies that moral truth is relative to humans, or at least to social animals. Non-human individuals who are not members of any society and, indeed, are not social beings at all will not be able to endorse true moral beliefs concerning their own moral obligations. On Copp's society-centred account, there simply cannot be a truth-condition for moral propositions that can be fulfilled in their case.

Although I believe that the Darwinian Dilemma refutes all varieties of meta-ethical realism, I shall not further pursue these issues here. What I would like to conclude is merely that the *only* versions of meta-ethical realism that can survive

---

[96]   Ibid., p. 200.

[97]   Cf. Sharon Street, 'Reply to Copp: Naturalism, Normativity, and the Varieties of Realism Worth Worrying About', *Philosophical Issues* 18, *Interdisciplinary Core Philosophy* (2008), 207–28, at pp. 217–22, for another argument to this effect.

[98]   Cf. Copp, 'Darwinian Skepticism about Moral Realism', p. 200: 'Since societies have the same basic needs, moral codes that are authoritative relative to different societies will tend to be similar in content. Yet societies can be in different circumstances, so the "best" moral codes for different societies are unlikely to be exactly the same.' Copp seems to assume that there always is one 'best moral code' for a specific society, but that is not at all obvious. What should one say about truth-conditions if there are multiple 'best moral codes'?

evolutionary explanations of our human moral sense are versions in which the truth-conditions of moral propositions are linked somehow to what is adaptive for humans.[99] Let me call this the Thesis of Adaptive Truth (TAT). This thesis will be crucial to my argument in the next and final section.

The Predictive Power of Theism

At the beginning of this chapter, I briefly discussed Francis Collins' contention that human awareness of what he calls 'the Moral Law' should be explained by theism, so that theism is confirmed by the existence of our moral sense. Let us now wonder under what conditions theism can be said to explain something at all. In general, a hypothesis h can explain an empirical phenomenon e only if h makes e more likely than it would otherwise be, that is, according to a hypothesis $\sim h$. As a consequence, a hypothesis cannot be explanatory unless we can somehow determine its likelihood $P(e|h)$, that is, the probability of e given h. Let us call the set of these likelihoods with regard to all relevant e_i's the 'predictive power' of the hypothesis h. Can we determine the predictive power of theism concerning some specific phenomenon e?

Traditionally, theism is defined as the thesis that God exists, where God is said to be a bodiless personal spirit who is omniscient, omnipotent, perfectly free and perfectly good. Because God is said to be omnipotent, the likelihood $P(e|h)$ will be equal to one if we assume that God intended to bring about e. On this assumption, the theistic explanation of e will defeat all rival explanations of e, such as evolutionary ones, for which the likelihood $P(e|h)$ is between 0 and 1 (apart from the problem of its prior). But how can we know that the assumption is true? It seems that we can never know this, because God's freedom is said to be absolute and our limited minds do not have any access to the mind of God, which is hidden to us (if God exists at all). So, how can we fathom God's intentions?

We might think that God has revealed His plans to us humans in some revelation, such as the Bible, the Koran, the Book of Mormon, etc. But there are many reasons for denying that 'receiving revelations' are a reliable source of knowledge. Numerous passages in alleged revelations have been refuted by well-tested scientific results. Historical research reveals that the contents of quite a number of revelations, such as some books of the Old Testament, stem from earlier sources, which are not acknowledged as revelations by the relevant religious authorities. Surely, we will refuse to believe witnesses who claim that they saw something themselves if their testimony turns out to be based upon hearsay. Furthermore, we might expect that an omniscient God would have revealed truths to us humans which are so intricate and new that the receiving populations could not have discovered them by themselves. But this is not the case in any alleged

---

[99] Unless, of course, we endorse some theistic theory of guided evolution, for which there are no empirical arguments whatsoever.

revelation. There are many contradictions in revelations that cannot be resolved easily by accommodating interpretations. As such, it is much more probable that the revelations have been produced by various human authors than that they were communicated to us by an omniscient God. Finally, religious authorities such as the Pope claim that only their own revelation is a true one.[100] However, it seems to be incoherent to pretend that one's own revelation is genuine, while also holding that the epistemic source of 'receiving revelations' is utterly unreliable because it produced false revelations in all other cases. In short, we cannot legitimately rely on revelations in order to discover God's intentions.

Of course, theism cannot be a good explanation of a phenomenon *e* if we *arbitrarily* ascribe to God the intention to bring about *e*, or if we ascribe this intention to Him merely because we know that *e* exists. Attributing the intention should be based upon grounds that are independent of our knowledge of *e*.[101] Is there any alternative to revelations for acquiring such independently attested information about God's plan? Most religious believers will implicitly rely on their moral intuitions whenever they ascribe intentions to God. Is God not defined as being perfectly good? Should we not expect Him accordingly to intend things that we humans regard as good? The idea is, then, that we can have access to God's plan, at least to some extent, by relying on our human moral intuitions. Elsewhere, I have called this the Moral Access Thesis (MAT).[102]

The MAT presupposes a very strong version of meta-ethical realism. The fundamental moral norms or standards that hold for us humans must also hold for God, at least in part. In any case, these standards must not only exist independently of all human evaluative attitudes, but their content must also be independent of human needs or interests. Such a strong version of meta-ethical realism or objectivism has been defended by some philosophers of religion, such as Richard Swinburne.[103]

Swinburne's positive argument for his moral objectivism is not very convincing. He concludes that it must be true because there are established procedures for reaching agreement in moral matters.[104] However, the existence of established procedures for reaching agreement is not a sufficient condition for what we agree upon being true or false in this strongly realist sense. We may have procedures for reaching agreement on political decisions, for example, whereas decisions cannot

---

[100] Cf. the *Declaratio Dominus Iesus*, published by the *Congregatio pro Doctrina Fidei* of the Vatican in 2000.

[101] Cf. Elliott Sober, *Evidence and Evolution. The Logic Behind the Science* (Cambridge: Cambridge University Press, 2008), § 2.12.

[102] In Chapter 9.3 of my book *God in the Age of Science? A Critique of Religious Reason* (Oxford: Oxford University Press, forthcoming).

[103] Richard Swinburne, *The Coherence of Theism*, revised edn (Oxford: Oxford University Press, 1993), Chapter 11, pp. 188–209; and Richard Swinburne, *The Existence of God*, 2nd edn (Oxford: Oxford University Press, 2004), Chapter 5.

[104] Swinburne, *The Coherence of Theism*, pp. 205–6.

be called true or false, let alone true or false in the sense of Swinburne's moral objectivism.

It is not only the case that Swinburne's argument for meta-ethical realism or objectivism is unconvincing. The position is also very implausible in itself. Swinburne's idea is that because God is omniscient, He will know all moral truths. Since these truths allegedly hold independently of all human evaluative attitudes and interests, they will have normative force for God as well. God, being perfectly free, will always choose to do what is morally best or, if there is not one best action, He will choose to do what is good. And because we humans have some grasp of these objective moral truths, we also have some access to God's intentions. As a consequence, we have evidence for the content of God's intentions that is independent of our knowledge of what in fact exists, as should be the case if theism is to have any predictive power.

However, if my argument in the preceding section is correct, the strongest version of meta-ethical realism that is compatible with the TEC is a version like the one developed by David Copp, according to which the truth-conditions of moral propositions are essentially linked to the needs of human societies. As a consequence, the true norms of morality will not apply to God because, according to theism, God is unique in His kind, instead of being a social animal. It follows not only that the MAT is false, so that theism does not have any predictive power, and Collins' attempt to explain our moral awareness by the hypothesis of theism fails for this reason, but also that we do not know what we are talking about when we say that God is perfectly good. God may always choose to do what is best according to *His* standards. But these standards will not be the true moral standards that hold for *us*, and we can have no idea what God's moral standards are, if any.[105]

---

[105] The first version of this chapter was presented at the eighth conference of the British Society for the Philosophy of Religion on 'God and Morality' at Lady Margaret Hall, the University of Oxford, in September 2009. I am grateful to many participants for their instructive comments. A later version has been discussed in several research seminars in the Netherlands. I am particularly grateful to Anthony Booth, Thomas Müller, Rik Peels, Sabine Roeser and the members of my research seminar on Analytic Philosophy for their helpful suggestions.

PART II
Evil and the Goodness of God

The Parameters of Omnibenevolence

Chapter 9

God, Omniscience and Understanding Evil

Dan O'Brien

According to St Anselm, God is the greatest being that can be conceived – 'that-than-which-a-greater-cannot-be-thought' – the omni-God: omniscient, omnipotent and omnibenevolent. If God is omniscient, then he knows the meaning of every statement, the content of every thought: he knows that I believe that Miles Davis played the trumpet and that I desire to hear 'Blue in Green'. If he understands everything, he also understands sinful thoughts: he knows, for example, that Adam lusts for Eve. 'Shall not God search this out? For he knoweth the secrets of the heart' (Psalms 44:21).

However – and this is a key claim for which I must provide argument – to understand the sinful thoughts of others, one has to be able to empathize with their thinking; one has to be able, in one's imagination, to think those thoughts for oneself. Thus, if God can understand such moral defects, then He must be able, in His imagination, to have morally imperfect thoughts. To think in this way, though, is morally reprehensible. Omniscience and moral perfection are therefore incompatible, and so it would seem that the traditional God of Christianity cannot exist.

Torin Alter[1] discusses, and criticizes, an argument that on the surface is similar to mine. He calls this the argument from evil desires. An omniscient being would know what it is like to have an evil desire. However, in order to have such knowledge, it is necessary for one actually to have had such desire; yet the having of such evil desires is incompatible with moral perfection, an attribute of God. Omniscience and moral perfection are incompatible and therefore the omni-God cannot exist. This argument, though, relies on the controversial empiricist claim that one can only grasp what it is like to have certain mental states if one actually has them oneself. God can only grasp what it is like to have an evil desire – He can only have this knowledge – if He actually has such desires. Various writers, including Alter, deny this claim.[2]

My argument differs from that of Alter in two important ways: it does not focus on *what it is like* to have an evil desire and it does not depend on empiricist principles. I focus on the understanding of the content of evil desires and I am

---

[1]   Torin Alter, 'On Two Alleged Conflicts Between Divine Attributes', *Faith and Philosophy* 19 (2002), 47–57.

[2]   See, for example, Frank Jackson, 'Postscript on Qualia', in *Mind, Method and Conditionals* (New York: Routledge, 1998).

neutral on whether such understanding depends on experience in the way that empiricists claim (the empathetic abilities involved could be innate).[3, 4]

First, then, I must show why understanding the thoughts of another involves thinking like them. Simulation theorists in the field of cognitive science provide empirical evidence for this claim; I, however, shall focus on *a priori* considerations.

Empathy and Understanding

Descartes proposed the ontological real distinction between two distinct types of substance: mind and body. Gregory McCulloch,[5] in a paper on Quine, highlights the epistemological real distinction. In coming to understand others, in interpreting them as minded individuals, one uses a different methodology and acquires a different mode of knowledge from those involved in one's understanding of the physical world. One's knowledge of the physical world is from 'side-on', as John McDowell puts it.[6] In science we posit objective law-like relations between various observed and theoretical phenomena. God can therefore be omniscient with respect to the physical world: he can know all the regularities there are to know. However, knowledge of other minds cannot be acquired from side-on. McDowell, McCulloch, Collingwood[7] and Quine[8] claim that we do not interpret intentional states in this way; rather, we attempt to get into the minds of those we interpret by empathizing with them. Understanding someone's words involves being able to think the thoughts that they entertained when they said them.

We can see why empathy is essential for understanding by turning to Quine and McCulloch. Empathy plays an essential role in Quine's account of the interpretation of each other's utterances. He focuses on what he calls radical translation: the

---

[3]   I shall ignore theodicies in which apparent evils are taken to be 'in reality, goods' when seen in the 'full cosmic context' (John Hick, *Evil and the God of Love* (Houndmills: Palgrave Macmillan, 1966), p. 15) and accounts in which evils are seen in terms of the privation of goods.

[4]   My argument is also distinct from a particular kind of argument concerning God's inability to sin, one that explores the incompatibility between omnipotence and God's moral perfection. See T.J. Mawson, 'Omnipotence and Necessary Moral Perfection are Compatible: A Reply to Morriston', *Religious Studies* 38(2) (2002), 215–23; Wes Morriston, 'Omnipotence and Necessary Moral Perfection: Are They Compatible?', *Religious Studies* 37 (2001), 143–60; and Nelson Pike, 'God's Omnipotence and God's Ability to Sin', *American Philosophical Quarterly* 6 (1969), 208–16. My argument, in contrast, explores the incompatibility between omniscience and moral perfection.

[5]   Gregory McCulloch, 'From Quine to the Epistemological Real Distinction', *European Journal of Philosophy* 1 (1999), 30–46.

[6]   John McDowell, *Mind and World* (Cambridge, MA: Harvard University Press, 1994).

[7]   Robin George Collingwood, *The Idea of History* (Oxford: Clarendon, 1946).

[8]   Willard van Orman Quine, *Word and Object* (Cambridge, MA: MIT Press, 1960).

coming to understand the utterances and thoughts of an alien community from scratch. All we have to go on is the behaviour of the native speakers. And this, he claims, is also true of our understanding of each other. Radical translation highlights the nature of all understanding. In communicating with one another all we have to go on is the behavioural evidence:

> In general the underlying methodology of the idiom of propositional attitudes contrasts strikingly with the spirit of objective science at its most representative … in indirect quotation we project ourselves into what, from his remarks and other indications, we imagine the speaker's state of mind to have been, and then we say what, in our language, is natural and relevant for us in the state thus feigned … what is involved is evaluation, relative to specific purposes, of an essentially dramatic act.[9]

As the native utters 'gavagai', we consider what we would have said *if we were him*. We may perhaps have been drawn to utter 'rabbit' and so we forward this as a translation of his utterance. To check whether this is a good translation, we can try out 'gavagai' in other situations in which we take 'rabbit' to be appropriate. If signs of approval are elicited from the natives, then we will make a start on our translation manual; if not, then 'rabbit' would be rejected and further empathetic acts would have to be attempted.

Following McCulloch, let us consider the home case in which we come to understand an utterance made by someone of our own linguistic community. As we interpret the words of a friend, we do not just ascertain that he makes a certain noise: 'ra – bit'; rather, we interpret him as saying that *a rabbit is over there*. One must understand what one's friend *means* by 'rabbit'. In order to interpret the thoughts of a thinker, we must understand the content of the propositional attitude ascriptions that they make. 'Only if I can *understand your words in your way* can I gain full-blooded understanding of you as a subject of propositional attitudes.'[10] Similarly with the natives: to ascribe propositional attitudes to them, one must come to understand 'gavagai' in the way that they do. When one has, one can then go about finding expression for this in one's home idiom. 'The true measure of understanding is the view from inside, not the take-home message.'[11] One understands and then one translates. Interpretation is thus an empathetic exercise since we must take on the native's way of understanding his words and not simply use our own.

There is therefore an important distinction between how we attempt to understand each other and how we attempt to understand the physical world, and it is empathy that grounds this distinction. When interpreting a physical system, we work 'from the outside', applying our own concepts to the observational

---

[9]   Ibid., pp. 218–19.

[10]   McCulloch, 'From Quine to the Epistemological Real Distinction', 34.

[11]   Ibid., 42.

evidence. In order to interpret the mental states of a thinker, however, we must attempt to instantiate the very cognitive makeup that he or she is manifesting. Folk psychology is, in Quine's words, an 'essentially dramatic idiom'.[12]

It might be thought that these are contingent claims about how we come to have knowledge of other minds: we may find it good translation practice to empathize with the native, but there are in principle other ways of coming to learn what they are talking or thinking about. However, this is not so: Quine's reflections are the source of the interpretationist approach to interpretation and the mind, the interpretationist claim being that we have no notion of the mind apart from that it is the kind of thing that can be accessed through interpretation. There is a conceptual relation between minds and interpretation. Further, the interpretation of minds necessarily involves empathy. There is nothing about a certain noise ('gav-a-guy') that carries with it its own interpretation; that would be imbuing noises with a magical connection to the world. In order to interpret what someone means by that utterance, we have to see how the word 'gavagai' is used. Further, Quine argues that there are innumerable ways that we could match the native's use of 'rabbit' with words of our own language. He takes this to entail that the native's language (and our own) have no meaning.[13] McCulloch, however, rightly rejects this sceptical conclusion whilst keeping Quine's insight with regards to empathy. Determinate lines cannot be drawn – from the 'side' – between our concepts and those of the native, but, in empathizing with the native, we can see from the 'inside' that 'gavagai' refers to rabbits and not to other possible translations.

How, then, does this relate to God and His understanding of us? God does not speak or think in English and so we are natives to Him. He may, however, have access to more evidence for interpretation than we do with respect to the native.[14] We only have the behavioural evidence to go on, but God may know the states of our brains and/or the states of our spirits when we think our thoughts. However, just as there is nothing about the sound 'gav-a-guy' that wears its meaning on its sleeve, there is also nothing about certain brain or spirit states that does either. God, too, must ascertain how we use our language, how it is that we apply our thoughts to the world. This is the core of Wittgenstein's rejection of Cartesianism. God's knowledge of human thought should not be seen as akin to God having an access-all-areas pass to our private Cartesian theatres, reading off the meanings of the symbols He finds paraded there. 'If God had looked into our [Cartesian]

---

[12]   Quine, *Word and Object*, p. 219.

[13]   Quine also argues for the inscrutability of reference; this is a distinct route to the claim that our thoughts do not have determinate content. See Willard van Orman Quine, *Pursuit of Truth*, revised edition (Cambridge, MA: Harvard University Press, 1992), pp. 50–52.

[14]   It could be argued that the model of radical translation, on which I base my argument, is not appropriate since God created us. To resist this claim, though, think about our own children: we bring them into being, but sometimes we do not understand their actions or their thinking, that is, until we attempt to empathize with them.

minds he would not have been able to see there whom we were speaking of.'[15] Further, following McCulloch's earlier response to Quine's scepticism, we must assume that God thinks in terms of concepts – in, say, Godese. And, again, there will be innumerable ways that our thoughts can be translated into those articulated in Godese. Therefore, God – in order to understand us – must embrace our perspective.[16, 17] This, I shall claim in the next section, is at odds with His moral perfection.

As mentioned above, Alter's argument is based on empiricist premises and on the notion of what it is like to have an evil desire. My argument, however, is based on *a priori* claims concerning the nature of interpretation.[18] Alter's claims depend on the distinction between the content of a desire and the experiential quality of having that desire. He acknowledges the importance of content – 'What makes a desire evil is its content, or the combination of its content and the circumstances (broadly construed) in which one possesses it'[19] – and he uses this claim to argue against the empiricist account of understanding. Evil desires do not have a distinctive phenomenology and so God can come to know what it is like to have an evil desire by combining His understanding of an evil desire which, being omniscient, He can have, with His knowledge of the general phenomenology of desire which He can also have given His possession of virtuous desires. God 'would understand the propositional content of the relevant desire. And, again, he knows what it's like to have a desire. Therefore, he should be able to combine those two items of knowledge and thereby come to understand what it's like to have the desire in question'.[20] My argument, however, concerns the stage where God comes to understand evil desires; it is

---

[15]   L. Wittgenstein, *Philosophical Investigations*, ed. G.E.M. Anscombe, R. Rhees and G. von Wright (Oxford: Blackwell, 1953), IIxi, p. 217.

[16]   McCulloch talks of empathy enabling us to access further facts – phenomenological facts – that allow us to see a thinker as having thoughts with determinate content. Even God can only have access to such facts if He empathizes with our thinking.

[17]   Science is sometimes said to adopt a God's-eye view; it attempts to describe the world *sub species aeternitatis*. In Dan O'Brien, *A Critique of Naturalistic Philosophies of Mind* (with a foreword by Professor C. Hookway) (New York: Mellen Press, 2007), I argue that folk psychology is at odds with the God's-eye view and thus that science cannot provide a reductive account of the mind. Here I argue that there are certain aspects of folk psychology – the morally imperfect thoughts of others – that cannot be viewed from the perspective of the Christian God. Both arguments concern the God's-eye view. My earlier argument, though, considers it strictly as a metaphor, whereas the argument of this chapter is concerned with a more literal reading of such a perspective.

[18]   This may sound odd given that my thoughts are developed from those of Quine who of course rejects the very notion of the *a priori*. Full-blooded Quineans, however, can take my claims not to be *a priori*, but to be those that are deep within our web of belief, far from the periphery where claims can be tested against our experience.

[19]   Alter, 'On Two Alleged Conflicts Between Divine Attributes', p. 52.

[20]   Ibid, p. 53.

this, I claim, that is inconsistent with the attributes of an Anselmian God. Alter's argument cannot therefore be run; God cannot come to understand what it is like to have an evil desire as a result of His ability to understand such desires combined with His experience of virtuous desires, and this is because He cannot come to understand evil desires.

However, it could be objected that *we* may have to think someone else's thoughts in order to understand them, but God does not; he can have direct cognitive access into their minds. Alter 'see[s] no reason to doubt that God could directly perceive the contents of human consciousness – by telepathy'.[21] Such a response would be a powerful one if it were a contingent fact about understanding that it involves empathy. We may understand others in this way, but God need not. As already stated, though, the arguments I have focused on are *a priori*. My conclusions concern the essential nature of understanding. They concern what understanding consists in for you, me and everyone, including God. This is not to say that God must understand us in just the same way as we understand each other, by, say, literally observing our gesticulations and hearing what we say. God's understanding, as Alter claims, may involve some kind of telepathy. This telepathy, though – if it is to constitute *understanding* – must involve God coming to have thoughts with the same content as us; He must adopt our point of view. This must be true even if God's knowledge of our minds is direct and/ or immediate.

A related objection to my argument claims that we cannot say that God's understanding involves the empathetic sharing of our thoughts because we cannot say anything about God's understanding at all. Divine cognition is completely different from our own and we are incapable of grasping its nature. 'Great is the Lord, and greatly to be praised and his greatness is unsearchable' (Psalms 145:3). Divine cognition is veiled behind 'a cloud of unknowing'. Demea, the mystic in Hume's *Dialogues*, claims that:

> we ought never to imagine, that we comprehend the attributes of this divine Being, or to suppose, that his perfections have any analogy or likeness to the perfections of a human creature. Wisdom, thought, design, knowledge; these we justly ascribe to him; because these words are honourable among men, and we have no other language or other conceptions, by which we can express our adoration of him. But let us beware, lest we think, that our ideas any wise correspond to his perfections, or that his attributes have any resemblance to these qualities among men.[22]

---

21 Ibid., p. 51.

22 David Hume, *Dialogues Concerning Natural Religion* in *Dialogues and Natural History of Religion* [1779], ed. J.C.A. Gaskin (Oxford: Oxford University Press, 1993), p. 44.

There must, however, be some core features shared by our understanding and God's understanding, otherwise there would be no sense to the claim that we are talking about understanding at all when we talk of divine understanding. If we have no grip at all on divine understanding, then how is this cognitive act distinguished from, say, divine imagination or divine emotion? We can, of course, think of divine understanding as God's way of coming to know the truth, in this case the truth about our thoughts and desires; the mystery, though, is how He does this. I shall say little in response to this objection, only that the onus would seem to be on those who accept the mystery; I have a model of how it is possible to understand the minds of others and, lacking an alternative account, it would seem reasonable also to apply this to the case of God and to see what conclusions can be drawn.

Understanding Sinful Thoughts

My argument depends on the claim that embracing the perspective of someone who thinks sinful thoughts endangers one's own moral status and that this is also so with respect to God. In order to make this claim plausible, I shall consider not just sinful thoughts but thoughts that might be called evil. This helps to focus the issue. One reason for this is that one of my arguments is based on the phenomenology of understanding sin, and the phenomenology associated with evil thoughts is more striking.

First, we do not always understand the actions and thoughts of evil people. We sometimes only adopt the side-on perspective; from there we can determine what we think that person will do and we can apportion moral blame to their actions. We do this in our actual encounters and when we read or watch fiction. I predict that the crazed man will reach for the axe when his family get too much for him because that is generally what such characters do (in the movies at least). Here we may not make the cognitive effort to understand the evil protagonist. It is plausible that at some point up the scale of atrocity we are prepared to say that we simply do not understand the actions of certain people. Sometimes, though, it seems we can take on the evil thoughts of others, in actual encounters, in understanding history and in reading fiction. Let's try … Just how could the axe-wielding murderer have done that …?

Well, I imagine that I have work deadlines, that work is my life, that the noise coming from downstairs is leading me to distraction … that I will never get the work done … If only it would stop, if only I could find a way to shut them up…

In such cases I do not actually desire to kill those downstairs; rather, I imagine having such a desire. I must be able to do this if I am to understand the thoughts of someone so driven. We, as Quine says, 'project ourselves into what … we imagine the speaker's state of mind to have been'.[23] And I have argued that God must

---

[23]   Quine, *Word and Object*, p. 219.

also be able to do this.[24] Such cognitive exercises, though, are carried out in the imagination: I do not actually have such desires – I imagine having them – and I do not intend to act in line with such desires. The claim still needs to be made, then, that such empathy is in itself sinful or morally imperfect in some way.

It could be claimed that empathy has an effect on one's behavioural dispositions, that sharing thoughts with sinful or evil people will invariably lead to one's own behaviour being subverted. Think of a typical character in a detective film, living and working in the underworld: his attempts to understand and empathize with criminals lead to the corruption of the thoughts and behaviour of this once honest cop. Such ways of thinking, even in one's imagination, may become entrenched. This is a plausible psychological conjecture, but one that is of no help with respect to my argument; that is, if one only sees moral imperfections arising as one's actual intentions and behaviour become affected. Rather, for my purposes – for the argument to endanger the moral perfection of God – it is the very act of empathizing, before any subsequent effect on intention and behaviour, that must be seen as morally tainted. For my argument, I need to claim that in coming merely to understand criminals, detectives become more like them. Relatedly, Carlin Barton, in the introduction to her book on the psyche of the ancient Romans, writes:

> I worry that I may have tried to confront and to understand things that should not be understood, to articulate things better left unsaid. I have worried that if one understands horror it is because, in one sense, one is a sadist. To the extent you understand, you confess … [I]t is … possible that their ways of ordering the world may have 'infected' me; I may have become, in the course of writing this book, like that which confounds me.[25]

For evidence that empathetic understanding endangers moral perfection, I shall turn to scripture which, in places, suggests that the kind of imaginative exercises involved in understanding evil may be sinful. Consider first Matthew 5, where Jesus says 'whoever looks at a woman to lust for her has already committed adultery with her in his heart'. Here, however, it is left open whether the would-be adulterer actually intends to commit adultery or merely imagines doing so. Yet in Genesis 8:21, it is more explicit that imagination itself, even without intention, can

---

[24]   One could perhaps argue that God can still be omniscient because He can know, for example, that Adam lusts for Eve without *understanding* that he does or why he does. One way to fill out this distinction between knowledge and understanding would be to claim that the latter has to involve, in this case, an appreciation of why it is that Adam lusts for Eve. God, not given to lust, cannot have such understanding. My argument, though, involves the claim that knowledge – even without understanding – requires empathy. I cannot grasp what the concept 'lust' refers to unless I can, in my imagination, take up the perspective of a lustful creature.

[25]   Carlin Barton, *The Sorrows of the Ancient Romans: The Gladiator and the Monster* (Princeton, NJ: Princeton University Press, 1993), p. 8.

be sinful: 'the imagination of man's heart is evil from his youth'. And in Genesis 6:5: 'God saw that the wickedness of man was great in the earth, and that every imagination of the thoughts of his heart was only evil continually.' It is not only our actions and intentions that should obey God, but all our thoughts and imaginings, as claimed in 2 Corinthians 10:4–6:

> For the weapons of our warfare are not carnal but mighty in God for pulling down strongholds, casting down arguments and every high thing that exalts itself against the knowledge of God, *bringing every thought into captivity to the obedience of Christ*, and being ready to punish all disobedience when your obedience is filled. (Emphasis added)

The claim that understanding evil is sinful may also be supported by the phenomenology of understanding such thoughts. Sinfulness is associated with metaphors involving cleanliness. Sins pollute, defile, stain and blemish. Consider, then, the discomfort that one can feel when thinking about historical or fictional evil. One talks of being polluted; one wishes one had not read or seen that – not because it gives one an outside perspective on something distasteful or immoral, but because it gives one the inside perspective. The phenomenology of such understanding is suited to the religious notion of sin. Sinners need to be 'purged' or 'cleansed'; they need to be 'pure' again.[26]

Omniscience, Understanding Evil and the Maximal God Thesis

My conclusion is that in order to understand us, God must take on our point of view – empathize with our thinking – but this, in the context of evil thoughts, is incompatible with His moral perfection. There is a certain kind of argument against the Anselmian or omni-God thesis that attempts to show the inconsistency between the divine attributes. The omni-God of Christianity does not therefore exist since there cannot be a being that has all the properties usually ascribed to the omni-God. My argument could be taken as having this structure. Alternatively, it could be taken to support the strategy recently adopted by Yujin Nagasawa. The inconsistency arguments show that we must rethink the nature of the Anselmian God: Anselm's God and the God of Christianity do not have to be *omni*potent, *omni*scient and *omni*benevolent. Instead, we must adopt '*The Maximal God Thesis*. God is the being that has the maximal consistent set of knowledge, power

---

[26]   William Wringe, in 'Is Understanding Evil Morally Dangerous: Fiction, Emotion and Moral Contagion', in D. Medicott (ed.), *Their Deeds Were Evil: Understanding Atrocity, Ferocity and Extreme Crimes* (Amsterdam: Rodopi Press, forthcoming), discusses the phenomenology associated with reading literature concerning evil characters and actions.

and benevolence'.[27] God could be omniscient but, as my argument has shown, He would then be lacking in moral perfection; or He could be morally perfect and thus He must fall short of omniscience – the latter combination being perhaps more consistent with Christian teachings.[28]

What reasons are there to prefer this approach? First, Nagasawa argues that his response to the inconsistency arguments is more 'economical' than attending to each objection on its own terms. One could, for example, reject my claims concerning empathy and thus the alleged inconsistency between understanding and moral perfection. The omni-God thesis would still then be afloat. There are, though, various other inconsistency arguments that need, and will need, to be addressed. However, Nagasawa '[tries] to develop a radically new and more economical response to Anselmian theism, one that aims to eliminate the force of the arguments against it *all at once*'.[29]

Secondly, this response can be seen as sharing the virtues of a certain account of how philosophical problems should be solved. McDowell argues that solutions – or what he calls exorcisms – are better if they allow one to maintain the claims that feed the philosophical problem in question:

> a proposed exorcism is more satisfying to the extent that it enables us to respect, as insights, the driving thoughts of those who take the familiar philosophical anxieties to pose real intellectual obligations (our driving thoughts when we find ourselves beset by anxieties), even while we unmask the supposed obligations as illusory.[30]

In this case the insights would be that understanding necessarily involves empathy and that God is the greatest being that can be conceived. Both these thoughts can be maintained if one accepts Nagasawa's thesis. McDowell's suggestion, though,

---

[27]   Yujin Nagasawa, 'A New Defence of Anselmian Theism', *Philosophical Quarterly* 58 (2008), 577–96.

[28]   Other philosophers give up on omnipotence in response to God's inability to sin. See John Bishop, 'Evil and the Concept of God', *Philosophical Papers* 22 (1993), 1–15; Peter Geach, *Providence and Evil* (Cambridge: Cambridge University Press, 1977); Wes Morriston, 'Omnipotence and the Anselmnian God', *Philo* 4(1) (2001), 7–20. Nagasawa's position is a generalization of their partial retreat from the omni-God thesis.

[29]   Nagasawa, 'A New Defence of Anselmian Theism', p. 585. My argument is that the omni-God cannot exist because it is impossible to understand evil and be morally perfect. One could respond here by tweaking one's definition of omniscience. God is omniscient because He knows everything that it is logically possible for God to know. It is not logically possible for God to understand evil thoughts – because, by definition, He is morally perfect – and thus His omniscience is not compromised by His failure to come to know the morally imperfect thoughts of His creation. For an analogous approach with respect to omnipotence, and for objections to it, see Nicholas Everitt, *The Non-Existence of God* (London: Routledge, 2004), pp. 264–7.

[30]   McDowell, *Mind and World*, pp. xxii–xxiii.

assumes that we are dealing with insights. If, however, either the claim concerning empathy or that concerning God does not deserve 'respect', then an exorcism that maintains these claims would seem to be unsatisfactory. Philosophical argument, though, is supposed to persuade. I may have emphasized that my argument is *a priori*, but *a priori* claims are just as challenged as empirical theories. And, realistically, I doubt that my argument would lead any theist to reject his belief in God. Nagasawa's thesis is therefore attractive since, in the context of his approach, my argument is more likely to engage with those who are sympathetic to the claims concerning empathy and the existence of the Anselmian God, with those who see these as insights. God may be the greatest being of which we can conceive, and one way to articulate His greatness is to accept that He is limited in His understanding of some of His creation, yet He is morally perfect.

If one accepts some such account, then there are interesting consequences for the mutual understanding (or lack of) between God and man. The traditional picture involves an epistemic barrier between us and God – the cloud of unknowing. God, being omniscient, understands His creation, yet many of God's ways are mysterious to us. However, I am suggesting that there is mutual unknowing: we cannot understand some of the ways of God and God cannot understand some of the ways of man.[31, 32]

---

[31]   This may lead to problems for the view that we have a relationship with God, one in which God helps us, guides us and judges us. In order to do these things, it would seem that He must understand us.

[32]   I would like to thank audiences at the British Society of the Philosophy of Religion conference, Oxford, the Glasgow Philosophy of Religion workshop and the Oxford Brookes Human Nature research group seminar. Thanks also to Yujin Nagasawa for helpful comments.

Chapter 10
What Makes Generosity Sometimes Unjust?

Nicholas Wolterstorff

Sometimes one's bestowal of a good on someone other than oneself, or one's distribution of some good among a number of persons, is morally required of one; it is one's duty. On other occasions it is not out of duty but out of generosity that one bestows or distributes some good. Yet gratuitous generosity sometimes perpetrates injustice. Though one would wrong no-one if one did not bestow or distribute the good, in bestowing or distributing the good, one does wrong someone. The question whose answer I want to pursue in this chapter is what makes gratuitous generosity sometimes unjust?

The Parable of the Labourers in the Vineyard

Two of the most famous examples in Western literature of gratuitous generosity that some people in the story found unjust, but that the narrator clearly did not, are Jesus' Parable of the Prodigal Son (Luke 15) and his Parable of the Labourers in the Vineyard (Matthew 20). The former has captured the artistic imagination of the West far more than the latter. Because most readers find the generosity exhibited in the latter more problematic than that exhibited in the Parable of the Prodigal Son, and because it is less well known, let me remind the reader of how the Parable of the Labourers in the Vineyard goes.

The owner of a vineyard hired some day labourers early in the morning, saying that he would pay them the going daily wage. He hired others at nine o'clock, telling them that he would pay them whatever was just (*dikaios*). He hired an additional group around noon, another around three o'clock and a final group around five o'clock. When the working day was over, he instructed his manager to pay the workers, beginning with those hired last and ending with those hired first.

Those hired last were given the going daily wage. Those hired first took note and expected considerably more. But everybody was paid the same. As such, they grumbled. They had worked long hours through the heat of the day, whereas the five o'clockers had worked only one hour when the heat was moderating. It was not fair to give equal pay for such unequal work. It was an in-your-face injustice.

'Friend,' said the landowner to one of the grumblers, 'I am doing you no injustice; did you not agree with me for the usual daily wage? Take what belongs to you and go; I choose to give to this last the same as I give to you. Am I not allowed to do what I choose with what belongs to me? Or are you envious because I am generous?'

Jesus obviously approves of the action of the landowner. My guess is that most readers who do not simply accept what Jesus said because he said it believe that the grumblers had a case. The landowner was not obligated to be charitable to anyone; his obligation was to pay the workers what was due them for the work they had done. But if he was going to go beyond his obligations and be generous, then he was obligated to be just in his generosity. And the policy that he settled on seems patently unjust: a big dollop of charity to those who worked only one hour and none to those who worked all day. The response of the landowner to the grumblers ignores this point. Yes, of course he is permitted to be generous; nobody said he wasn't. But he is not permitted to be unjust in his generosity.

It is not hard to imagine a scenario in which the charge of injustice is somewhat mitigated. Suppose the landowner was aware of the fact that these workers all had families dependent on them and that the going daily wage was barely enough to support a family. That is what led him to act as he did; he cared about the families of these workers. This interpretation fits the point about the kingdom of God that Jesus was using the parable to make. It is important to everyone that they have a place in the kingdom. That is why God treats the late-coming Gentiles the same way as the Jews who have laboured long and faithfully in the vineyards of Torah.

The early workers have an obvious response. If all along it was the landowner's intention to give everybody an amount equal to the going daily wage, whether they had earned it or not, why didn't he announce that to everybody at the beginning? Then each labourer could freely decide how much work he wanted to put in.

Of course, the landowner was no fool; he knew that if he openly presented this option to all the day labourers at the beginning of the day, he would not have enough workers to get the work done. Thus, he manipulated the situation in order both to get the work done and to be seen as generous. The result of his curious combination of generosity to some with earned pay to the others was that he wronged the early workers; he perpetrated injustice.

Though Christian commentators agree with Jesus in his estimation of the landowner, they are all over the place in stating just what it was in the behaviour of the landowner that is admirable. Some take the landowner at his word, that he did the early workers no injustice, though I know of no-one who explains exactly why that is the case. Others say that the grumblers were right, they were treated unjustly, but that love trumps justice. Let me quote a few sentences from Anders Nygren's interpretation: 'If it were really a question of merit and worthiness, then the labourers who complained were undoubtedly in the right. It is impossible to make a simple addition of the exercise of kindness and the non-infringement of justice ... The principle of justice requires a due proportion between work and wages ... It is futile to try to eliminate from this Parable that which is offensive in it from a juridical point of view. The offence only ceases when the principle of justice itself is eliminated as inapplicable to the religious relationship ... Where spontaneous love and generosity are found, the order of justice is obsolete and invalidated'.[1]

Emil Brunner's interpretation is essentially the same. Having spent several chapters in *Justice and the Social Order* affirming the importance of our natural sense of justice, he says that this 'natural sense of justice is violated ... by Christ's parable of the labourers in the vineyard ... [I]t is love, the incomprehensible gift, bound to no law of retributive justice and standing in absolute contrast to what we must call just in the things of this world, which is shown here as God's manner of action ... The substance of the parable is not the *justitia civilis* but the *justitia evangelica* which consists precisely in the cessation of all deserving, in the denial of all lawful claims, and is hence the antithesis of the law of worldly justice'.[2] Neither Nygren nor Brunner explains how he interprets the insistence of the landowner that he is not being unjust, *adikos*, to the early workers.

I will come back to the parable at the end of the discussion.

Examples that Refute the Aristotelian Paradigm

Our concern here is solely with those cases in which the distribution of some good to one or more parties is not required by justice but is an act of pure generosity – cases in which none of the recipients would have been treated unjustly had no distribution been made. Refusal to make the distribution might reflect poorly on the character of the person who declines the opportunity to be generous, but it would not constitute wronging anybody.

Anyone acquainted with the Western philosophical tradition will at this point immediately think of Aristotle's formula for justice in distributions: justice in distributions always takes the form of equality of some sort, while injustice always takes the form of inequality of some sort. I judge that the statement of Aristotle's idea that Joel Feinberg gives in one of his articles is more illuminating of what Aristotle had in mind than are Aristotle's own formulations. When divisible goods are being distributed, says Feinberg, 'the Aristotelian paradigm [is that] justice requires that relevantly similar cases be treated similarly and relevantly dissimilar cases be treated dissimilarly in direct proportion to the relevant differences between them'.[3] Injustice in such cases consists in 'arbitrary and invidious discrimination of one kind or another: a departure from the requisite form of equal treatment without good reason'.[4]

---

[1]   Anders Nygren, *Agapé and Eros* (London: SPCK, 1953), pp. 87–90.

[2]   Emil Brunner, *Justice and the Social Order*, trans. Mary Hottinger (New York and London: Harper and Brothers, 1945), p. 111.

[3]   Joel Feinberg, 'Noncomparative Justice', *Philosophical Review* 83(3) (July 1974), 297–338, at p. 310.

[4]   Ibid., p. 299.

Is the Aristotelian paradigm, as formulated by Feinberg, correct? Does it give us what we are looking for? Does it pinpoint what it is that makes generosity sometimes unjust?

Let's be clear what we are asking here. I hold the traditional view that treating someone justly requires consists of rendering to that person what is due him or her. The question before us now is not whether the Aristotelian paradigm is an alternative account of justice that ought to be taken seriously, nor is it whether the Aristotelian paradigm is an account of justice that proves, on analysis, to be the same as the traditional one. The question is whether the Aristotelian paradigm explains why it is that, in some generous distributions, one or more persons are not receiving what is due them – why it is that one or more persons are wronged.

A couple of preliminary comments should be made at this point. There is a difference in how the Aristotelian paradigm is formulated in the two sentences that I quoted from Feinberg. The idea expressed in the first sentence is that justice in distributions consists of treating relevantly similar cases similarly and relevantly dissimilar cases dissimilarly. The idea expressed in the second sentence is that justice in distributions requires that similar cases be treated similarly unless one has a good reason for doing otherwise – or, as Feinberg puts it in other places, unless one has a *morally relevant* reason for doing otherwise. The first sentence speaks of relevant similarities and dissimilarities. The second speaks of morally relevant reasons. According to the first formulation, dissimilarity in one's assignment of goods has to be justified by pointing to some relevant dissimilarity among the potential recipients, otherwise the assignment is unjust. According to the second definition, dissimilarity in one's assignment of goods among potential recipients has to be justified by some morally relevant reason, otherwise the assignment is unjust.

The difference is only skin deep. The idea behind both formulations is the following. Suppose that one has some good that one wishes to distribute and suppose that there are a number of persons for whom it would be a good. Justice would then require that one distribute it equally or proportionately among those persons unless one has some morally relevant reason for excluding some or giving some less; a morally relevant reason will always consist of some morally relevant difference between the included and the excluded. What makes a distribution unjust is that it is a departure from equality or proper proportionality that cannot point to a morally relevant difference. Either there is no reason – the distribution is arbitrary – or the reason is not a morally relevant reason; for example, one withholds the benefit from those people there because they have a skin colour one does not like.

Reflection on a few cases makes clear that if the Aristotelian principle is to have any plausibility whatsoever, one has to be exceedingly lax and generous in what one is willing to count as morally relevant similarities and dissimilarities. Often the relevant similarities and dissimilarities will not be in the persons as such but in one or another relational property that they possess or lack.

To give an example: come Christmas, I give gifts to those to whom I am especially attached, family and friends. The children in my neighbourhood aren't much different from my own children; nonetheless, I do not give them gifts. And my neighbour isn't much different from my friend; however, I do not give him a gift either. We all agree that there is nothing unjust in this sort of partiality. So, if the Aristotelian principle is to hold for such cases, we have to regard the possession and lack of the relational property of *being someone to whom I am attached* as constituting a morally relevant similarity and dissimilarity. This is just one of many examples of the point.

The example can be used to make another preliminary point. When selecting Christmas gifts for my children, my attention is focused entirely on doing my best to ensure that they will more or less equally prize the gifts I give them; the thought that I am giving presents only to my own children and not to the children in my neighbourhood never crosses my mind. But in applying the Aristotelian principle, one has to attend not only to relevant similarities and dissimilarities within the distribution class on which one is focused, but also to relevant similarities and dissimilarities between those within that class and those outside. It is especially when one attends to the latter similarities and dissimilarities that one comes to realize how lax and generous the idea of a morally relevant reason has to be if the Aristotelian principle is to come out true. Of course, if the good that one is distributing is non-divisible, then the distinction between these two sets of similarities and dissimilarities disappears; in such cases, there are no similarities and dissimilarities among the members of the distribution class, since the class has only one member.

Enough by way of preliminaries. Does the Aristotelian paradigm explain what makes the just exercises of generosity just and the unjust exercises unjust? Well, suppose that I am seated at my desk, getting ready to write cheques for my end-of-the-year charitable contributions. Over the course of the year I have sorted out the appeals for funds that came my way, filing those from organizations that seemed to me to serve a worthy cause and to be needy of funds, and tossing the others into the wastebasket. Now I open my file and find that I have collected appeals from 30 organizations, to none of which I feel any particular attachment.

As I am wondering how to proceed, the Aristotelian paradigm comes to mind. I conclude that what it tells me to do is to rank these organizations in terms of some combination of worthiness and need, and then proportion my contributions accordingly. But as I am reflecting further on whether to employ this understanding of the paradigm as my guide, it occurs to me that I have been almost entirely passive up to this point. I have made no attempt to search out needy and worthy organizations. I have simply taken the appeals that arrived in the mail and sorted them into two categories. But surely there are many needy and worthy organizations that happen not to have had me on their mailing list. Is that a morally relevant reason for treating them differently from those that do have me on their list? I am not sure; I find that I do not have a very good grip on this concept of a morally relevant reason. But it doesn't seem like a morally relevant reason. It is hard to see why one would think it was, other than that one wants to keep the Aristotelian paradigm from coming out false for this case.

I dismiss these unsettling thoughts and return to asking myself whether I should follow the Aristotelian paradigm for the organizations whose appeals I have kept. Should I rank them in terms of some combination of worthiness and need, and then proportion my contributions accordingly? For no particular reason, I decide that this year I do not want to spread my charity thin in the way that this would require. I will select just a few, four or five perhaps, and concentrate my charity on them.

Now I have to select those few. I carefully read once again the brochures in my file, this time looking for anything I can seize on as a morally relevant reason for tipping my decision one way or another. After several hours of this, I find myself paralyzed; I cannot choose. So in desperation I assign numbers to the various organizations and make my choice by rolling dice. Or perhaps I hit on graphic design as the deciding factor and give my money to the five organizations whose brochures strike me as the most attractive. Or perhaps I notice that a few of these organizations list the members of their boards of directors; I find this apparent openness appealing and decide to give my money to them. Or I notice that four of them have their home offices in my state; that tips me towards them. Or I recall that I visited Africa in the course of the year and was very moved by what I experienced there, so I decide to give all my money this year to organizations that work in Africa. It is easy to go on in this vein and imagine other such ways of making my decision.

So far as I can see, none of these ways of making my decision constitutes treating any organization unjustly. If those I pass over become aware that I have passed them over, they will regret my doing so, but they cannot claim to have been wronged. Yet the Aristotelian paradigm has surely not been satisfied. In no case did I have a morally relevant reason for choosing as I did; in no case was my departure from equal treatment based on morally relevant similarities and dissimilarities among the organizations. In each case my choice was more or less whimsical and arbitrary. How is the location of an organization's home office or the aesthetic quality of its brochure relevant?

Alternatively, if one declares that the fact that an organization came up with a winning number on a roll of the dice is a morally relevant reason for including it within my benefactions, then surely the idea of a morally relevant reason is no longer doing any work; it is not explaining anything. One's only reason for calling such a fact morally relevant is that one wants to prevent the Aristotelian paradigm from implying that the form my generosity took in this case was unjust.

Feinberg suggests that we are offended by arbitrary discriminations and find them unjust because they are 'offensive to reason': 'The principle that relevantly similar cases should be treated in similar ways, put in just that general way, is a principle of reason, in much the same way as Aristotle's principles of identity, contradiction, and excluded middle are "laws of thought." It is *absurd* to treat relevantly similar cases in dissimilar ways.'[5] We are, of course, offended by many arbitrary discriminations and we do find many of them unjust. But, as for myself, the examples of arbitrary discrimination that I have given seem to me not at all offensive or unjust; they do not violate some principle of reasons. And they represent merely the tip of the iceberg.

Suppose someone offers to fund a scholarship at his or her alma mater and insists that the criteria for eligibility include the requirement that the candidate was born in the same small Minnesota village that the donor came from. The university authorities will try to talk him or her out of such a quirky stipulation; however, in doing so, they cannot claim that it would be unjust. Or suppose some millionaire decides to dispose of some of his or her wealth by tossing $100 bills out of his or her Manhattan hotel room; is anybody wronged by this erratic behaviour? Or suppose the Gates Foundation decides to concentrate its AIDS endeavours on Africa because the first person suffering from AIDS that Bill Gates met was born in Africa. This is hardly a morally relevant reason, but is anybody wronged?

And then there are all the cases of arbitrary random assignment of indivisible goods. Suppose I decide to bequeath my automobile to one of my children. After trying and failing to find some 'rational' way of deciding to whom to give it, I resort to chance. I have my children pull straws, throw dice, or whatever. Those who lose in the draw will naturally be regretful, but they cannot claim to have been wronged.

So far as I can see, the Aristotelian formula is patently mistaken. Its grip on Western thought is not because of its truth but in spite of its falsehood.

Some Factors that Make Generosity Unjust

My conclusion thus far is negative. The Aristotelian paradigm was offered as an explanation of why certain exercises of generosity are just and others are unjust. The paradigm says that what makes a selective exercise of generosity just is the presence of a morally relevant reason for including these persons here but excluding those there from one's benefaction, even though the latter group would also benefit from the benefaction. And it says that what makes a selective exercise of generosity unjust is the absence of a morally relevant reason for including these persons but excluding those, when those would also benefit. We have found cases of just generosity whose justice the paradigm does not illuminate, since the paradigm implies that those cases are unjust. It would be desirable if we could get beyond this negative conclusion and gain some insight into why some benefactions are just and some are unjust. And let's keep in mind that it is possible that though the Aristotelian paradigm does not explain all cases, it does explain some.

Let's approach the matter from the side of injustice and look at some examples of unjust generosity in the hope of discerning what makes them unjust.

---

[5] Ibid., p. 319.

Suppose I have promised to bequeath the art prints that I own to my children and suppose further that, after considerable discussion, we have agreed on a distribution that makes all the children equally happy. Then, in the course of a party that I throw for my neighbours one evening, one of the neighbours admires one of my prints, and I, pleased by his admiration, impulsively say 'Here, it's yours'. Flush with good feelings and a bit too much wine, I then grandly announce that everybody is free to select one of my prints and take it home with them. When everybody is gone, I have none left. Only next morning do I remember, to my horror, that I had promised them to my children.

My generosity is clearly a violation of justice. But being flush with good feelings for these people on this occasion seems a morally relevant difference between them and everybody else. Had I not made the promise to my children, my generosity to my neighbours would not have been unjust, and a defender of the Aristotelian paradigm would have pointed to my good feelings for these people as the relevant similarity among them and the relevant dissimilarity from everybody else. So, having a morally relevant reason for making one's distribution as one did proves not to be sufficient for justice. What made my distribution unjust was not that I lacked a morally relevant reason for making the distribution as I did; what made it unjust was that, in being generous to my neighbours, I broke a promise to my children. My breaking of my promise is what made my generosity unjust, not my departure from equal treatment of everybody who might benefit from my paintings without a morally relevant reason for my departure.

Consider the following example. Sam is a bachelor who likes to offer sweets every now and then to children on his street. None of these children has a right to receive sweets from Sam; giving out sweets is gratuitous generosity on his part. And Sam is not wronging anyone by giving sweets to these children; he has not promised the sweets to anyone. Let us also agree that he is not wronging the children in the next street by giving sweets only to those who live on his street – though for the Aristotelian it is a nice question why living on this street rather than on that street counts as a morally relevant principle of discrimination.

But Sam has taken a strong dislike to one of the children on the street, Roger. Why he dislikes Roger is not entirely clear to him. He has no reason to think that Roger has a bad character, Roger has always treated him politely; moreover, Sam has never seen Roger being mean to other children. But there is something about the look on Roger's face that turns Sam off; perhaps he dislikes that look because of some episode buried deep in his memory. In any case, whenever Sam distributes sweets, he sees to it that Roger gets none.

Sam's charity is patently unjust; in making his distribution as he does, he wrongs Roger. Why? Why is his exclusion of Roger from his benefactions unjust whereas his exclusion of the children on the neighbouring street is not unjust? Suppose Sam had thrown all the sweets up into the air and that, in the ensuing scramble, everybody managed to get some except Roger. Add to this the fact that Roger is as agile as any of the other children. This outcome would be unfortunate – one hopes that some of the children would take pity on Roger and give him some of theirs – but it would not be unjust. Sam's exclusion of Roger from his generosity was unjust because it was motivated by inexcusable ill-will. No such ill-will motivated his exclusion of the children in the neighbouring street from his largesse, and no such ill-will would account for Roger winding up with no sweets had Sam tossed them all up into the air.

Consider, next, a case Feinberg presents that is more or less of the opposite sort. Imagine a father who is making out bequests to his two sons, *A* and *B*. 'Let us suppose', says Feinberg, 'that *A* and *B* are roughly of the same age, size, health, appearance, abilities, beliefs, and ideals, that each has the same basic financial needs and that the bequests more than fulfil them in each case.' And now suppose 'that the father leaves everything else after those basic needs have been met – say, one million unsuspected dollars – to *A* simply because he likes *A* better'.[6] Feinberg thinks that this would be a case of injustice. I agree; I think son *B* is wronged by such treatment.[7]

Why? If *B*'s needs are adequately met by the bequest from his father, why is he wronged? Isn't the father permitted to dispose of the extra million dollars as he wishes? Suppose he had donated all of it to some charitable organization. As such, *B* would not have been wronged. So why is he wronged if the father gives the million dollars to *B*'s brother?

It's the father's favouritism that is the culprit. The bestowal of the million dollars on *A* is an act of favouritism on the father's part; *B* is wronged by that favouritism. Parents sometimes like one of their children more than another; perhaps they usually do. I dare say that ideally they would like all their children equally. However, the fact that often they do not is not as such a blot on their moral character. But when a parent's liking of one child more than another takes the form of favouritism in the distribution of goods, then the disfavoured child is wronged. An important normative component in the role of parent in our society – it may be different in other societies – is that parents do their best to be even-handed in promoting the flourishing and respecting the worth of their children. Favouritism is a violation of this role-obligation.

One way of interpreting Jesus' Parable of the Prodigal Son is that the elder son is accusing the father of favouritism for his scoundrel brother; although he does not actually say that the father's favouring of the younger son is an injustice to him, clearly that is the idea. As the elder son is coming in from the fields, he hears the noise of a party in the family home. He asks someone what is going on and learns that a party is being thrown to celebrate the return of his dissolute younger brother. The elder brother is very angry and refuses to join the party. The father goes out and pleads with him to join the festivities. The elder son responds: 'Listen! For all these years I have been working like a slave for you, and I have never disobeyed your commands; yet you have never given me even a young goat

---

[6]   Ibid., p. 315.

[7]   Feinberg takes the example from A.D. Woozley, who thinks it would not be a case of injustice.

so that I might celebrate with my friends. But when this son of yours came back, who has devoured your property with prostitutes, you killed the fatted calf for him!' (Luke 15:29–30).

The father does not concede the charge of favouritism and then go on to contend that no injustice was done. Instead, he contests the charge: the elder son is misinterpreting the situation. It is not favouritism that led him to throw the party. Remember, 'all that is mine is yours. But we have to celebrate and rejoice because this brother of yours was dead and has come to life, he was lost and has been found' (15:31–2).[8]

Finally, consider the following example.[9] A small manufacturing company is holding its annual Christmas party. Since the company has been unusually profitable this year, the owner has decided to share the wealth and give out bonuses; he has never done that before. So, at a certain point in the festivities, he stops the music, says that he has a surprise announcement and declares that he will now hand out bonuses. He explains that for some time he contemplated proportioning the size of a person's bonus to his or her position in the company, the quality of his or her work and so forth, but eventually he decided that things were getting too complicated. Give them all a $5,000 bonus, he decided. So he calls the workers forward one by one, in alphabetical order. But he fails to call out Joseph's name, Joseph being the only person of colour who works for the firm. Some of the workers notice the omission and call it to the attention of the owner. The owner blandly replies, 'You're right; I did skip Joseph. There's no bonus for Joseph', whereupon he sits down.

Joseph rightly feels hurt and angry. I would say that he has been wronged; the way in which the owner dispensed his generosity was unjust. But why? Neither Joseph nor anyone else had a bonus coming; nobody would have been wronged had the owner not given any bonuses. So why is Joseph wronged by not receiving a bonus? The answer, once again, is obvious. Joseph has been snubbed, demeaned, treated as if he were of less worth than the other workers; there is no other way to read the situation. The owner might have chosen some random procedure for distributing bonuses to only some of the people in the firm; those who did not win a bonus in the lottery would be regretful, but they could not claim that they had been wronged. It was the owner's demeaning of Joseph in how he distributed his generosity that made his distribution unjust.

Let me pull things together. Feinberg states the Aristotelian paradigm as declaring that injustice, in the sorts of cases we are considering, consists of 'departure from the requisite form of equal treatment without good reason'.[10] It is the absence of a morally relevant reason for differentiating between the included

---

[8]   There is a fascinating and pointed contrast between the elder son referring to the one who returned as 'this son of yours' and the father referring to him as 'this brother of yours'.

[9]   My example is an adaptation of an example of Scott Dolff given in conversation with the author.

[10]   Feinberg, 'Noncomparative Justice', p. 299.

and the excluded that accounts for the injustice of unjust exercises of generosity. Extrapolating from the cases we have considered, I suggest that it is seldom the absence as such of a morally relevant reason that accounts for the injustice of an unjust distribution. The implicit assumption – that the default option in the exercise of generosity is that everybody who can benefit is to be treated equally – is false. Even if we expand the notion of a morally relevant reason so far that it no longer has any explanatory content, benefactors do not need morally relevant reasons for distributing their benefactions as they do. Without violating justice, they can employ quirky reasons or resort to chance procedures.

I submit that there is no one thing that explains the injustice of unjust generosity. Sometimes what makes a distribution unjust is that distributing the largesse to these people breaks a prior obligation to distribute it to other people. Sometimes what makes a distribution unjust is that a nefarious reason is guiding the distribution or that it amounts to treating one person as of less worth than others when they are in fact of equal worth. No doubt, if we continued looking at examples, we would find yet other sources of injustice in generosity.

Generosity Not Made Unjust by the Violation of Rights that it Generates

An implication of the Aristotelian principle as it applies to generosity is that, where the good is divisible and nobody has a prior right to a share in the benefactor's generosity, the generosity generates in certain people a right to a share in the good. Once the benefactor begins his or her distribution, then he or she finds that he or she has generated, in those who are relevantly similar to the initial recipients, the right to a share that is equal or proportionate to the share that the initial recipients received. If any receive, then now all who are relevantly similar have a right to receive.

But if the conclusion that I drew just above is correct, this implication is mistaken. It is not in general true that generosity generates new rights and that it is the violation of those generated rights that accounts for injustice in generosity. Roger had a prior right not to be treated with culpable ill-will; it was the violation of that prior right that accounted for the fact that he was wronged. Son *B* had a prior right not to be the victim of his father's favouritism; it was the violation of that prior right that accounted for the fact that he was wronged. Joseph had a prior right not to be treated as of less worth than his fellows on account of his being a person of colour; it was the violation of that prior right that accounted for the fact that he was wronged by the owner's omission of him in the distribution of bonuses. Generosity, to be just, must attend to the rights that we already have.

Our Conclusions Hold for Generosity in the Form of Mercy

None of my examples has been an example of generosity in the form of mercy. Mercy comes in two forms. One form is mitigation of the severity of punishment; the other is alleviation of the plight of the unfortunate. Does mercy in either of these two forms require different conclusions from those I have drawn?

I think not. Start with mercy of the former sort, mitigation-mercy. Examples of this sort of mercy that come immediately to mind are pardons of prisoners issued by governmental officials – in the USA, by the President of the country and by the governors of the states. We, the citizens of the USA, expect that the President, with the assistance of the Department of Justice, will be reasonably systematic in selecting the most worthy candidates for pardon. If the President departs from that expectation by tossing coins or by allowing his choice to be determined by favouritism or prejudice of one kind and another, we are disturbed and regard the process as unfair and unjust. But suppose that in some kingdom there is the long-standing practice of the king employing a random procedure for selecting 10 prisoners for release each New Year's Eve. So far as I can see, no-one is wronged by such a procedure; justice is not violated.

Generosity in the form of alleviating the plight of the unfortunate is no different. It should be noted that mercy in the form of alleviation of hardship is not always an exercise of gratuitous generosity; sometimes it is obligatory. The Samaritan in Jesus' Parable of the Good Samaritan was, I would say, obligated to come to the aid of the wounded man, as were the priest and the Levite. And I have a so-called *imperfect* duty to show mercy to some of the unfortunates who accost me with their pleas for aid as I walk about Manhattan. But not all such mercy is obligatory; some goes above and beyond the call of duty. A good deal of volunteer work is like that – volunteering to help out at the local soup kitchen, volunteering to help out in a nearby retirement home and so forth. Does volunteering to help out on one occasion imply that if one fails to help out on all relevantly similar situations, one is acting unjustly? Of course not.

Was the Owner of the Vineyard Unjust?

Let's return to the story with which we began. Did the owner of the vineyard wrong anyone by the highly unusual way in which he combined generosity to some with earned pay to the others? Everybody but the five o'clock workers disliked the owner's combination of generosity to some with earned pay to the others; the early workers disliked it intensely. But was anyone wronged?

I fail to see that anyone was. The landowner did not act out of ill-will toward anyone, nor did he act out of favouritism. Did he then perhaps break an implicit agreement between himself and the early workers? Had he led them to believe that the only principle on which he would act was equal pay for equal work and unequal pay for unequal work? He had not led them to believe this. He was entirely open with the early workers about the basis on which he would pay them: the going daily wage for those who worked the full day, a just wage for those who arrived a bit later. He kept his word. Did his actions perhaps demean the early workers, treating them as of less worth than those who came at five o'clock? Not as far as I can see.

The owner did not cite a morally relevant reason for the unusual way in which he dispensed his charity. In fact, he did not cite any reason at all for the peculiar pattern of his largesse; he merely declared that he was permitted to be generous. But, as we have seen, selective generosity may be just even in the absence of any morally relevant reason for one's selection. The early workers strongly preferred that the owner pay each person what he had earned and then, if he wished to be generous, give everybody an equal-sized gift. Better yet would have been proportioning the size of the gift to the length and onerousness of the work. But the fact that they strongly preferred these arrangements does not establish that the landowner wronged them in not choosing one of those alternative arrangements.

And as to the religious import of the parable: *pace* Nygren and Brunner, God's generosity does not transcend justice by violating justice; it transcends justice by doing what justice requires and more. We are to do likewise.

Chapter 11

God's Love and the Problem of Hell

Ioanna-Maria Patsalidou

Eleonore Stump's article 'Dante's Hell, Aquinas' Moral Theory, and the Love of God' offers an interesting defence of God's love and the problem of hell. The question that Stump attempts to answer is: how is divine love supposed to be shown to those who are damned in hell?[1] The problem, Stump thinks, presupposes a certain notion of goodness.[2] Only by properly defining the notion of God's goodness can we reconcile it with the existence of hell. She finds the proper definition of God's goodness in the writings of Thomas Aquinas and, in particular, in his meta-ethical principle of the identification of 'being' and 'goodness'.[3] She endorses his moral theory and, in particular, his concept of love, and considers the results of bringing this theory to bear on the problem raised by Dante's hell. Stump proposes an 'improved' view of hell inspired by Dante's hell to show that in all the suffering of the damned in hell, God's love is at work.[4]

In the first part of the chapter I present Stump's account of hell. In order to understand how Stump brings Aquinas' moral theory to bear on the problem of hell, it is essential that we examine Aquinas' principle of the identification of 'being' and 'goodness' and his concept of love. First, I will expose the main concepts of Aquinas' moral theory – being, goodness and love – and then I will explain how Stump adopts these into her account of her improved view of Dantean hell. In the second part of the chapter I identify some weaknesses within Stump's theory. I argue that she does not show that the existence of the damned in a Dantean hell

---

[1]   Eleonore Stump, 'Dante's Hell, Aquinas' Moral Theory, and the Love of God', *Canadian Journal of Philosophy* 16(2) (1986), 181–98, at p. 183.

[2]   Stump says that if we did not think that inflicting finite pain for infinity were some sort of evil, then there would be no problem in reconciling divine love with God's existence. Or, again, if it could be proved that hell is not compatible with the existence of a good God, where, for example, good here means 'pleasure-maximizing', it would not be a problem for Christians, since they have never defended the existence of such a God. See ibid., p. 183.

[3]   There are two main Christian theories concerning what is to count as good. Stump thinks that both face some serious criticisms regarding the connection of moral values and God, which cannot be overcome. Only Aquinas' theory of morality can escape these problems and give a response to the problem of hell. For more, see ibid., pp. 183–4; and Eleonore Stump and Norman Kretzmann, 'Being and Goodness', in Scott MacDonald (ed.), *Being and Goodness* (New York: Cornell University Press, 1991), pp. 98–128.

[4]   Stump, 'Dante's Hell', p. 198.

is sufficient for God to be good to them and love them. Annihilation, on the other hand, as the fate of the damned is sufficient for God to be good to them.

Aquinas' Moral Theory

The Theory of 'Being' and 'Goodness'

For Aquinas, the terms 'being' and 'goodness' are the same in reference, but differ only in sense.[5] Aquinas argues:

> The essence of goodness consists in this that is in some way desirable. Hence the philosopher says: Goodness is what all desire. Now it is clear that a thing is desirable only in so far as it is perfect, for all desire their own perfection. But everything is perfect so far as it is actual. Therefore it is clear that a thing is perfect so far as it is being; for being is the actuality of every thing, as is clear from the foregoing. Hence it is clear that being and goodness are the same really. But goodness expresses the aspect of desirableness, which being does not express.[6]

'Being' in Aquinas' theory refers to being. It signifies that something actually is; that something exists.[7] Every thing, Aquinas argues, has a nature, a substantial form which is essential to it. In describing the nature of a thing, we specify the species or genus to which it belongs to. For example, a human being is a rational animal. For Aquinas, every thing that exists is a thing of some species; it is a thing of a certain kind.

Aquinas argues that a thing's being determines the genus within which the thing's species belongs, but that it also differentiates the thing's species from other species of that genus. Each thing's substantial form includes at least one power, capacity or potentiality which is an essential characteristic peculiar to and constitutive of the thing's species.[8] To employ the classical example: the genus 'animal' is specified to the species 'human being' by the differentia 'rationality'. A thing's specific essence (being) is always described by the genus and the differentia characterizing that particular species.[9]

Every thing that exists is good to some degree [in some form] but a thing cannot be called wholly good merely on the basis of the degree of goodness it possesses,

---

[5] *ST* Ia.5.1.

[6] Ibid.

[7] Stump points out that actual is opposed to what is potential rather to what is merely possible. See Stump and Kretzmann, 'Being and Goodness', p. 99.

[8] Aquinas holds that every form is a source of some activity or operation which he calls the differentia or specific potentiality of a thing. See *SCG* I.42.10; *SCG* III.7.7.

[9] Stump, 'Dante's Hell', p. 188.

because something is wholly good when it actualizes its specific potentiality. Even if a thing has some amount of being just by existing, it will always fall short of being so long as it does not actualize its specifying potentiality.[10]

A thing's being is progressively perfected (it progressively fulfils its nature) by exercising its specific capacity. By actualizing a differentia or capacity, a thing's being is increased. Since being is related to the nature of the thing which has being, by fulfilling its nature its goodness is increased. The goodness of a thing is tied fundamentally to its fulfilment of its nature.[11] A thing is perfect insofar as it is fully developed and its specifying potentialities have been actualized.[12] Aquinas says that 'the goodness of anything is its actuality and perfection'.[13] In this way, the terms 'being' and 'goodness' have the same referent, that is, the actualization of a thing's specifying potentiality. On the one hand, the actualization of its specifying potentiality is its existence as such a thing – having being. On the other hand, the actualization of its specifying potentiality is, to the extent of actualization, that thing's being whole. And it is in this sense that the thing is said to have goodness.[14]

The theory of 'being' and 'goodness' which Aquinas proposes is incomplete without a notion of love. On Aquinas' theory, to love something is in part to desire for the goodness of the thing loved. In the next section I will present Aquinas' notion of love and explain its purpose in Stump's account.

God's Love

Aquinas holds that the ultimate proper object of love is God, who is the highest good absolutely.[15] But God's goodness is also revealed in every human person, given that for Aquinas every human being is made in the image of God. Thus, the proper object of love also includes human beings. In Aquinas' view, then, love is primarily the love of persons.[16]

According to Aquinas' account of the nature of love, love is a passion which stimulates the lover to desire:[17] 1) the good of the beloved[18] and 2) union with

---

[10]   *ST* Ia.5.3; see also ibid., p. 190.

[11]   Stump, 'Dante's Hell', p. 189.

[12]   Aquinas uses the term 'perfect' in a metaphysical manner. See Stump and Kretzmann, 'Being and Goodness', p. 102; see also *ST* IaIIae 3.2; *ST* IaIIae. 49.4; *SCG* I.39.

[13]   *SCG* I.37.4; *SCG* I.38; *ST* Ia.5.1. See also Stump and Kretzmann, 'Being and Goodness', p. 100.

[14]   Stump and Kretzmann, 'Being and Goodness', p. 101.

[15]   *ST* Ia.6.2. See also *ST* I-II.27.1; *ST* I-II.27.2; *ST* Ia.20.1.

[16]   Eleonore Stump, 'Love, by all Accounts', *Proceedings and Addresses of the American Philosophical Association* 80(2) (2006), 25–43, at p. 27. For more, see Eleonore Stump, 'Suffering, Theodicy, and Defense', in *Wandering in Darkness – Narrative and the Problem of Suffering* (Oxford: Oxford University Press, 2010), p. 92.

[17]   *ST* Ia.20.1.

[18]   *ST* I-II.26.4; *ST* I-II.28.4.

the beloved.[19] Love tends towards the good that a person wishes to someone and towards that to which he wishes some good.[20]

First, Aquinas holds that to love a person is to will good for that person,[21] and the good of the beloved is that which truly promotes the beloved's well-being. To wish good for someone is to wish for the beloved those things which do in fact contribute to his or her flourishing.[22] So, for example, a rugby coach who desires to humiliate his players verbally because he thinks that humiliation is good for them, i.e. to motivate them to play better, is wrong on this formula; his desire to humiliate his players does not count as a desire of love, whether or not he thinks it does. Secondly, Aquinas holds that inasmuch as the lover loves the beloved, he wills good for the beloved and also union with the beloved. Since the lover desires good for the beloved, the union he seeks with the beloved should be one which contributes to the flourishing of the beloved.

Even if the two desires are interconnected, they are different in character. To desire good for the beloved does not depend on any intrinsic features or relational features of the beloved.[23] On the other hand, the desire for union with the beloved is dependent on the intrinsic features or relational features of the beloved.[24] The desire for union with the beloved requires that the lover shares something of himself with the beloved. Love is not the very relation of union, but that union is the result of love.[25]

God's love for human beings involves Him doing whatever is open to Him to do to ensure the most good for them.[26] To desire the good of anything, according to Aquinas, is to desire the actualization of the specifying potentiality of a thing's nature; it is to desire the fulfilment of its nature. God's love for human beings consists in treating them according to their nature and so helping them to develop. On Aquinas' theory, the specifying potentiality of human nature is rationality. A human being is good as a human being he or she exercises and actualizes this capacity which is specific to human beings. Human beings gain 'being' and 'goodness' by becoming more perfect specimens of humanity. Actions which

---

[19]   *ST* I-II.26.2 ad 2 and *ST* I-II.28.

[20]   *ST* I-II.26.4.

[21]   *ST* Ia.20.1.

[22]   Stump points out that Aquinas' account does not require that the lover understand the good for the beloved as something which promotes the beloved's well-being 'since a person may fail to recognize the object of his desire under one or another description of it'. Aquinas holds that since there is an objective standard of goodness, the measure of value for the goodness in love is also objective. The things which the lover desires as the good for the beloved have to be things which do contribute to the beloved's flourishing. In Stump, 'Love, by all Accounts', p. 28.

[23]   Ibid., p. 30.

[24]   Ibid.

[25]   *ST* I-II.26.2.

[26]   Stump, 'Dante's Hell', p. 192.

accord to rationality increase 'the extent to which the agent has goodness as a human being'.[27] Only acts that accord with rationality contribute to a human being's moral goodness, and as far as a good human being is a moral one, a rational action is always a moral action.[28] An action which is performed contrary to reason is a wrong action. For this reason, Aquinas describes a human virtue as a stable disposition, a settled tendency to act in accordance with one's nature – to act morally.[29]

God loves human beings by helping them to maximize their capacity for reason,[30] which is to love the good and act in accordance with it. But the ultimate good is God, so the nature of human beings is fulfilled by loving and obeying God. Stump holds that a necessary condition for union with God is the state of freely willing only what accords with God's will. If this is the case, God cannot ensure that all His human beings will be saved in the end. So what would God do with those who have rejected Him freely? If God prevented them from acting in the ways they do and thus saved them from eternal damnation, He would be acting contrary to their will and, to that extent, would destroy the nature of human beings.[31] Loss of being and hence of goodness entailed by preventing human beings from acting in evil ways is a greater loss of being than whatever loss may be incurred by the evil God permits.[32] If, on the other hand, God decides to annihilate the wicked, His action will be an unloving one because annihilation is the complete removal of being. Love desires the goodness of things, and since 'being' and 'goodness' are identical, annihilation will be an unloving act. Stump argues that God shows that He loves His human creatures by preserving them in being in hell and by allowing them to express as much of their vicious dispositions as possible, which have become a *second nature* to them. Stumps finds this idea expressed in Dante's *Inferno,* which I present in the following section.

Stump's Account of Hell

The damned, according to Dante, are the people who have by free choice willed things contrary to their nature and acquired stable dispositions to act in ways contrary to reason. They have become habituated to irrational acts; they have not acquired virtues in their earthly lives but vices.[33] Following Aquinas, Stump holds that a vice is a stable disposition, a settled tendency to act contrary to one's nature,

---

[27]   Stump and Kretzmann, 'Being and Goodness', p. 103.

[28]   Stump and Kretzmann, 'Being and Goodness', p. 103; see also Stump, 'Dante's Hell', p. 190.

[29]   Stump, 'Dante's Hell', p. 192.

[30]   Ibid.

[31]   Eleonore Stump, *Aquinas* (London: Routledge, 2003), p. 459.

[32]   Ibid, p. 459. See also *ST* Ia.48.3.

[33]   Stump, 'Dante's Hell', p. 195.

i.e. reason.[34] A vice is destructive of the being of someone habituated by it. Having a stable disposition and acting on it is itself a kind of nature commonly referred to as *second nature*.[35] It is 'an acquired cast of character which is produced over a period of time by our free choices and which is difficult to change'.[36] So, what will God do with those who will not will union with Him?

In Dante's view of hell, what God does with the damned in hell is to treat them according to their second nature. Stump claims that hell is a place in which the damned are confined so as to not do more harm to the innocent.[37] God shows that He acknowledges the evil nature of the damned and He cares for it:

> because by keeping the damned from doing further evil, he prevents their further disintegration, their further loss of goodness and of being; he cannot increase or fulfil ... [their being]; but by putting restraints on the evil they can do, he can maximize their being by keeping them from additional decay.[38]

By keeping them from decrease of being, Stumps holds that God shows love for the damned; Aquinas' kind of love. If goodness is identical with being, then God can be good to unbelievers simply by allowing them to exist.[39] As long as the damned continue to exist, their existence is good and thus God is good to them.

Moreover, Stump holds that hell is a place provided by God to the damned where they can still act and will in accordance with their evil nature. Hell is not a place of punishment inflicted by God but it is 'the condition to which the soul reduces itself by a stubborn determination to evil, and in which it suffers the torment of its own perversions'.[40] The pains and suffering imposed on the damned are not imposed by God, but the pain is the result of those who surround them in hell and what they do to themselves. So, for example, for a person who exhibits a wrathful behaviour in his earthly life and ends up in hell, the closest he can come to the natural functioning of a human being is to act in wrath. By keeping him in a place in which he can act in wrath, God allows him as much being, and thus as much goodness, as the damned are capable of. By maximizing the good of the damned, He shows that He loves them.

---

[34] Ibid., p. 192.

[35] Ibid., p. 195.

[36] Ibid.

[37] Ibid., p. 196.

[38] Ibid., pp. 196–7.

[39] God is good to human beings and in particular to the damned, by virtue of creating them.

[40] *Dante: The Divine Comedy: Hell*, trans. Dorothy L. Sayers (London; Penguin Classics, 1949), p. 68.

What is Wrong with Stump's Account of Hell?

So far I have explained how Stump uses Aquinas' meta-ethical principle and his notion of love to hold that God shows love to the damned in the Dantean hell. However, her account does not escape criticism. In this section I argue that Stump fails to show that God shows love to the damned. I will support this claim by arguing that it is not clear that the being of the damned is preserved, but it seems that there is further deterioration of being. From this I argue that if there is further loss of being, then the continued existence of the damned in hell is not sufficient for God to be good to them. Thus, it would be preferable for the damned to be annihilated than to be kept in existence.

It is Not Clear that Being is Preserved in Hell and that There is no Further Disintegration

Stump claims that hell is the place in which the damned are located in order prevent them from harming more innocent people. By keeping the damned from harming the innocent, God prevents (restrains) them from doing further evil and thus prevents their further deterioration of being. I will argue that it is not clear that being is preserved in the Dantean hell. On the contrary, it seems that there is further deterioration of being. I give two reasons in support this:

1. The damned do further evil in hell. By doing further evil, they lose more being.
2. It is not obvious that the second nature of the damned is fulfilled.

1. The damned do further evil in hell   In the Dantean hell, the damned are confined in different places according to the second nature that they have acquired for themselves. Those, for example, who have given into wrath during their earthly lives will be consigned to a place with like-minded people. The damned can then act according to their second nature and the sufferings and pain which they undergo emerge from their behaviour, as well as the behaviour and acts of others around them. So, for example, we are told that Philippo Argenti, who has been wrathful in his earthly life, is attacked and torn apart by other wrathful people. For Stump, this case of the wrathful is not a case of the damned doing further evil. Her claim suggests that the damned cannot affect anyone with their evil actions as long as the persons affected are the damned and so no further evil is done. I argue that since the damned are allowed to act according to their second nature and harm each other, this suggests that they do further evil, and if they do further evil, there is no guarantee that there will be no deterioration of being.

I would like to draw a parallel between the situation of the damned and that of prisoners in a high security prison. Criminals, murders, rapists and others who fit the description of, let us say, an evil person are confined in high-security prisons. One of the main reasons for which these people are confined to prison is to prevent them from harming more people – to prevent them from committing further crimes/ evils against others.[41] However, official figures show that those who are sentenced to prison do not refrain from committing more crimes.[42] Serious prison violence such as homicide and inmate assault is common in prisons. Can we say that the prisoners do no further evil just because they do not harm 'innocent' people? I do not think so. The prisoners continue to commit serious crimes against each other and so continue to do more evil.

Let us consider the following example. Suppose that Alex is in jail for violence against elderly people. The court decided that it would be best for him to serve time in jail in order not to harm more elderly people and so do further evil. However, Alex turns against other inmates and causes severe bodily harm to some of them. Moreover, his actions cause anxiety and distress to other inmates who try to avoid close encounters with him. The fact that he does not cause harm to the innocent and his evil actions are towards other criminals does not give less value to the nature of evil done and suffered. It does not mean that he does not do further evil. Therefore, we can say that his evil nature is not really preserved, but it can deteriorate to an even worse nature since he can still harm others. And the more evil his nature becomes, the more his being deteriorates. Furthermore, his actions not only affect his nature but also the nature of his inmates. Researchers have shown that violence in prisons can result in psychological tensions such as stress, tension, anxiety, depression and hostility.[43] These in turn can result in more violence. For example, someone who has been charged with rape can, when he finds himself in these conditions, commit murder. So Alex's actions can affect the psychological behaviours of his fellow inmates. The inmates' nature then can be affected in a way that will contribute to the deterioration of their being.

Stump seems to suggest that because the damned continue to act according to their second nature in a place with like-minded people, evil is contained. They can do further evil only when they harm innocent people. But from the above case involving prisoners, we can see that the crimes which are committed against other prisoners are taken to be further instances of evil and so more evil is done. That the evil performed is confined within a prison does not suggest that the prisoners do no further evil by inflicting pain – physical or/and psychological – on their fellow inmates. Returning to the Dantean hell, we learn that the damned can turn

---

[41]   Other key reasons are to punish, to rehabilitate or to reform.

[42]   Sheldon Ekland-Olson, 'Crowding, Social Control, and Prison Violence: Evidence from the Post-Ruiz Years in Texas', *Law & Society Review* 20(3) (1986), 389–422, at p. 392.

[43]   See ibid., pp. 389–92. Researchers have shown that violence in prisons can result in psychological tensions induced by crowded conditions. In overcrowded places such as prisons, the prisoners are exposed to the risks of assault and homicide. A consequence of this is the enhancement of stress, tension, anxiety, depression and hostility. The close proximity for long periods of time, along with the need for self-preservation and avoidance of victimization, can lead to violence on behalf of the inmates.

on each other and inflict tremendous pain on one another (see the Philippo Argenti story). Since the damned act according to their second nature and turn against each other, we can say that they do further evil in the same way as the inmates do to each other in prison. As long as the damned can harm others, we can say that it is possible that there will be further disintegration of being in hell. Moreover, those who suffer harm face no different fate. It is possible that the sufferers will form other psychological behaviours such as fear, envy, anxiety, etc., which, instead of helping them to maximize their being, causes it to deteriorate.

Moreover, as the damned perform more evil actions, they become more and more enslaved to their passions and desires, and as they become more and more enslaved to their passions and desires, they lose their freedom. In Aquinas' view, the good within human beings is connected with their capacity for rationality. An essential constituent of rationality is freedom of will. As long as human beings act according to reason, they perform free actions and they also increase their being. But we can say that the damned behave in the same way as a drug addict. Addicts are not capable of using their freedom of will because they are enslaved to their desires, and so it is said that they act in irrational ways. Since freedom of will is an essential part of rationality, the more the damned are enslaved to their passions, the more irrational they become and so the less being they have. A decline of freedom is a decline of being.[44]

2. It is not obvious that the damned's second nature is fulfilled   In Dante's hell, the damned are given to their deepest desires and they can act on and fulfil these desires without harming the innocent. But what Stump claims is not possible with certain vices.[45] There are some vices which require i. .ocent victims for their proper expression. For example, a paedophile lusts for children and his second vicious nature can only be fulfilled if his desires are fulfilled. In other words, his desire can only be fulfilled if there are children in hell. Or suppose that someone finds great pleasure in being violent towards mentally disabled people. If the

---

[44]   Stump's account has drawn the attention of few philosophers. Jonathan Kvanvig offers two criticisms against her account. His first criticism is similar to mine – he argues that it is not clear that being is preserved in Hell. Since the damned are allowed to express their evil second nature, they become increasingly corrupt and thus fall away from the ideal of primary human nature, which is rationality. There is no reason, says Kvanvig, to think that the damned have already become as corrupt as humanly possible by the time they arrive in hell. His second criticism deals with the concept of freedom. He says that as the damned become more corrupt, they lose more and more of their freedom. The problem is that if freedom is part of human nature, then a decline of freedom is a decline of being. The damned slowly lose being. Thus, it is not obvious that annihilation is a worse fate than hell. For more detail on Kvanvig's criticisms, see Jonathan L. Kvanvig, *The Problem of Hell* (Oxford: Oxford University Press, 1993), pp. 123–9.

[45]   I make the same objection as Kelly Clark. See Kelly Clark, 'God is Great, God is Good: Medieval Conceptions of Divine Goodness and the Problem of Hell', *Religious Studies* 37(1) (2001), 15–31.

damned who lust for children or the damned who find pleasure in being violent towards mentally disabled people are placed with like-minded people, then it is difficult to see how their second nature is going to be fulfilled. The existence of innocent people in hell is necessary in order for them to fulfil their desires.

I argue that the satisfaction of one's desires is required for the fulfilment of one's nature. In the case of the damned, desires that are eternally frustrated will possibly result in a loss of being. Let us consider the following case, presented in Dante's *Inferno*. Dante enters the circle of the lustful in which those who have sinned by excess of sexual passion, those souls who in life made pleasure their hope, are tossed upon a howling wind forever. In particular, he sees Paolo and Francesca.[46] The couple drifted into self-indulgence and were carried away by their passions during their earthly life, and now they drift forever, spinning through the air. Paolo and Francesca lust after each other and want to be together, but they can never be because the wind drives them apart. If their second nature is being lustful but they everlastingly drift apart and never have each other, their second nature is not and will never be fulfilled. It is not enough to lust for each other; the fulfilment of their nature can only be the result of satisfying their lust for each other.[47] If the fulfilment of their second nature lies in the successful satisfaction of desires, then in drifting apart they can never fulfil that nature.

The lust which Paolo and Francesca have for one another, one might say, could persist forever and so their nature of being lustful continues forever. But I do not think that this is necessarily true. Even if their being can be preserved for some time, it is nevertheless possible that it will not be preserved forever. If Paolo and Francesca lust after each other for all eternity, it is possible that their lustful nature will be transformed into a wrathful nature. Unfulfilled desires can lead to wrath. In hell, Dante observes that the pair cries out lamentations and insults to God as they are blown about. If their desire for each finds no expression in action, then their desire gets frustrated. We can say that there will be a point at which the pair will be in wrath. It is possible that their second nature – being lustful – will not be preserved but will deteriorate to a wrathful nature. If this is the case, then I think that it is safe to say that there is deterioration of being.

The isolation model which Stump proposes does not guarantee that there will be no further disintegration of being. First, I argued that the damned do further evil in hell and they harm themselves and others around them. By doing further evil, their being is decreased. Secondly, I argued that it is not obvious that the damned's second nature will be fulfilled in every single case. The continuous unsuccessful completion of some vices will lead to lesser and lesser vices and will possibly result in a loss of being. Stump claims that in hell God preserves the being of the damned and so He shows love to them. But if, as I have shown, the being is not

[46]   Dante, *The Divine Comedy: Hell*, trans. Dorothy L. Sayers (Harmondsworth: Penguin Classics, 1949), Canto V, Circle II: The Lustful, pp. 99–101.

[47]   Clark holds that 'it is not enough to lust; one's desires must eventuate in actions for human fulfilment'. See Clark, 'God is Great, God is Good', p. 25–6.

preserved, then it will be difficult for Stump to hold that God loves them in the way she thinks He does. Where does this lead us? I will argue in the next section that the Dantean damneds' good is not enough of a good to show that God loves them. Annihilation, on the other hand, is a better fate for them. God will show the damned that He loves them if He annihilates them rather than isolates them in hell.

How is Existence in Hell Better than Non-existence?

Stump, following Aquinas, holds that human beings can achieve goodness and fulfil their nature when they act according to reason. A person who lives his or her life according to reason is a good and a happy person. To act and live according to reason is what is objectively good for every human being. However, this does not suppose that every human being knowingly desires a life lived according to reason. Wishing what is ultimately good is to desire union with God and only those who exercise their specifying potentiality – reason – can do so. However, to the extent to which a person does not think that the ultimate good consists in acting according to reason, there will also be a sense in which it is true to say of a person who wants happiness that, subjectively considered, he or she does not want a life lived according to reason.[48] So a human being cares about two things: on the one hand, he or she cares about his or her well-being, his or her flourishing. On the other hand, he or she cares about 'what has great value for [him or] her in virtue of her commitment to it'.[49]

Since there is both an objective and a subjective good that human beings care about, Stump says that there are two sides of suffering as well. Part of what it is to suffer is to prevent someone from being what he or she ought to be, that is, to prevent him or her from flourishing. On the other hand, to cause someone to suffer is to prevent him or her from fulfilling his or her desires. Therefore, Stump holds that suffering is bad because it undermines or destroys what the sufferer cares about, his or her own flourishing, his or his desires, or both.

Let us connect this way of reasoning with the suffering of the damned in hell. Hell as a place where the human potentiality cannot be exercised and the being of the damned cannot be increased is a place of suffering and so it is something bad for the damned. By being in a place with like-minded people in which they can never wish and attain what is objectively good for them, the damned could never be happy in the sense that they cannot live according to the objective good, to the will of God. The evil which the damned endure in hell constitutes suffering for them because it goes contrary to (or undermines) human flourishing. In hell they

---

[48]   Stump, 'Suffering, Theodicy, and Defense', p. 9.

[49]   Ibid., p.10. Stump says that someone can care about something which is not equivalent to what one ought to be: 'Instead, it picks out something a person is deeply committed to, whether or not that is what would constitute his flourishing or even be compatible with it. We care about our own flourishing, but that is not all we care about.'

can never be what they ought to be, they can never increase their being, and the qualities which constitute their flourishing are absent.[50]

Moreover, I argued that it is not clear that the desires of the damned are fulfilled and so their second nature is fulfilled. I argued that if their desires are not fulfilled, then some of the damned (if not all) will become wrathful. By becoming worse, the being of the damned deteriorates. If their desires are not fulfilled, then we can say that even in their second nature the damned will suffer. Suffering which stems from the lack of fulfilment of desires is the subjective side of suffering. So it looks as though the damned suffer by not being able to attain either what is objectively or subjectively good for them. Why, then, would their existence in hell be better than their non-existence? Aquinas says something interesting about non-being which I shall use to support my claim that annihilation is better than existence in hell.

Aquinas holds that a total lack of being would be an absolute evil. However, although not to be is (*prima facie*) evil, it is also a good when it reduces unhappiness. Thus, it is better not to be than to be in cases in which non-being is desirable on the ground that it reduces suffering. Aquinas says:

> I answer that, Not to be may be considered in two ways. First, in itself, and thus it can nowise be desirable, since it has no aspect of good, but is pure privation of good. Secondly, it may be considered as a relief from a painful life or from some unhappiness: and thus 'not to be' takes on the aspect of good, since 'to lack an evil is a kind of good' as the Philosopher says (Ethic. v, 1). In this way it is better for the damned not to be than to be unhappy ... Although 'not to be' is very evil, in so far as it removes being, it is very good, in so far as it removes unhappiness, which is the greatest of evils, and thus it is preferred 'not to be.'[51]

And elsewhere he says:

> Non-being is desirable, not of itself, but only relatively – i.e. inasmuch as the removal of an evil, which is removed by non-being, is desirable. Now the removal of an evil cannot be desirable, except so far as this evil deprives a thing of some being. Therefore it is being which is desirable of itself, while non-being is desirable only relatively, viz., inasmuch as one seeks some being of which one cannot bear to be deprived; and thus it happens that even non-being can be spoken of as relatively good.[52]

The damned in hell act according to their second nature and there is nothing God or they can do to increase their being. From what has been said above, the prevention of someone from fulfilling his or her nature constitutes suffering for him or her and so it is something evil. Furthermore, I argued that there are cases

---

[50] Ibid., p. 8.

[51] *ST* Suppl.98.3.

[52] *ST* Ia.5.2.

in which the desires of the damned, that is, what they take to be subjectively good, will not be fulfilled and this will lead to further deterioration of being and thus more suffering. If there is no possibility for increase of being and if there is further loss of being and rationality due to the fact that some desires will not be fulfilled, then the continued existence of the damned and their suffering/unhappiness is not sufficient for God to be good to them. Therefore, it would be preferable not to be than to be, because the damned are in such circumstances that their suffering, which results from privation of the subjectively and the objectively good, is worse than their non-existence. It seems that a reduction of unhappiness, even when it is accompanied by a loss of being, is good. Unless Stump shows that their second nature is fulfilled, then the continued existence of the damned is not sufficient for us to say that God is being good to them and also is not a sufficient good to override the good of annihilation.

Conclusion

In this chapter I have exposed the main concepts of Aquinas' moral theory – being, goodness and love – and I have explained how Stump adopts these into her account of an improved Dantean hell. I have identified and presented some weaknesses in her account and I argued that the Dantean hell which she portrays does not guarantee that there will be no further deterioration of being. Moreover, I have argued that if there is deterioration of being, then the existence of the damned in hell is not sufficient for God to be good to them and so annihilation may be a better fate for the damned.

God and Moral Responsibility

Chapter 12

The Origin of Evil and the Benefits of Sin

Vasil Gluchman

There was a wide spectrum of attitudes towards sin and evil within Slovak Lutheran ethics of the eighteenth and nineteenth centuries, ranging from a pillorying of any human sin or evil as the Devil's deed, through a sympathetic attitude towards human weaknesses and faults, to a teleological conception that justifies sin and evil as a means of human moral development. The differentiation of attitudes towards sin and evil in Slovak Lutheran ethics in these centuries was predominantly an outcome of the internal development, or internal conditions, in the Lutheran Church in that given period. They were, for instance, influenced by the course of conflicts between pietism and orthodox Lutheranism in the eighteenth century, or between rationalism and orthodoxy in the nineteenth century.

The views of Samuel Hruškovic (1694–1748) and Pavel Jakobei (1695–1752) provide examples of the first attitude towards sin and evil in the eighteenth century. In *Vlastný* životopis [*Own Biography*] (1720), Hruškovic writes that he commits sins every day and, for that, he deserves eternal hellish punishment.[1] To the Devil he attributes all deeds that do not arise from a pure and true heart.[2] Similarly, Jakobei understands sin as the Devil's trap into which man can easily fall; it is, however, very hard to get out of the Devil's net. He thinks that the Devil, our enemy, strikes at us from all around and instigates many sins, which makes many people devote themselves to gluttonous feasting and drinking, shameless lust, envy, pride and avarice, which they, possibly, do not even consider to be sin.[3] He calls for a return to extremely cruel punishment for debauchery, as used in Ancient Rome in the times of the Emperor Aurelian, that is, tearing apart the bodies of adulterers or executing them as was done in the Middle Ages.[4] According to Jakobei, if one gives into debauchery and shamelessness only once, it contaminates one's whole heart, and even if, later on, one wishes to make it right, this can hardly be done. We should rather avoid sin early on and be careful with the whole of our bodies: the heart to cleanse us of all impurity, the eyes not to look on vanity, the ears not to listen to obscene and indecorous talk, and the hands

---

[1] Samuel Hruškovic, *Vlastný životopis* (Liptovský Svätý Mikuláš: Transocius, 1943), p. 11.

[2] Ibid., p. 16.

[3] Pavel Jakobei, *Welmi Důležité Přjčiny, pro které čtyř neyhlawněgššich a v tyto poslednj časy neyobičegněgšších hřichů.. wárowati se máme* (Modra, 1724), pp. 2–3.

[4] Ibid., p. 21.

not to reach where inappropriate, but rather to work and avoid idleness which is the Devil's domain. We should also beware of our feet so as not to enter bad circles. We have to remember what Augustine said: whoever wants to avoid sin has to retreat from the sources. Thus, man has to keep an eye on his whole body so as not to overfill it by abundant gluttony and drinking, since drunkenness brings debauchery and this opens all doors to adultery and sodomy. That is why it is best for man to enter into matrimony as early as possible, as matrimony is God-created as an aid to drive away various ill desires. Matrimony, according to St Paul, is the sacred school for all human life, where we can learn a lot and get used to good.[5]

Above all, Jakobei attributes to the Devil arguments, envy, restlessness and disharmony; the Devil takes pleasure in disturbing peace in the spiritual, secular and *domestic realms. We can see how many conflicts there are in clerical administration, in religion and the elements of Christian religion, and within secular administration, where no*-one believes or yields to the other, and such conflict gives rise to wars and rebellions in all countries. Also, married couples keep arguing and fighting; brothers and sisters, friends and neighbours are like cats and mice. Jakobei holds that this is nothing more than a darned Devil's deed trying, in all sly ways possible, to rouse disharmony and quarrels among people, as well as misery, grief and sorrow.[6] The Devil is present in arguments, envy, trouble and disharmony, and he makes an effort to turn these into great evil in all establishments, be they spiritual, clerical or private. If the Devil enters religious administration, teachers and preachers try their best to save their own honour or to take revenge, they blame and besmirch each other, which harms the church. It is due to these arguments that the true Holy word is lost and heresy enters in. When the Devil gets among secular lords and counts, then the proverb applies that whenever masters fight, servants' heads will fall. When the Devil enters a household, the husband and wife, the parents, start arguing and this brings many other wounds and murders.[7]

* * *

Augustín Doležal (1737–1802), who was a Lutheran pastor and an important representative of the Slovak Enlightenment, presents a completely different position on sin and evil. He can be considered as a representative of rationally-oriented enlightenment philosophy in Slovakia. The evidence of such a statement is the work *Pamětná celému světu Tragoedia...* (1791) [*The Whole World Memorial Tragedy...*]. In this work, which is based on a biblical story, he tried to explain several theological, philosophical, ethical and social problems of his times. Through the literary form, he sought rational answers to the question of how evil can exist in a world which is the result of God's act of creation. Today,

---

[5] Ibid., pp. 26–7.

[6] Ibid., pp. 29–30.

[7] Ibid., pp. 32–4.

his contribution to Slovak philosophy and ethics is mentioned only tangentially.[8] However, Leibniz's influence on Doležal, and Doležal's philosophy and ethics in their own right, are worth further consideration.[9] Doležal produced one of the most important literary works of the end of the eighteenth century in Slovakia, a work that has indisputable importance for the history of ethics in Slovakia and the history of Slovak Lutheran ethics in particular.

Doležal's work has been analysed or subjected to much criticism by a number of Slovak and Czech literary historians, especially in the twentieth century, including Jaroslav Vlček, Jan B. *Čapek*, *Štefan* Krčméry and Eva Fordinálová. The work of Eva Fordinálová is, to this day, the most detailed literary-historical analysis and criticism of the given piece, containing interesting and important philosophical reflections. In a similar fashion to *Čapek* before her, Fordinálová observes that it is a predominantly philosophical piece of work.[10] *I would like to focus more on moments and aspects of Doležal's writings that were not primarily under her attention*, i.e. the philosophical and ethical dimension of the work from the point of view of understanding good and evil.

Doležal's choice of topic was most likely influenced by his university studies in Altdorf, where the impact of Gottfried Wilhelm Leibniz (1646–1716) and Christian Wolff (1679–1754) was evident. In Doležal's *Tragoedia*, the influence of Leibniz's ideas, especially his work *Theodicy* (1710), could be profoundly felt. In particular, Doležal was able to find a number of positive features and values that emerged for humanity from the story of Adam and Eve and the origin of evil and sin.

Doležal, through Adam's lips, notes that God tried to prevent man from falling into sin in different ways, for example, by forbidding him to eat from a certain tree in the Garden of Eden. While it is right externally to permit sin (in the sense of enabling its possibility), this is not moral permission.[11] To prevent man from committing sin or evil, God would have had to create logs instead of humans. 'As the Lord is our Spirit, His work is divine, His essence is moral as are His intentions! Should he who governs holy morality also block the path

---

[8]   Ján Bodnár, Milan Burica, Dalimír Hajko, Richard Marsina, Teodor Münz, Marianna Oravcová, Terézia Palovičová, Július Sopko, Viktor Timura and Elena Várossová, *Dejiny filozofického myslenia na Slovensku, vol. 1* (Bratislava: Veda, 1987), pp. 218–20; Teodor Münz, *Filozofia slovenského osvietenstva* (Bratislava: SAV, 1961), pp. 227–8; Samuel Štefan Osuský, *Prvé slovenské dejiny filozofie* (Liptovský Svätý Mikuláš: Transocius, 1939), p. 388.

[9]   Gluchman, Vasil, *Etika na Slovensku – minulosť a prítomnosť* (Bratislava: H&H, 2008), pp. 55–68.

[10]   Eva Fordinálová, *Stretnutie so starším pánom alebo Tragédia Augustína Doležala* (Martin: Osveta, 1993), p. 236; Jan Blahoslav Čapek, *Augustin Doležal a jeho Tragoedia* (Prague: Učená Spoločnost Šafaříkova v Bratislavě, 1931), p. 17.

[11]   Augustín Doležal, *Pamětná celém světu Tragoedia, anebožto Veršovné vypsánj žalostného Prvnjch Rodičů Pádu...* (Uherská Skalica: Jozef Antonin Škarnycl, 1791), pp. 197–8.

to moral freedom violently? All morals, be they bad or holy, when imposed in a violent way, lose the value of their freedom...'[12] This expression is fundamental to the explanation of the existence of evil in the world. Man rather than God is responsible for the existence of sin or evil in the world. God did not want to be an immoral tyrant and despot; he left man with the possibility of freedom, and so evil exists. In principle, this is Leibniz's motif, but Leibniz presented it in a more sophisticated way than Doležal. Doležal has Seth ask whether God can be blamed for the sin of the first parents, and replies: has anyone seen a king constantly follow his subjects? Subjects should do as the King orders especially when the King gives them the authority.[13] The reason for sin and evil resides in the existence of man's free will.

Later, Adam asks the following question: in the case of no existence of sin in the world, how could man know about the majesty, justice and holiness of God who can save sinful mankind as well?[14] According to Doležal, a more logical question can be formed as to whether sin and evil exist in order that God display His goodness and power over evil. Based on the teleological approach to the existence of evil in the world, its purpose is the glorification of God and His ability to deal with evil. To a certain extent, this view was canvassed even earlier, when Doležal stated that the wisdom and effectiveness of a landowner can be best manifested when he is able to solve the problems connected with landowning. One might expect Doležal to have Adam and Eve persuade their son Seth of the harmfulness of evil. However, Doležal, together with Adam, finally arrives at the surprising statement (exactly in accordance with Leibniz): if Eve and Adam did not sin, all businesses would lose their value, there would be no theology because we all would confess the same religion and philosophy. There would be no doctors or pharmacists if all could carry their own medicine in their own bodies; no soldiers would be needed if we all would follow holy justice.[15] When we sinned for the first time, God gave various authorities as kings, emperors, princes, counts, dukes, etc. to the world. We have district governors, district vice-governors, notaries, lawyers, reeves, etc.[16] 'Even in sin it is praiseworthy that it was done like that by God's majestic power!'[17]

Seth had already seen something positive in the sin, *viz,* man's ability to know evil. Adam conveys all that mankind would lack were it not for the sin. He fully expresses Leibniz's idea, although in artistic form, that God allowed evil in the form of the first sin of Adam and Eve for the benefit of our greater good. He shares Leibniz's view that a world or society consisting only of good people is worse than a society or world where bad people live alongside the good, and that, by

---

[12]   Ibid., p. 198.

[13]   Ibid., p. 58.

[14]   Ibid., p. 199.

[15]   Ibid., p. 202.

[16]   Ibid., pp. 208–9.

[17]   Ibid., p. 209.

overcoming evil, greater good arises.[18] In the best possible world, goodness springs from overcoming evil.[19] I would add that, at times of struggle with evil, man and society develop, whereas in a state of permanent goodness, it would stagnate.

To Seth's doubts as to whether it would be better for mankind not to know sin, his father Adam noted that it would be foolish to think of the world as entirely miserable, bad and stillborn because of moral mistakes.[20] One should take into consideration all human vocations, businesses, positions, offices, jobs, crafts and virtues. All human occupations that are performed by people should be considered and it would be evident that, without the first sin, there would not be any of those occupations. A great number of professions and necessities exist, such that even a sinner can be joyful when doing them and can strive in piety to reach heavenly pleasure.

At the same time, in connection with knowledge, Adam states that the primary sin was ultimately not all bad because, thanks to it, mankind has discovered a great amount of information that has helped nature itself. Adam, in the same context, claimed that because we have sinned, we must exercise our brain; what we did not know before, we know now, having sinned.[21] Ironically, one could add: the snake was right when he persuaded Eve that the forbidden tree was the tree of knowledge and that people would understand what they did not understand, that they would know what they did not know. Adam admitted this, but not directly. The climax is, however, an almost heretical idea: Adam claims apologetically: 'this world is so good and beautiful that even the life of death itself can radiate. And would that no wrong had ever been done, one would not be aware that God made sin into a virtue'.[22]

Seth notes that it is not enough only to have good intentions but that it is also necessary to act well. Someone can intend good but can act sinfully or harmfully.[23] Adam picks out his son's ideas about the importance of intention or motive for action or action evaluation, and claims that will is enough for virtue in all cases where an act cannot be performed.[24] The fact that will itself is sufficient for virtue in cases where the action cannot be performed is very important. It is a third approach to motive, intention or will in Doležal's work.

Adam frequently states the need to avoid actions that one's soul most resists. The better we know the reasons to avoid an action, the bigger the sin we are committing if we perform that action.[25] According to Doležal, the biggest sin

---

[18]   Gottfried Wilhelm Leibniz, *Theodicy: Essays on the Goodness of God, the Freedom of Man and the Origin of Evil* (London: Routledge & Kegan Paul, 1996), p. 198.

[19]   Ibid., pp. 137; 186, 190, 195, 197 and 378.

[20]   Doležal, *Pamětná celém světu Tragoedia*, p. 200.

[21]   Ibid., p. 220.

[22]   Ibid., p. 225.

[23]   Ibid., p. 142.

[24]   Ibid., p. 162.

[25]   Ibid., p. 190.

resides in deliberate action that is in conflict with God's order or prohibition. In this thought, Doležal surpasses Leibniz. He holds that it is the failure in obedience, not the results of the action, that determines the level of sin. The more deliberate and intentional the disobedience, the bigger the sin and evil performed. The worse the intention, the greater evil we commit, and the extent of the punishment is equal to such action. This is a very interesting moment in Doležal's concept of evil and intention. It can be stated that he admitted the existence of several levels of evil, mainly depending on the extent of deliberate or intentional action.

According to Doležal, a sinful world does not need to be only a place of suffering but also a place of delight and pleasure. It seems that it was God Himself who, although expelling Adam and Eve from paradise, did not punish them fatally; however, He offered them enough space or opportunity for pleasure and enjoyment, not only in spiritual but also in physical form, as, for instance, in the form of natural beauties. At one point in the text, Eve explains why it is possible that, together with Adam, even after their sin, she is experiencing joy and pleasure in the world. Eve notes that God said that despite profanation of his gift of being in paradise, man would not stay completely without his grace and God would redeem him from his sinfulness. He would fulfil his requests to reach the state of full joy even in his present state of sorrow. The condition is that man should have full hope in God's glorious name, should serve and sacrifice himself every day of his life and then he would live to see salvation.[26] That Doležal did not consider sexual love as a sin, but, on the contrary, regarded it as joyful for people is another proof of his concept.[27]

Finally, I would like to note that while, in most cases, primary sin is interpreted as a prime example of man's disobedience to God, in Doležal's work it can, in a certain sense, be seen as an attempt by man to gain autonomy from God (although only an unintentional one). It can possibly be interpreted as an eternal temptation or an eternal desire for knowledge, and as exposing that which had hitherto been undiscovered or unknown. Humanity is attracted by mystery, by unsolved or unanswered questions, and, as Doležal appreciated, while the primary sin resulted in evil, it was, even more so, the origin of much good. It may sound rather heretical to state what Doležal only implied that 'thanks' to the primary sin or desire for knowledge, for the discovery of the new and unknown, man became a full person able to realize his potential, to develop his knowledge and skills. Without this sin, he would have stayed in paradise forever and become stultified; in everything, he would have depended on God who would perform, judge and think on his behalf. God, in Doležal's deistic interpretation, permitted the evil of the primary sin for man's emancipation. Man, in a certain sense, grows through problems that are caused by him and by the fact that he steps beyond an apparent line between what is and is not permitted. One can agree with Eva Fordinálová[28] that Doležal's work

---

26   Ibid., p. 243.

27   Ibid., p. 305.

28   Fordinálová, p. 231.

talks about man, his failures and victories, about searching for himself in activity, about man who rejoices, who suffers, who becomes wise thanks to obstacles and effort, to pain and losses that are necessary.[29]

---

[29] This article is a part of VEGA 1/0327/11 research project *History of ethical thinking in Slovakia*. It was also prepared with the support of *Martin Luther Bund society* (Germany) and *Department of Theology and Studies of the Lutheran World Federation* in Geneva (Switzerland) for research project on the history of Slovak Lutheran ethics to the end of the nineteenth century.

Chapter 13
God and Moral Responsibility

Alicja A. Gescinska

Introduction

Although Max Scheler (1874–1928) was seen by many of his contemporaries as one of the most important intellectual forces in European philosophy, the interest in his thought rapidly decreased soon after his death. In general, Scheler's philosophy has received little attention, at least not the attention one would think worthy of a major intellectual force in philosophy. One could refer here to Hans-Georg Gadamer, who, rather sharply, expressed his discontentment with the lack of recognition that Scheler's writings receive, even in Germany: 'It is almost unbelievable, but when you nowadays ask a young man about it, or even an older one, who is interested in philosophy, he hardly knows who Scheler was.'[1]

Scheler's later works (1922–8) especially have been sadly misunderstood and under-estimated. In these writings Scheler abandoned Catholicism and developed a panentheistic world-view with an utterly original concept of God (*Gottwerdung*) which is hardly compatible with Catholicism. As far as I am concerned, most of the attempts to explain this metaphysical swing in Scheler's thought and to grasp its essence and significance seem to have been rather unsuccessful. This can partly be ascribed to the fact that most of Scheler's readers and critics were immensely disappointed that he broke with the Catholic Church. For about a decade, Scheler had been the most important German Catholic philosopher. His influence and intellectual authority were such that many people converted to Catholicism after reading his writings.[2]

One can understand how disappointed many were in Scheler's 'metaphysical swing' towards panentheism, and the emotional reactions it provoked severely hindered any objective analysis of Scheler's *Späte Schriften* (*Late Writings*). They were immediately dismissed as inferior to anything he had written before and the reasons for this alleged qualitative decline in his thought were solely sought in his private life. Jan Nota, for example, one of the experts on Scheler, described Scheler's ideas of this period as cold and methodologically unsatisfactory in

---

[1] Hans-Georg Gadamer, 'Max Scheler: Der Verschwender', in Paul Good (ed.), *Max Scheler im Gegenwartsgeschehen der Philosophie* (Bern: Francke Verlag, 1975), pp. 11–18, at p. 11. (Translations in this article are those of the author.)

[2] The most well-known example of this is of course Edith Stein, who had known Scheler personally and sketched a beautiful portrait of the man in her diaries.

comparison with his earlier works, and, like many critics, argued that Scheler's turbulent private life and 'sexual activities' (he wanted a divorce from his second wife, while the divorce from his first wife had already caused a huge scandal) were to be held responsible for this. This was the *communis opinio* of most readers of Scheler's writings, as is illustrated in Louis de Raeymaeker's comments on Scheler's abandonment of Catholicism, saying that he had done so 'not because of reasons of a philosophical kind [but that Scheler] felt obliged to adapt his system to his loose life'.[3]

Furthermore, it has always been *bon ton* to describe Scheler as an inconsistent, rather impulsive thinker, who changed his views from one day to the next. His drastic parting from Catholicism was therefore dismissed as an impulse. Dietrich von Hildebrand, Howard Becker and many others have all attributed Scheler's metaphysical change to 'some inadequacy of the man himself'.[4]

In any case, it was generally assumed that Scheler did not have good reasons for his metaphysical swing and that his reasons were not of a philosophical kind. This negative evaluation of his *Späte Schriften* is not only characteristic of his Christian contemporaries and critics. Martin Buber critically commented upon Scheler's metaphysical swing as 'one of the countless gnostic attempts to strip the mystery from the biblical God',[5] and some of the most important contemporary connoisseurs of Scheler's philosophy have criticized these writings in a remarkably sharp way, albeit that their rejection of his late metaphysics had nothing to do with any moralizing judgments about his private life. Eugene Kelly, for example, wrote in his praiseworthy *Structure and Diversity* that he has 'never forgiven Scheler for this late turn to metaphysics',[6] even characterizing this late turn as 'ultimately misbegotten'.[7]

I will argue in this chapter that Scheler's last writings are certainly not necessarily less valuable than his earlier works. First, I will try to prove that his *Späte Schriften* are in remarkable concordance with his earlier writings, at least from the perspective of his ethical views and system, and certainly do not represent such a dramatic rupture as is often put forth by those who have never been able to 'forgive' him for his metaphysical swing. The main part of this chapter will therefore consist of an analysis of the moral implications that are inherent in Scheler's renewing concept of God, as it is obvious that his concept of *Gottwerdung*, which was central in his late metaphysics, does not leave morality

---

[3]   Louis de Raeymaeker, *De philosophie van Scheler* (Mechelen: Het Kompas, 1934), pp. 26–7.

[4]   Peter H. Spader, *Scheler's Ethical Personalism: Its Logic, Development, and Promise* (New York: Fordham University Press, 2002), p. 177.

[5]   Martin Buber, 'The Philosophical Anthropology of Max Scheler', *Philosophy and Phenomenological Research* 6 (1945), 307–21, at p. 313.

[6]   Eugene Kelly, *Structure and Diversity: Studies in the Phenomenological Phenomenology of Max Scheler* (Dordrecht: Kluwer Academic Publishers, 1997), p. 195.

[7]   Ibid., p. 176.

untouched. I will stress the fact that these moral implications remarkably coincide with the core of Scheler's earlier ethical system, as developed in his magnificent *Der Formalismus in der Ethik und die Materiale Wertethik* (*Formalism in Ethics and Non-Formal Ethics of Values*). Furthermore, not only are Scheler's *Späte Schriften* compatible with the essence of his earlier ethics, but there is also a great consistency in them, even though they are often characterized as merely a collection of distinct essays. His so-called *metanthropology* accords with his political, epistemological and ethical views. It is beyond doubt that the recognition of the internal and overall consistency of Scheler's writings leads to a better comprehension and fuller appreciation of his latest creative period.

Secondly, and more generally, I will try to explain why Scheler changed his metaphysical views. As I have already indicated, some say this is due to his turbulent private life and sexual activities. It has been said that Scheler's new metaphysical conception in fact mirrors his own powerlessness in the face of his sexual urges. I find this criticism rather disrespectful. It does not explain Scheler's swing. Nor does the alleged 'innate philosophical inconsistency' of Scheler explain his profound change of thought.

God and Morality: From Ethics to Metaphysics

An Anthropocentric Concept of God

Before I can advance to an analysis of how Scheler's new metaphysical position related to his earlier writings, I will briefly outline the essence of this new position, which Scheler elaborated above all in *Die Stellung des Menschen im Kosmos* (*The Place of Man in the Cosmos*), which also echoes several of his other later writings. The work starts with a digression on the distinction between the nature of man and that of animals, a digression that is perhaps not very interesting and remains rather speculative. However, bearing in mind that Scheler was often regarded as an inconsistent thinker, it is important to notice how this digression in fact reflects his everlasting interest in defining the nature and place of man, and that it not only relates to his anthropological but also, as I shall further demonstrate, to his metaphysical and ethical views.

Die Stellung des Menschen im Kosmos becomes more interesting when Scheler relates the distinction he made between two primal principles – a powerless *Geist* (Spirit) and a powerful *Trieb* (Force) – to the relationship between God and man. According to Scheler, it is not God who *delivers* us from evil, but it is man who has to *deliver* God from the eternal tension between Force and Spirit. Only man – as an acting person (*Aktvollziehendes Wesen*) – can realize a mutual penetration of these two universal attributes and God is the outcome of this penetration. God is realized by and through man (*Gottwerdung*). God is not, until he is set free by man:

> The primal relationship between man and *Weltgrund* consists in the fact that this *Weltgrund* realizes itself directly in man. The place of this self-realization [...] is man. The human self and the human heart is the place of God's becoming (*Ort der Gottwerdung*).[8]

Scheler explicitly refutes the idea of man as God's slave or subject. Man is God's *Mitbildner*, His 'co-creater' or 'co-builder'. This in short is the essence of Scheler's metaphysics and concept of *Gottwerdung*. The main bone of contention for Catholic readers was of course the idea that God is in Himself incomplete as his existence and fulfilment would have to depend on what people do. Johannes Hessen, who wrote a very good introduction to Scheler's thought, has nicely expressed the immense gulf between such a concept of God and that of traditional theisms:

> Every kind of God who is Himself incomplete, and yearns for completion and salvation, is all too human to be a God. It is the model of *Faust* in a macrocosmic expansion. Such a God is not the God of the real religious consciousness.[9]

The Origins of the Concept of Gottwerdung

As I have already said, many displeased Catholic critics and readers of Scheler tried to explain away Scheler's metaphysical swing and his anthropocentric concept of God by a one-sided 'psychologizing' of his philosophy, as if nosing in Scheler's private life was the only way to understand his thoughts. This tendency is for example very evident in Nota's interpretation of the powerful *Trieb* and the powerless *Geist* in Scheler's metaphysics as merely a metaphysical reflection of Scheler's inability to resist his own sexual urges. Such 'psychologizing' has no doubt contributed to the general devaluation of Scheler's philosophy after his death, as the arguments of philosophers whose world-views depend on their own libido generally do not seem very convincing.

Of course, it does not show much respect for Scheler as a philosopher to claim that he changed his metaphysics in such a fundamental way as he did due to merely personal (and above all sexual) motives. Anyone who takes Scheler seriously as a philosopher must assume that he must have had good philosophical reasons for abandoning traditional theism by formulating a panentheistic concept of God.

When Scheler first asked Hessen what he thought of his new concept of God, Hessen uttered all sorts of doubts and strongly criticized the concept itself; 'However, such consideration could not seriously alter Scheler's belief in his new

---

[8]   Max Scheler, 'Die Stellung des Menschen im Kosmos', in his *Späte Schriften* (Bern: Francke Verlag, 1976), pp. 7–71, at p. 70.

[9]   Johannes Hessen, *Max Scheler: Eine kritische Einführung in seine Philosophie* (Essen: Von Chamier, 1948), p. 126.

convictions, as they were too deeply rooted in the depth of his being.'[10] A similar idea was also put forth by Peter Spader in his very insightful *Scheler's Ethical Personalism*. Spader argues that Scheler's metaphysical change was in fact the logical consequence of his consistency as a moral philosopher. Change was the necessary result of his 'ethical concerns'.

Although Spader correctly argues that Scheler's ethical beliefs caused his metaphysical swing towards panentheism, I do not entirely agree with Spader when he claims that it was more precisely the problem of evil that caused this swing. Spader argues that Scheler's ethical system did not allow him to give an answer to the question of why so much evil resides in the world without entirely altering his metaphysical position:

> This [problem of evil] is, of course, a problem for any theism, but given Scheler's
> ethical beliefs in the moral role of the infinite person and the connection between
> the moral values of the person and the realization of high and low nonmoral
> values, it was particularly devastating for Scheler's ethics.[11]

Such a statement seems rather bold: Spader says in fact that Scheler's ethical system in *Der Formalismus* does not allow for an explanation of the problem of evil, without dramatically changing metaphysical positions, as if one could not acknowledge Scheler's value theory as a Roman Catholic, an assumption that has been rejected by many Catholic readers of *Der Formalismus*. At the time this book inspired several German Catholic theologians, such as Tillman (*Die Idee der Nachfolge Christi*) and Schmidt (*Organische Aszeze*), and it exerted a great influence on Karol Wojtyla.[12]

I agree with Spader that the foundation of Scheler's new metaphysics is to be sought in his ethics, but disagree that 'the problem of evil' can explain Scheler's metaphysical swing or that it was in any way a substantial cause of its development. Moreover, Scheler never dealt with the problem of evil that extensively and never suggested that it caused his metaphysics to change, as Spader admits.[13]

---

[10]   Ibid., p. 127.

[11]   Spader, *Scheler's Ethical Personalism*, p. 187.

[12]   Wojtyla argued, in his *Habilitationsschrift* as well as in several short essays, that Scheler's attempt to construct a philosophical *Grundlegung* for a Christian, personalist ethics was not entirely succesful, and pointed to some important dissimilarities between, on the one hand, Scheler's views on love, *model persons* (like Jesus Christ) and moral obligation and, on the other, Christian ethics and the Gospel. It must be noticed that Wojtyla's interpretation of Scheler is not always entirely correct, although this does not alter the fact that Scheler exerted a great influence on the philosophical development of the man who was to become Pope John Paul II.

[13]   Ibid., p. 191.

The Primacy of Ethics

If one wishes to detect a causal relationship between Scheler's ethical beliefs and his metaphysical shift, it makes sense to take into account the considerations that are central to his ethics. Yet, it is not easy to determine what those considerations exactly are. Scheler's oeuvre is a labyrinth of thoughts in which one can easily get lost, due to the fact that he wrote so much and did not always structure his thoughts thoroughly (although he promised to do so more than once).

However, at least three aspects of Scheler's ethics seem to hold a prominent place and are relevant here: the human person, the human (moral) act and human responsibility. It is fair to say that these three themes form the core of his ethical system, not as distinct moral or philosophical phenomena, but as three parts of a close-knit unity.

Der Formalismus offers a hierarchical theory of values. Moral values are realized *on the back of* non-moral values. There is, according to Scheler, an objective hierarchy of non-moral values, and moral values are realized whenever one chooses to realize a higher non-moral value (for example, intellectual development) instead of a lower one (for example, pleasure). In this theory, the importance of man, the human person is enormous: man has to create, so to speak, the Good. The human person is *the* locus of morality. The human person, defined by Scheler as an acting person, an act-accomplishing being (*aktvollziehendes Wesen*), occupies a central place. The human person is the place where moral values see the light of day. The Good occurs when the human person voluntarily chooses to perform these acts which he or she assumes are of a higher (non-moral) order then their (non-moral) alternatives.

Moral values always depend on the human person and are thus explicitly defined as *Personwerte*. Scheler's *tour de force* is that he so defines moral values without slipping back into any sort of moral subjectivism. In a study of Karol Wojtyla's ethics, Rocco Buttiglione very nicely expressed the role of the human person in Scheler's thought and its general significance in the history of philosophy:

> The fundamental orientation is toward an ontology of the interior order, at the center of which is the person. The manifestation of the person and of the particular character of personal existence, within which values reveal themselves, is Scheler's great discovery.[14]

Scheler formulates an 'immanent transcendental' ontology of values, in which transcendence is derived from an objective order of values (moral objectivism) and in which immanence results from the great stress on the human person (I would use the term 'moral subjectivism' if that were not so misleading) and the human person as an *acting* person. The latter gives this ethical system and

---

[14]   Rocco Buttiglione, *Karol Wojtyla: The Thought of the Man Who Became Pope John Paul II* (Grand Rapids, MI: Eerdmans Publishing Co., 1997), p. 92.

ontology of values an utmost dynamic character. It is, I would like to remark, no coincidence that philosophers like Nikolaj Berdjaev, Karol Wojtyla and Vladimir Jankélévitch, who were all acquainted with Scheler's writings, have formulated a dynamical ethical theory in which a similar emphasis on the human person and act can be found. All these philosophers formulate an ethical theory in which man is confronted with an enormous moral responsibility and autonomy.

Due to the emphasis Scheler puts on the human act in order for morality to exist, this morality has an unmistakable dynamic character. The essence of morality lies in its being performed, which is why it seems correct to describe Scheler's ethical system as a *Philosophie der Tat*; it is an active philosophy which does not neglect the importance of the will (intention), but which stresses the importance of 'the human act' in the genesis of moral values. The Good is not, until it is done.

It requires both *Gesinnung* and *Handlung*; the mere act of willing needs to be connected with a concrete willingness and ability to act. Scheler states that a child may be willing that the stars drop from the sky into his or her own hands, but this pure act of willing does not tell us anything about the active realization of moral values, which requires an actual willingness and ability to perform moral acts (*Tunwollen* and *Tunkönnen*). Essential to the moral development and elevation of man – to the ontological and axiological existence of moral values – is the acting person. 'The primary phenomenon, which characterizes all spiritual maturing, is a continuous reference of the will to the sphere of acting [*die Sphäre des Tunlichen*]'.[15] The moral and spiritual nature of man depends on the ability to evolve from a mere act of willing to a concrete act of doing good. This is where man can testify to his goodness and virtue, for Scheler defines virtue as the *tatbereite und tatfähige Gesinnung*, again stressing the moral meaning of the human person and his agency.[16]

The dynamical concept of morality, as Scheler himself indicated in the preface to the third edition of *Der Formalismus*, led him to rethink his metaphysics. One could indeed wonder to what extent his dynamical concept of morality was compatible with a more traditional concept of God as the primary source of moral values and even as the fundamental instigator of man's moral acts.[17] How does a static concept of an almighty God relate to a dynamical conception of morality in which the human person is the locus of moral values? How does this relate to man's moral responsibility and autonomy, and Scheler's aversion to any sort

---

[15]   Max Scheler, *Der Formalismus in der Ethik und die Materiale Wertethik: Neuer Versuch der Grundlegung eines ethischen Personalismus* (Bern: Francke Verlag, 1966), p. 141.

[16]   Ibid., p. 144.

[17]   Such is, for example, the view of Karol Wojtyla/John Paul II, who insisted that the initiative towards establishing a relationship between God and man, by example in prayer (see, for example, Vittorio Messori's *Crossing the Threshold of Hope*) but also in doing good, always comes from God. The Pope was certainly influenced in this regard by his analysis of the mysticism of St John of the Cross, about whom he wrote his doctoral thesis.

of moral slavery and suppression? Obviously, these questions bothered Scheler considerably, and in *Die Stellung des Menschen im Kosmos* he explicitly expressed his rejection of the idea of man as God's slave or subject. Here we seem to come to the specific point where he implicitly acknowledges how his ethics and new metaphysics meet:

> Man appears in proportion to the structure of society as *a slave of God,* to whom he kneels by means of guile and humble prostration, seeking to move Him by petition and threat or with magic means ... All similar ideas must be rejected in the light of our philosophical endeavours relating the relationship between Man and the primal Ground of everything. And we have to reject it therefore, because we do not accept the theistic presupposition of a spiritual, almighty personal God. (Emphasis in original)[18]

In order to fully affirm his ethical views on man's moral responsibility and autonomy, Scheler used a different kind of metaphysical framework from those offered by traditional theisms. He tried to formulate a metaphysical framework which affirmed his ethical views, and it is consequently no coincidence that indeed many of the earlier writings and ethical views can be found in the renewing and controversial metaphysics of Scheler's *Späte Schriften*. The anthropological quest for the definition and moral value of the human person is, as it had always been, the driving force of Scheler's thought, and the Schelerian leitmotifs of love, knowledge, self-realization and so on, so central in this quest, are still manifestly at the fore after his metaphysical swing.

Furthermore, the dynamical character of morality – so central in Scheler's ethics and in many theories formulated by those who were, to a greater or lesser extent, adherents of Scheler's thought – finds its metaphysical equivalence in the concept of *Gottwerdung*. Where the human person – on the basis of Scheler's *Der Formalismus* – used to be responsible 'merely' for the realization of the Good, he is now explicitly held responsible for the realization of God: 'It is thus through the human person that God becomes.'[19]

Ever greater stress is thus put on the enormous responsibility and autonomy of man, who is responsible not only for the Good but also for God's existence. Scheler's thought is always insistent and urges us towards the realization of the Good. His philosophical struggle is perhaps above all a struggle against nihilism, moral indifference, relativism and passivity, which can all be described as forms of moral slavery (for it is only in doing good that man achieves and realizes his freedom). Scheler's ethics is a struggle against these forms of slavery, and it is no surprise that he explicitly dealt with this slavery in *Der Formalismus* in a chapter entitled 'The Essence of the Moral Person', in which he puts emphasis on the significance of the person's moral autonomy and responsibility. Slavery

---

[18]   Scheler, 'Die Stellung des Menschen im Kosmos', p. 70.

[19]   Spader, *Scheler's Ethical Personalism*, p. 194.

is opposed to the core of Scheler's ethical theory like fire is to water, and lacks precisely those things Scheler calls the essence of the moral person: responsibility, autonomy, *Tunwollen* and *Tunkönnen*.[20]

Scheler's views on the human *acting* person, his dynamical conception of morality, the Schelerian question of why people are actually motivated to do the Good (a question which is implicitly present in all his main ideas and concepts) and ultimately his concept of *Gottwerdung* relate to this struggle to preserve man's moral autonomy and responsibility. His ethics is therefore also a struggle against nihilism and moral inertia. He morally rejects man's passivity, apathy and inertia, and this is a salient feature of his entire oeuvre: from the early writings to the *Späte Schriften*. It is, for example, characteristic of his theory of resentment and the concept of *Ohnmacht*, which he defines as the cause of value distortions (i.e. resentment) and which he considers to be typified by Fyodor Dostoevsky's *underground man*, who is a victim of his own inertia and whose inertia leads to his moral downfall. In his theory of resentment, Scheler links a lack of interest, participation and action to moral decline – not only the person's individual moral decline but even that of society as a *Gesammtperson* (collective person). 'Scheler warns of the link between political apathy and the rise of despotism.'[21]

Since the person's agency is indispensible in order for moral values to come into existence, inaction itself, which (though not exclusively) can be a consequence of passivity, apathy and inertia, is a severe moral problem. Scheler's theory of resentment, the value theory elaborated in *Der Formalismus* and eventually the concept of *Gottwerdung* all entail an emphasis on the moral significance of the human person as an *aktvollziehendes Wesen*. The concept of *Gottwerdung* as such is in line with and undergirds the entire essence of Scheler's ethics. Scheler's metaphysical swing did not entail an abandonment of the earlier ethical beliefs but, on the contrary, strongly affirms these beliefs. In a way, one could conclude that Scheler's oeuvre proves Levinas right: the first philosophy is always ethics.

Internal Consistency of the *Späte Schriften*

On Knowledge

Having said this, I would like to conclude this chapter by emphasizing that Scheler's *Späte Schriften* are not just a collection of distinct essays. It has been said that Scheler had 'degenerated' from being a real philosophical system builder (*Der Formalismus* was a voluminous work which did not leave many philosophical disciplines untouched) to a philosopher who could not structure his

---

[20] Scheler, *Der Formalismus in der Ethik und die Materiale Wertethik,* pp. 472–5.

[21] Zachery Davis, 'A Phenomenology of Political Apathy: Scheler on the Origins of Mass Violence', *Continental Philosophy Review* 42 (2009), 149–69, at p. 152.

ideas thoroughly and therefore only continued to write short essays in which the internal consistency was seriously questioned.

If one were to recognize the internal consistency between these *Späte Schriften*, one could probably come to a better evaluation of them. First of all, it is important to realize how Scheler's ethics and renewing metaphysics were closely connected to his epistemological views. According to him, man is the only living creature capable of opposing its own *Trieb*, which allows him to evolve from *Dasein* (the *existence* of things) to *Sosein* (the *essence* of these things). Put simply, man is capable of evolving from mere existence to the true essence of being, owing to the fact that man is the place where *Geist* and *Trieb* meet. The main function of the human Spirit is *Ideierung* and this specific act leads to knowledge. Scheler gives the example of pain. When man experiences pain, he can direct his *Geist* towards something that surpasses mere reality (the pain itself). He can address certain philosophical and metaphysical questions: what is the source of this experience, what is pain, what is the source of the world *überhaupt*, etc.? Why is this world like it is (*Sosein*)? After having experienced reality, man – with his *Geist* – can evolve towards a deeper insight and a higher, ontological form of knowledge.[22]

This theory of knowledge is of the utmost importance in the totality of Scheler's image of God and man. Furthermore, Nota has correctly noticed that much of this theory of knowledge could already be found in the early writings, once more an indication that although Scheler rejected any theism in the end, he did not change that much as a philosopher.

The subject that knows has a certain desire to transcend reality, a desire that Scheler more than once described as (an act of) love. It is the love to direct one's *Geist* to the essence of being (*Sosein*); the love to resist or surpass *Trieb* and mere existence. This 'love' makes knowledge possible, since it generates an orientation towards the substantial. According to Scheler, there are three types of knowledge, the first of which is called *Herrschaftswissen* (mastery knowledge). This is the kind of knowledge that allows people to control or structure reality: nature, society, history, etc. It is the knowledge of positive sciences, aimed at mastering reality by the use of technology and applied sciences. It is a kind of knowledge which solely focuses on *Dasein*.

A more philosophical kind of knowledge is *Bildungswissen* (cultural knowledge). This type of knowledge allows us to detach ourselves from reality and question the reasons and origins of this reality. It allows us to see through the surface of things to their essences (*Wesensschau*). Whereas *Herrschaftswissen* is aimed at changing reality, *Bildungswissen* causes the human *Geist* to change and develop. This knowledge leads to *Bildung, Humanisierung, Menschwerdung*, i.e. the moral, cultural and intellectual formation of man as a human person.

The highest form of knowledge is not directed to the development of the human person itself but to the development of God. *Erlösungswissen* (redemption

---

[22]   J. Nota, *Max Scheler: Een worstelen om het wezen van den mens* (Utrecht/Brussels: Het Spectrum, 1947), pp. 163–9.

knowledge) is metaphysical and religious knowledge, and obviously relates to Scheler's concept of *Gottwerdung*. When man reaches this kind of knowledge, he can truly call himself *Mitbildner* or *Mitstifter* of God and the world process. Such a man is described by Scheler as a *Total Man* (*Allmensch*) and fulfils the most beautiful and important of all tasks: the realization of God and the Good through a balanced reconciliation of Spirit and Force. Thoughts and acts are unified in harmony and this harmony leads to an eternal peace in God.

I would like to add two things here so that Scheler's views will not be mistaken. First, this eternal peace in God must not be understood as a static end point of history, but rather as a goal without finality (which is also characteristic for the philosophy of Buber, Jankélévitch, Levinas and even for Kant's *Kingdom of Ends*). It is something we ought to strive for and keep striving for. We can never come to a point where we can rest on our laurels, contemplating our lives and history in a self-congratulatory way. Such an interpretation of this eternal peace in God would be completely contradictory to the essence of Scheler's ethics, which is, as previously stated, characterized by an eternal openness and activity. In his brilliant and under-estimated essay *Ordo amoris* (which can be seen as an addendum to *Der Formalismus*), Scheler states that the moral essence is only revealed in the moments we perform moral acts. Human love – as the essence of these acts – always has an infinite and incomplete character. It is a *wesensunendliche Prozess* due to the fact that every realization is only temporal. When we linger over what *is* and fail to see what *should be*, what is still to come and to be done, love no longer exists (once more, one could keep in mind that these thoughts can also be found in the works of Jankélévitch). Love, morality, God and eternal peace all have an active, dynamic character and need to be fulfilled not once, but over and over again.

Secondly, I would like to stress that Scheler's epistemology, ethics and metanthropology do not lead to any kind of 'renewed asceticism'. Due to the fact that Scheler explicitly stated that one needs to surpass and transcend reality in order to realize the highest form of knowledge, many have interpreted Scheler's epistemology as a plea for ascetism and for a denial of life. Ron Perrin, for example, wrote that Scheler's 'conception of the total man concludes in a new asceticism',[23] adding that Scheler had evolved from an initial vitalism into an extreme sort of intellectualism and spiritualism in which reality is thought away. Scheler's references to Buddhism have also been understood more than once as indications of this 'new asceticism'. I do wish to stress that such interpretations seem to neglect the dynamic character of Scheler's ethics and I do not see how Scheler's persistent emphasis on the human person as an acting person, who bears the responsibility to do good, can be compatible with such an asceticism.

To resume, the close relationship between knowledge and morality consists in the fact that Scheler elaborated a hierarchy of knowledge which corresponds with

---

[23] Ron Perrin, *Max Scheler's Concept of the Person: An Ethics of Humanism* (Basingstoke: Macmillan, 1991), pp. 123–4.

a hierarchy of values: the highest form of knowledge, metaphysical knowledge, is the knowledge that stimulates man towards the fulfilment of the highest and most beautiful of all moral values: *Gottwerdung*, the bringing into being of God.

On Politics

Although Scheler perhaps did not write any voluminous studies during the last years of his life, he was still a system builder whose ethical views related to his metaphysics and epistemological views. His epistemological views related to his concept of *Gottwerdung*, but so did his meta-anthropology and ethics. The same can be said of his political views. Scheler expressed these political views in the essay *Der Mensch im Weltalter des Ausgleichs* (*Man in an Era of Adjustment*). Perrin has correctly stressed that this work in fact returns to the problem of Spirit and Force and how they can be unified, by man, in politics and society.

There are indeed many characteristics of Scheler's ethics and metaphysics which can also be found in his political views. First, these views focus entirely on the harmonization of opposing principles and attributes. It is a politics of reconciliation, harmony and mutual understanding, and in this mirrors his metaphysics, in which the harmonization of *Geist* and *Trieb* occupies a central place. Secondly, the problem of personal and co-responsibility has once again directly and implicitly come to the fore in his political views, indicating that responsibility was not merely a pillar of Scheler's ethical theory but is also crucial in his views on politics and society. Thirdly, and more importantly, Scheler resumed the idea of a *Total Man*, who has the will, the love, the knowledge and the motivation to do the Good and realize God in *Der Mensch im Weltalter des Ausgleichs*. His ethical and metaphysical conceptions are thus explicitly present in his political views and ultimately determine his political goals and ideals.

Scheler's ideal of *Ausgleich* has unmistakable spiritual, philosophical as well as social and political components, which do depend on one another. Not only do Scheler's philosophical views determine his political views; these political goals in turn are fundamental in his striving towards a cosmopolitan metaphysics. As such, his political ideal of an *Ausgleich* is absorbed into a wider ethical goal: 'That this Adjustment may lead to a rise of personal value. This is above all the purpose of all politics.'[24]

Conclusion

I have thus far tried to argue on the one hand how Scheler's metaphysical swing is in fact the logical outcome of his earlier ethical views and on the other hand that his new metaphysical position was in harmony with the epistemological and political views he held in the last years of his life. I hope that this will not only lead

[24]   Scheler, 'Die Stellung des Menschen im Kosmos', p. 152.

to a better comprehension of his entire oeuvre but also to a re-evaluation of his last writings. Scheler's oeuvre is a labyrinth of thoughts, in which one can easily get lost. An internal harmony between these thoughts and writings is therefore not always easy to find and has given rise to the popular interpretation of Scheler as an inconsistent thinker who changed ideas too readily to be associated with any definite group of ideas. This popular critique seems incorrect and certainly unsatisfying when trying to explain the development of his thought.

Scheler was not an inconsistent philosopher. At most, he was a precipitate philosopher, who could have used more time to structure his ideas more clearly. In his thought there is a remarkable ethical consistency: love, moral responsibility, the dynamics of morality (by which I mean the realization of moral potentiality in an Aristotelian sense), the combination of sociological and phenomenological methods, anthropology and the human person all dominate his thought, from the beginning to the end. The fact that he abandoned Catholicism and changed his metaphysical views is no sign of any inconsistency but is rather the proof of his consistency as a moral philosopher who wished to define the human person as the locus of an ever moving and developing morality through the human act (man as an *Aktvolziehendes Wesen*). This dynamic conception of value required, in the end, a dynamic concept of God (*Gottwerdung*) and that is the path that Scheler was bound, in consistency, to take.

Whether one agrees with Scheler's metaphysics or not, the persistent value of his thought is his critique of any form of moral slavery. He was a convinced advocate of human dignity, autonomy and responsibility. Although his thought has received but little attention and seems to interest only a few people, his words have not lost any significance over the years and seem of great relevance in an era in which this dignity, autonomy and responsibility are curtailed by moral inertia, apathy and passivity. Scheler's concept of God and his concept of man both invite us to acknowledge that we cannot leave undone what has to be done.

Afterword

The Continuing Debate on Morality and God

John Cottingham

I am most grateful to Harriet Harris for her kind invitation to append a brief postscript to this collection. As President of the British Society for the Philosophy of Religion during the period of its 2009 Conference, which was devoted to the theme 'God and Morality', I was delighted when it was decided to take steps to publish a selection of the papers presented on that occasion and am even more delighted that the project has now been brought to fruition. We hope that the present volume will be the first of many to follow in the wake of the Society's biennial conferences. I know that all the contributors represented here would wish to join with me in thanking the Editor for the energy and efficiency with which she has steered this collection through to publication.

Since Dr Harris's own editorial introduction (pp. 1–28, above) provides an excellent conspectus of the ground covered by the various papers included in this book, and since I have already had the opportunity to set out some of my own views (in the paper that appears as Chapter 2), I shall confine myself here to a few brief observations about the state of our subject and the direction of future debate.

As is implied by Harris in her opening remarks, the place of philosophy of religion in our contemporary philosophical culture is a curious one. Developments over the last few decades have seen many philosophers of religion direct their attention to specifically Christian topics such as the Trinity, the Incarnation and the Resurrection. This move towards areas traditionally within the province of 'revealed' rather than 'natural' theology has, in the eyes of some critics, undermined the neutrality and critical detachment that ought to be the hallmarks of proper philosophical inquiry, and has risked turning the subject into a form of Christian apologetics. Put this way, the worry seems to be overdone: there is no clear reason why someone who is involved in a particular faith tradition should not be able to subject the concepts and doctrines of that tradition to proper philosophical scrutiny and critical analysis. It is true that the involvement and commitment that faith requires are not easily reconcilable with the detachment and impartiality that many see as the hallmarks of proper philosophizing; however, even the most hard-nosed analytical philosopher will be hard put to it to deny authentic philosophical value to some of the arguments in Anselm, say, or Augustine, despite the fact that both writers are committed Christians operating under the rubric of 'faith seeking understanding'. Yet, in spite of this, there remains something troubling about the recent rise of 'partisanship', as it might be called, in the philosophy of religion.

Extrapolating present trends forward, one might foresee a future 'ghettoization' of the philosophy of religion, so that it became a subject practised only by those already committed to Christian theism; should this happen, it is not hard to see the dangers it might pose for the health and vigour of the subject, or for its role within the wider philosophical community.

However, when we come to that part of the philosophy of religion which deals with the nature of morality, there seems much less danger of the subject ever retreating into the cosy domain of theological discussion among believers. In the practical realm of prescriptive or normative ethics, even were the subject to confine itself to what have been thought of as specifically 'Christian' virtues or values (such as humility, self-sacrifice or forgiveness), there would always be further philosophical questions to be raised about whether a Christian (or more generally a theistic) framework is actually needed to explain or underpin these values or whether they can be accommodated within a purely secular world-view. And as for the more theoretical realm of meta-ethics, it seems hard to imagine any specifically Christian or theistic account of the nature of goodness or of obligation that would not immediately invite comparison with other accounts on offer from naturalist or other non-theistic perspectives. So, sooner or later, any serious reflection about morality occurring in the philosophy of religion seems likely to bring the subject into critical contact with philosophical work going on elsewhere.

Cross-fertilization is generally thought to be a good thing in the world of ideas, and most theistically oriented moral philosophers would probably accept that bringing their views into juxtaposition with secular theories of morality can be a fruitful undertaking. However, the converse does not always seem to be the case, at least judging by the extent to which theistic accounts of goodness and obligation tend to be marginalized or ignored by many contemporary secular moral philosophers. This seems to be a regrettable situation, which it is up to philosophers of religion to try to change by engaging with the secular accounts and examining how they measure up, in terms of explanatory power and intuitive plausibility, when measured against theistic-based accounts.

There are I think at least two areas in particular where current work in moral philosophy might benefit from the stimulus afforded by juxtaposing secular views of goodness and morality with Christian-theistic accounts. The first, which surfaces in several of the chapters included in the present volume and which is highlighted by Harris in her introduction, relates to the recent surge of interest in evolutionary approaches to explaining human morality. To speak of 'recent' interest may seem odd, given that Darwinian ideas have been with us for a long time, but it is only comparatively recently that large numbers of philosophers seem to have been gripped by the vision of an 'empirical ecological' (to use Owen Flanagan's phrase) grounding for morality – one that will base the recipe for human flourishing and right conduct on a scientific study of our evolutionary history and of the traits (including social and altruistic propensities) that have conferred fitness on our species in the struggle for survival.[1] Such accounts do not merely aim to explain the origins of our moral sensibilities but purport to offer a grounding or justification for them. Yet, when set against theistic accounts of goodness and morality, such evolutionary accounts seem to encounter a *prima facie* problem about 'radical contingency', as Bernard Williams insightfully termed it.[2] Ethics, at least as conceived in the standard theistic framework developed over many centuries out of Judaeo-Christian and Platonic elements, takes us beyond the contingent flux of our biological and social development to standards that are necessary and unchanging. By contrast, any evolutionarily based ethics must presumably acknowledge that had our evolutionary history as a species been somewhat different our moral principles would have been different. And for those who wish to maintain any tolerably strong form of ethical realism and to say that there are right answers that generate the correct moral standards and principles to adopt, this fluidity and contingency looks deeply troubling.

Interpreted this way, one key issue in the clash between theistic and purely secular evolutionary accounts of morality may come down to whether one is willing to embrace radical contingency in the domain of the ethical. To be sure, this kind of collision between evolutionary and theistic accounts might perhaps be avoided, or its effects mitigated, if it should turn out that there is a parallel between how things work out in the moral domain and how they work out in the domain of natural science; that is, if evolution operates so as to favour *convergence* on the correct set of moral values, just as presumably we think, in the scientific case, that it operates so as to favour convergence on the right set of answers about physical reality. For the religious believer who accepts some version of the theory of evolution as the mechanism whereby God's creative activity is manifested, something like this convergence must presumably be what is to be expected (no doubt with some provisos about human sin and weakness, and the need for grace to help us orient ourselves towards the good). But from a secularist perspective, as Bernard Williams has persuasively argued, there seems in the ethical case to

---

[1]   Owen Flanagan, *The Really Hard Problem. Meaning in a Material World* (Cambridge MA: MIT Press, 2009), p. 61. Flanagan proposes an empirically based science of 'eudaimonics' that will use 'inductive, abductive, statistical, and probabilistic' reasoning to establish which are the 'best norms, values and practices' for human flourishing' (p. 121).

[2]   '[A] truthful historical account is likely to reveal a radical contingency in our current ethical conceptions. Not only might they have been different from what they are, but also the historical changes that brought them about are not obviously related to them in a way that vindicates them against possible rivals.' Bernard Williams, *Truth and Truthfulness* (Princeton, NJ: Princeton University Press, 2002), p. 20. See further J. Cottingham, 'The Good Life and the "Radical Contingency of the Ethical', in D. Callcut (ed.), *Reading Bernard Williams* (London: Routledge, 2008), Chapter 2, pp. 25–43.

be 'no coherent hope' of such convergence on a 'correct' set of moral values.[3] Whatever the solution to these complex problems, it seems clear that by juxtaposing the currently burgeoning secular evolutionary ethics with its theistic counterpart, we can uncover important underlying divergences between the two perspectives, with the beneficial result that certain key problems about the status and nature of morality are thereby thrown into stark relief.

The second (and by no means unconnected) area which brings theistic accounts into striking and potentially fruitful juxtaposition with secular accounts of morality concerns the issue of 'normativity', as it has come to be called: the authoritative power that moral values and obligations seem to exert upon us, whether we like it or not. The very idea of such objective normative values might, of course, be confused or erroneous, as a fair number of moral philosophers have held, taking their cue from the kind of 'error theory' of moral judgment espoused by John Mackie and others. But for those who are not prepared to dismiss as erroneous our powerful intuitive belief in an objective domain of value that exerts normative power over us, the question arises as to what, in the natural world or outside it, could explain or give rise to it.

There are many attempts to answer this question in the literature and this is not the place to canvass them. Religious accounts of normativity, to be sure, present difficulties of their own, many of them associated with the so-called 'Euthyphro problem', discussed in different ways in several of the chapters in the present collection. But, on the other side, it seems clear from the debates in moral philosophy over the last few decades that naturalistic approaches have serious difficulties when it comes to accounting for this peculiar feature of the human moral predicament – the fact that we are not simply creatures who have certain biological and social dispositions and impulses, but that we feel required, or called upon, to measure our lives against standards that do not appear to be of our making. Whatever the outcome of these debates turns out to be, the juxtaposition of theistic and non-theistic views once again seems a fruitful way of getting to the heart of the issues that are at stake.

It is never easy to predict the future direction of philosophical discussion, but it appears likely that the problem of normativity is likely to occupy centre stage in moral philosophy for some time to come. Some of the most stimulating recent work in this area has come from the writings of Christine Korsgaard, whose approach is rooted within the Kantian tradition and therefore is often seen as being at loggerheads with empirically based accounts of ethics such as that of Hume. But it is interesting to see that in her most recent work, Korsgaard offers (though she does not put it this way) a kind of synthesis of the Kantian and Humean

---

[3]   Bernard Williams, *Ethics and the Limits of Philosophy* (London: Collins/Fontana, 1985), Chapter 8, p. 136. Issues about contingency, realism and convergence are interestingly discussed by Herman Philipse in Chapter 8 of the present collection.

perspectives: values are 'human creations',[4] which are formed out of the raw material of our natural desires – thus far agreeing with Hume – but which are transformed and endowed with normative status in the complex process by which we 'constitute ourselves' as human agents. I mention this view not to embark on a discussion of the complex theory of normativity that Korsgaard develops, but simply to point to another approach that offers the opportunity for fruitful juxtaposition with theistic meta-ethics (which would adamantly reject any theory that suggests that we can somehow generate value and normativity through our own human resources alone). Korsgaard's ideas take us outside the direct scope of the present collection, but one central question they raise, which should offer rich food for thought for philosophers of religion, is whether the idea of self-constitution in the moral sphere succeeds in bypassing the need for God as a source of value. Does it really make sense to suppose that value can come into existence as the result of those actions whereby we constitute ourselves as agents, or can the true normativity of value only be found through an understanding of our *creatureliness* – the relation of dependency that we have to our creator?

In wrestling with our status, as a certain kind of evolved animal, yet one endowed with a degree of rationality plus a powerful sense of the normative demands of morality, we get to the heart of what makes moral philosophy worth doing. If the chapters included here are any guide, the struggle to resolve these issues provides rich opportunities for fruitful philosophical engagement, as well as demonstrating how the philosophy of religion continues to occupy a legitimate place at the heart of philosophical inquiry.

---

[4] Christine Korsgaard, *Self-Constitution* (Oxford: Oxford University Press, 2009), p. 209.

References

Adams, Douglas, *The Hitchhiker's Guide to the Galaxy* (London: Pan, 1979).

Adams, Nicholas, *Habermas and Theology* (Cambridge: Cambridge University Press, 2006).

Adams, Robert M., *Finite and Infinite Goods* (New York: Oxford University Press, 1999).

Adie, Kate, *The Kindness of Strangers: The Autobiography* (London: Headline, 2002).

Alston, William, 'Some Suggestions for Divine Command Theorists', in Norman Beaty (ed.), *Christian Theism and the Problems of Philosophy* (Notre Dame, IN: University of Notre Dame Press, 1990), pp. 303–26.

Alter, Torin, 'On Two Alleged Conflicts Between Divine Attributes', *Faith and Philosophy* 19 (2002), 47–57.

Anderson, Steven W., Antoine Bechara, Antonio R. Damasio et al., 'Impairment of Social and Moral Behavior Related to Early Damage in Human Prefrontal Cortex', *Nature Neuroscience* 2 (1999), 1032–7.

Angle, Stephen C., *Sagehood: The Contemporary Significance of Neo-Confucian Philosophy* (Oxford: Oxford University Press, 2009).

Anscombe, G.E.M., 'Causality and Determination', in G.E.M. Anscombe, *Metaphysics and the Philosophy of Mind* (Oxford: Blackwell, 1981), pp. 133–47.

Anscombe, G.E.M., 'Modern Moral Philosophy', reprinted in Roger Crisp and Michael Slote (eds), *Virtue Ethics* (Oxford: Oxford University Press [1958] 1997), pp. 26–44.

Arnhart, Larry, *Darwinian Natural Right: The Biological Ethics of Human Nature* (Albany, NY: SUNY Press, 1998).

Attfield, Robin, *Creation, Evolution and Meaning* (Aldershot and Burlington, VT: Ashgate, 2006).

Attfield, Robin, 'Darwin's Doubt, Non-deterministic Darwinism and the Cognitive Science of Religion', *Philosophy* 85 (2010), 465–83.

Audi, Robert, 'Divine Command Morality and the Autonomy of Ethics', *Faith and Philosophy* 24(2) (2007), 121–43.

Audi, Robert and William J. Wainwright, *Rationality, Religious Belief, and Moral Commitment: New Essays in the Philosophy of Religion* (Ithaca, NY: Cornell University Press, 1986).

Augustine, *The City of God*, trans. D. Wiesen (Cambridge, MA: Harvard University Press, 1968).

Barr, James, *Fundamentalism* (London: SCM, 1977).

Barr, James, *Biblical Theology: Old Testament Perspective* (Philadelphia: Fortress Press, 1999).

Barton, Carlin, *The Sorrows of the Ancient Romans: The Gladiator and the Monster* (Princeton, NJ: Princeton University Press, 1993).

Barton, John, *Understanding Old Testament Ethics* (Westminster: John Knox Press, 2003).

Bishop, John, 'Evil and the Concept of God', *Philosophical Papers* 22 (1993), 1–15.

Bodnár, Ján, Milan Burica, Dalimír Hajko, Richard Marsina, Teodor Münz, Marianna Oravcová, Terézia Palovičová, Július Sopko, Viktor Timura and Elena Várossová, *Dejiny filozofického myslenia na Slovensku, vol. 1* (Bratislava: Veda, 1987).

Bolhuis, Johan J. and D.D.L. Wynne, 'Can Evolution Explain How Minds Work?', *Nature* 458 (2009), 832–3.

Brelsford, Theodore, 'Lessons for Religious Education from Cognitive Science of Religion', *Religious Education* 100(2) (2005), 174–91.

Brickhouse, Thomas and Nicholas Smith, *Socrates on Trial* (Princeton, NJ: Princeton University Press, 1989).

Brown, Claire and Jerry L. Walls, 'Annihilationism: A Philosophical Dead End?', in Joel Buenting (ed.), *The Problem of Hell: A Philosophical Anthology* (Aldershot and Burlington, VT: Ashgate, 2010), pp. 45–64.

Brunner, Emil, *Justice and the Social Order*, trans. Mary Hottinger (New York and London: Harper and Brothers, 1945).

Brunschvicg, L. (ed.), *Blaise Pascal: Pensées et Opuscules* (Paris: Classiques Hachette, 1961).

Buttiglione, R. *La pensée de Karol Wojtyla* (Communio, Fayard, 1982).

Čapek, Jan Blahoslav, *Augustin Doležal a jeho Tragoedia* (Prague: Učená Společnost Šafaříkova v Bratislavě, 1931).

Carroll, Robert, *Wolf in the Sheepfold: The Bible as Problem for Christianity* (London: SPCK, 1991).

Carter, Alan, 'Evolution and the Problem of Altruism', *Philosophical Studies* 123 (2005), 213–30.

Chappell, Timothy, *Reading Plato's Theaetetus* (Indianapolis, IN: Hackett, 2005).

Chappell, Timothy, 'Moral perception', *Philosophy* 83 (2008), 421-438.

Cheetham, David and Rolfe King (eds), *Contemporary Practice and Method in the Philosophy of Religion: New Essays* (London: Continuum, 2008).

Clark, Kelly J., 'God is Great, God is Good: Medieval Conceptions of Divine Goodness and the Problem of Hell', *Religious Studies* 37(1) (2001), 15–31.

Clark, Stephen R.L., 'The Evolution of Language: Truth and Lies', *Philosophy* 75 (2000), 401–21.

Collingwood, Robin George, *The Idea of History* (Oxford: Clarendon, 1946).

Collins, Francis S., The Language of God. A Scientist Presents Evidence for Belief (New York: Free Press, 2006).

Copan, Paul, 'Morality and Meaning Without God: Another Failed Attempt', *Philosophia Christi* Series 2(6) (2003), 295–304.

Copp, David, 'Darwinian Skepticism about Moral Realism', *Philosophical Issues* 18 (2008), 186–206.

Cottingham, John, *Why Believe?* (London: Continuum, 2009).

Crenshaw, James, *The Divine Helmsman: Studies on God's Control of Human Events* (New York: KTAV Publishing House Inc., 1980).

Crisp, Oliver D. and Michael C. Rea (eds), *Analytical Theology: New Essays in the Philosophy of Theology* (Oxford: Oxford University Press, 2009).

Crisp, Oliver, 'On Analytical Theology', in Oliver D. Crisp and Michael C. Rea (eds), *Analytical Theology: New Essays in the Philosophy of Theology* (Oxford: Oxford University Press, 2009), pp. 33–53.

Cupitt, Don, *After God: The Future of Religion* (London: SCM, 1997).

Damasio, Antonio R., *Descartes' Error: Emotion, Reason, and the Human Brain* (New York: Grosset/Putnam, 1994).

Dante, Alighieri, *The Divine Comedy: Hell,* trans. Dorothy L. Sayers (Harmondsworth: Penguin Classics, 1949).

Darwall, Stephen, *The Second-Person Standpoint: Morality, Respect and Accountability* (Cambridge, MA: Harvard University Press, 2006).

Darwin, Charles, *The Origin of Species* (London: John Murray, 1872).

Darwin, Charles, *The Descent of Man and Selection in Relation to Sex* (1871). With an introduction by James Moore and Adrian Desmond (London: Penguin, 2004).

Davidson, Robert, *The Courage to Doubt* (London: SCM, 1997).

Davies, Andrew, *Double Standards in Isaiah* (Leiden: Brill, 2004).

Davies, Brian, *Introduction to the Philosophy of Religion* (Oxford: Oxford University Press, 2004, first published 1982).

Davis, Stephen T., Daniel Kendall and Gerald O'Collins (eds), *The Resurrection: An Interdisciplinary Symposium on the Resurrection of Jesus* (Oxford: Oxford University Press, 1997).

Davis, Stephen T., Daniel Kendall and Gerald O'Collins (eds), *The Trinity: An Interdisciplinary Symposium on the Trinity* (Oxford: Oxford University Press, 2003).

Davis, Stephen T., Daniel Kendall and Gerald O'Collins (eds), *The Incarnation: An Interdisciplinary Symposium on the Incarnation* (Oxford: Oxford University Press, 2004).

Davis, Stephen T., Daniel Kendall and Gerald O'Collins (eds), *The Redemption: An Interdisciplinary Symposium on Christ as Redeemer* (Oxford: Oxford University Press, 2006)

Dawkins, Richard, *The Selfish Gene,* 2nd edn (Oxford: Oxford University Press, 1989).

De Brés, Guy, 'The Belgic Confession', in P. Schaff (trans. and ed.), *The Creeds of Christendom*, vol. 3 (New York: Harper & Brothers Publishers, 1877).

De Waal, Frans, *Peacemaking Among Primates* (Cambridge, MA: Harvard University Press, 1989).

De Waal, Frans, *Good Natured: The Origins of Right and Wrong in Humans and Other Animals* (Cambridge, MA and London: Harvard University Press, 1996).

De Waal, Frans et al., *Primates and Philosophers. How Morality Evolved* (Princeton, NJ: Princeton University Press, 2006).

Dennett, Daniel, *Darwin's Dangerous Idea: Evolution and the Meanings of Life* (London: Penguin, 1995).

Destrée, Pierre and Nicholas D. Smith (eds), *Socrates' Divine Sign: Religion, Practice, and Value in Socratic Philosophy*. Special issue of *APEIRON: A Journal for Ancient Philosophy and Science* 38(2) (June 2005) (Kelowna, BC: Academic Printing and Publishing, 2005).

Doležal, Augustín, *Pamětná celém světu Tragoedia, anebožto Veršovné vypsánj žalostného Prvnjch Rodičů Pádu* (Uherská Skalica: Jozef Antonin Škarnycl, 1791).

Dummett, Michael, 'Truth' (1959), in Michael Dummett, *Truth and Other Enigmas* (Cambridge, MA: Harvard University Press, 1978).

Eichrodt, Walter, *Theology of the Old Testament,* vol. 2 (Philadelphia: Westminster Press, 1967).

Ekland-Olson, Sheldon, 'Crowding, Social Control, and Prison Violence: Evidence from the Post-Ruiz Years in Texas', *Law & Society Review* 20(3) (1986), 389–422.

Everitt, Nicholas, *The Non-Existence of God* (London: Routledge, 2004).

Farber, Paul Lawrence, *The Temptations of Evolutionary Ethics* (Berkeley, CA: University of California Press, 1994).

Feinberg, Joel, 'Noncomparative Justice', *Philosophical Review* 83(3) (July 1974), 297–338.

Flack, J.C. and F.B.M. de Waal, 'Any Animal Whatever: Darwinian Building Blocks of Morality in Monkeys and Apes', *Journal of Consciousness Studies* 7 (2000), 1–29.

Fordinálová, Eva, *Stretnutie so starším pánom alebo Tragédia Augustína Doležala* (Martin: Osveta, 1993).

Frame, John, 'Euthyphro, Hume, and the Biblical God', http://www.frame-poythress.org/frame_articles/1993Euthyphro.htm, accessed 1 August 2011.

Frege, G., *The Basic Laws of Arithmetic* [*Die Grundgesetze der Arithmetik*, vol. I, 1893], trans. M. Furth (Berkeley, CA: University of California Press, 1964).

Fretheim, Terrence, *The Suffering of God: An Old Testament Perspective* (Philadelphia, PA: Fortress Press, 1984).

Geach, Peter, 'Aquinas', in G.E.M. Anscombe and P.T. Geach, *Three Philosophers* (Oxford: Blackwell, 1961), pp. 61–125.

Geach, Peter, *Providence and Evil* (Cambridge: Cambridge University Press, 1977).

Gericke, Jaco, 'Beyond Reconciliation – Monistic Yahwism and the Problem of Evil in Philosophy of Religion', *Verbum et Ecclesiae* 26(1) (2005), 64–92.

Gibbard, Alan, *Wise Choices, Apt Feelings* (Cambridge MA: Harvard University Press, 1990).

Girard, René, *Violence and the Sacred*, trans. Patrick Gregory (Baltimore, MD: Johns Hopkins University Press, 1977).

Girard, René, *The Scapegoat* (Baltimore, MD: Johns Hopkins University Press, 1989).

Girard, René, *Things Hidden Since the Foundation of the World: Research Undertaken in Collaboration with Jean-Michel Oughourlian and G. Lefort* (Stanford, CA: Stanford University Press, 1987).

Gluchman, Vasil, *Slovak Lutheran Social Ethics* (Lewiston, NY: Edwin Mellen Press, 1997).

Gluchman, Vasil (ed.), *Morality of the Past from the Present Perspective: Picture of Morality in Slovakia in the First Half of the Twentieth Century* (Newcastle: Cambridge Scholars Publishing, 2007).

Gluchman, Vasil, *Etika na Slovensku – minulosť a prítomnosť* (Bratislava: H&H, 2008).

Gould, Stephen Jay and Richard Lewontin, 'The Spandrels of San Marco and the Panglossian Paradigm: A Critique of the Adaptationist Programme', in Elliott Sober (ed.), *Conceptual Issues in Evolutionary Biology*, 2nd edn (Cambridge, MA: MIT Press, 1998), pp. 73–90.

Gould, Stephen Jay and Elizabeth S. Vrba, 'Exaptation: A Missing Term in the Science of Form', in David L. Hull and Michael Ruse (eds), *The Philosophy of Biology* (Oxford: Oxford University Press, 1998), pp. 52–71.

Greene, Joshua D., R. Brian Sommerville, Leigh E. Nystrom et al., 'An fMRI Investigation of Emotional Engagement in Moral Judgment', *Science* 293 (2001), 2105–8.

Greene, Joshua D. and Jonathan Haidt, 'How (and Where) Does Moral Judgment Work?', *Trends in Cognitive Sciences* 6 (2002), 517–23.

Griffith-Dickson, Gwen, *The Philosophy of Religion* (London: SCM, 2005).

Griffith-Dickson, Gwen, *Human and Divine: An Introduction to the Philosophy of Religious Experience* (London: Duckworth, 2000).

Haidt, Jonathan, 'The Emotional Dog and its Rational Tail: A Social Intuitionist Approach to Moral Judgment', *Psychological Review* 108 (2001), 814–34.

Hamilton, W.D., 'The Genetical Evolution of Social Behaviour I and II', *Journal of Theoretical Biology* 7 (1964), 17–52.

Hare, John E., *God and Morality: A Philosophical History*, (Chichester and Oxford: Wiley-Blackwell, 2009).

Hare, John E., 'Goodness', in Charles Taliaferro and Chad Meister (eds), *The Cambridge Companion to Christian Philosophical Theology,* (Cambridge: Cambridge University Press, 2010), pp. 66–80.

Harris, Harriet A. 'Ambivalence over Virtue', in Jane Garnett et al. (eds), *Redefining Christian Britain: Post-1945 Perspectives* (London: SCM, 2006), pp. 210–21.

Harris, Harriet A., *Fundamentalism and Evangelicals* (Oxford: Clarendon, 2008).

Harris, Harriet A. and Christopher J. Insole (eds), *Faith and Philosophical Analysis: The Impact of Analytical Philosophy on the Philosophy of Religion* (Aldershot and Burlington, VT: Ashgate, 2005).

Harrison, Victoria S., 'The Pragmatics of Defining Religion in a Multi-cultural World', *International Journal for Philosophy of Religion* 59(3) (2006), 133–52.

Harrison, Victoria S., *Religion and Modern Thought* (London: SCM, 2007).

Harrison, Victoria S., 'Philosophy of Religion, Fictionalism, and Religious Diversity', *International Journal for Philosophy of Religion* 68 (2011), 43–58.

Harrison, Victoria S., 'Embodied Values and Muslim-Christian Dialogue: "Exemplar Reasoning" as a Model for Inter-religious Conversations', *Studies in Interreligious Dialogue* 21(1) (2011), 20–35.

Hedley, Douglas, *Living Forms of the Imagination* (London: T&T Clark, 2008).

Heekeren, H.R., I. Wartenburger, H. Schmidt et al., 'An fMRI Study of Simple Ethical Decision-Making', *Neuroreport* 14 (2003), 1215–19.

Helm, Paul, *Divine Commands and Morality* (Oxford: Oxford University Press, 1981).

Herrmann, Eberhard, *Scientific Theory and Religious Belief: An Essay on the Rationality of Views of Life* (Kampen: Kok Pharos, 1995).

Hessen, J., *Max Scheler: Eine Kritische Einführung in Seine Philosophie* (Essen: Verlag Dr. Hans V. Chamier, 1948).

Hick, John, *Evil and the God of Love* (Houndmills: Macmillan, 1966).

Hilbert, D., *Grundlagen der Geometrie* (Leipzig: Teubner, 1899)

Hilbert, D., *Foundations of Geometry*, trans. E. Townsend (La Salle, IL: Open Court, 1959).

Holdcroft, David and Harry Lewis, 'Consciousness, Design and Social Practice', *Journal of Consciousness Studies* 8 (2001), 43–58.

Hruškovic, Samuel, *Vlastný životopis* (Liptovský Svätý Mikuláš: Transocius, 1943).

Hume, David *A Treatise of Human Nature* [1739/40], ed. P. H. Nidditch (Oxford: Clarendon, 1978).

Hume, David, *Dialogues Concerning Natural Religion* in *Dialogues and Natural History of Religion* [1779], ed. J.C.A. Gaskin (Oxford: Oxford University Press, 1993).

Jackson, Frank, 'Postscript on Qualia' in Frank Jackson, *Mind, Method and Conditionals* (New York: Routledge, 1998).

Jakobei, Pavel, *Welmi Důležité Přjčiny, pro které* čtyř *neyhlawněgššich* a v *tyto poslednj* časy *neyobičegněgššich hřichů.. wárowati se máme* (Modra: 1724).

James, William, *The Varieties of Religious Experience* (1899), http://www.psychwww.com/psyrelig/james/james4.htm#65, accessed 1 August 2011.

Joyce, Richard, *The Evolution of Morality* (Cambridge, MA: MIT Press, 2006).

Kant, Immanuel *Groundwork of the Metaphysics of Morals* (1785), trans. Mary Gregor (Cambridge: Cambridge University Press, 1997).

Katz, Leonard D., *Evolutionary Origins of Morality. Cross-Disciplinary Perspectives* (Thorverton: Imprint Academic, 2000).

Kelly, E., *Structure and Diversity: Studies in the Phenomenological Philosophy of Max Scheler* (Dordrecht: Kluwer Academic Publishers, 1997).

Kenny, A., *What is Faith?* (Oxford: Oxford University Press, 1992).

King, Martin Luther, 'Pilgrimage to Nonviolence', in J.M. Washington (ed.), *A Testament of Hope* (San Francisco: HarperCollins, 1986).

Kinsey, Alfred C., Wardell B. Pomeroy and Clyde E. Martin, *Sexual Behaviour in the Human Male* (W.B Saunders Company, 1948; renewed Bloomington, IN: Indiana University Press, 1975).

Kinsey, Alfred C., Wardell B. Pomeroy, Clyde E. Martin and Paul H. Gebhard, *Sexual Behaviour in the Human Female* (W.B Saunders Company, 1953; renewed Bloomington, IN: Indiana University Press, 1981).

Kitcher, Philip, 'Psychological Altruism, Evolutionary Origins, and Moral Rules', *Philosophical Studies* 89 (1998), 283–316.

Knierim, Rolf, *The Task of Old Testament Theology* (Grand Rapids, MI: Eerdmans, 1995).

Knight, Douglas, 'Old Testament Ethics', *Christian Century* 100 (20 January 1982), 55–9, http://www.religion-online.org/showarticle.asp?title=1276, accessed 1 August 2011.

Kraal, Anders, *First-Order Logic and Classical Theism: Toward Logical Reorientation* (Uppsala: Universitetstryckeriet, 2010).

Kraal, Anders, 'Logic and Divine Simplicity', *Philosophy Compass* 6(4) (2011), 282–94.

Krailsheimer, A., *Pascal: Selected Works* (London: Penguin, 1966).

Krčméry, Štefan, *Dejiny literatúry slovenskej*, vol. 1 (Bratislava: Tatran, 1976).

Krčméry, Štefan, 'Literárne súvislosti (Milton – Leibnitz – Doležal – Madách)', *Sborník Matice slovenskej pre jazykozpyt, národopis, dejepis a literárnu históriu* 6 (1928), 1–10.

Kretzmann, Norman, 'Abraham, Isaac and Euthyphro', in Eleanore Stump (ed.), *Hamartia* (Toronto: Mellan, 1983), pp. 27–50.

Kretzmann, Norman, 'Abraham, Isaac, and Euthyphro: God and the Basis of Morality', in Eleanore Stump and Michael Murray (eds), *Philosophy of Religion: The Big Questions* (Oxford: Blackwell, 1999).

Kvanvig, Jonathan L., *The Problem of Hell* (Oxford: Oxford University Press, 1993).

Lamb, W.R.M. and H.N. Fowler, *Plato: Statesman, Philebus, Ion.* (Cambridge, MA: Harvard University Press, 1925).

Lathi, David C., 'Parting with Illusions in Evolutionary Ethics', *Biology and Philosophy* 18 (2003), 639–51.

Le Poidevin, Robin, *Arguing for Atheism: an Introduction to the Philosophy of Religion* (Abingdon: Routledge, 1996).

Leibniz, Gottfried Wilhelm, *Theodicy: Essays on the Goodness of God, the Freedom of Man and the Origin of Evil* (London: Routledge & Kegan Paul, 1996).

Levinas, Emmanuel, *Difficult Freedom: Essays on Judaism*, trans. Seán Hand (London: Athlone Press, 1990).

Liebeschutz, H., 'Boethius and the Legacy of Antiquity', in A.H. Armstrong (ed.), *The Cambridge History of Later Greek and Early Medieval History* (Cambridge: Cambridge University Press, 1970), 538–64.

Loades, Ann, 'Philosophy of Religion: Its Relation to Theology', in Harriet A. Harris and Christopher J. Insole (eds), *Faith and Philosophical Analysis: The Impact of Analytical Philosophy on the Philosophy of Religion* (Aldershot and Burlington, VT: Ashgate, 2005), pp. 136–47.

Long, A.A., *From Epicurus to Epictetus: Studies in Hellenistic and Roman Philosophy* (Oxford: Oxford University Press, 2006).

Lucas, J.R, *The Freedom of the Will* (Oxford: Clarendon, 1970).

Luther, Martin, 'Large Catechism', in F. Bente (ed. and trans.), *Triglot Concordia: The Symbolical Books of the Evangelical Lutheran Church: German-Latin-English* (St Louis, MN: Concordia Publishing Hose, 1921).

Mackie, J.L., *Ethics: Inventing Right and Wrong* (Harmondsworth: Penguin, 1977).

Mackie, J.L., *The Miracle of Theism: Arguments For and Against the Existence of God* (Oxford: Clarendon, 1982).

Maine, Henry, *Ancient Law: Its Connection with the Early History of Society, and its Relation to Modern Ideas* (London: John Murray, 1861).

Matthews, George, 'Euthyphro Problem', in Ted Honderich (ed.), *The Oxford Companion to Philosophy*. (Oxford: Oxford University Press, 1995), p. 253.

Mawson, T.J., 'God's Creation and Morality', *Religious Studies* 38(1) (2002), 1–25.

Mawson, T.J., 'Omnipotence and Necessary Moral Perfection are Compatible: A Reply to Morriston', *Religious Studies* 38(2) (2002), 215–23.

McCabe, Herman, *Faith within Reason* (London: Continuum, 2006).

McCulloch, Gregory, 'From Quine to the Epistemological Real Distinction', *European Journal of Philosophy* 1 (1999), 30–46.

McDowell, John, *Mind and World* (Cambridge, MA: Harvard University Press, 1994).

McEvilley, Thomas, *The Shape of Ancient Thought: Comparative Studies in Greek and Indian Philosophies* (New York: Allworth Press, 2006).

McPherran, Mark, *The Religion of Socrates* (University Park, PA: Pennsylvania State University Press, 1997).

McPherran, Mark, 'Recognizing the Gods of Socrates', in Mark McPherran (ed.), *Wisdom, Ignorance and Virtue: New Essays on Socrates, Apeiron*, Supplemental Volume 28 (1997), 125–39.

McPherran, Mark, 'The Aporetic Interlude and Fifth Elenchos of Plato's *Euthyphro*', *Oxford Studies in Ancient Philosophy* 25 (2003), 1–38.

McPherran, Mark, 'Introducing a New God: Socrates and his *Daimonion*', in Pierre Destrée and Nicholas D. Smith (eds), *Socrates' Divine Sign: Religion, Practice, and Value in Socratic Philosophy*. Special issue of *APEIRON:*

A Journal for Ancient Philosophy and Science 38(2) (June 2005) (Kelowna, BC: Academic Printing and Publishing, 2005), 13–30.

Midgley, Mary, 'Gene-Juggling', *Philosophy* 54 (1979), 438–58.

Midgley, Mary, 'Why Genes?', in Hilary Rose and Steven Rose (eds), *Alas, Poor Darwin* (London: Jonathan Cape, 2000), pp. 67–84.

Mill, John Stuart, *Utilitarianism* (1861), in John Stuart Mill and Jeremy Bentham, *Utilitarianism and Other Essays*, ed. Alan Ryan (London: Penguin Books, 2004).

Miller, Alexander, *An Introduction to Contemporary Metaethics* (Cambridge: Polity Press, 2003).

Moore, G.E., *Principia Ethica* (1903), revised edn, edited with an introduction by Thomas Baldwin (Cambridge: Cambridge University Press, 1993).

Morriston, Wes, 'Must There Be a Standard of Moral Goodness Apart from God?', *Philosophia Christi* Series 2(3) (2001), 127–38.

Morriston, Wes, 'Omnipotence and Necessary Moral Perfection: Are they Compatible?', *Religious Studies* 37 (2001), 143–60.

Morriston, Wes, 'Omnipotence and the Anselmnian God', *Philo* 4(1) (2001), 7–20.

Mouw, Richard, *The God Who Commands* (Notre Dame, IN: Notre Dame University Press, 1990).

Mumford, Stephen, 'Modelling Powers as Vectors', unpublished paper, presented to the Cardiff Branch of the Royal Institute of Philosophy, 2008.

Münz, Teodor, *Filozofia slovenského osvietenstva* (Bratislava: SAV, 1961).

Murphy, Mark, 'Divine Command, Divine Will, and Moral Obligation', *Faith and Philosophy* 15 (1998), 3–27.

Murray, Paul (ed.), *Receptive Ecumenism and the Call to Catholic Learning* (Oxford: Oxford University Press, 2008).

Nagasawa, Yujin, 'A New Defence of Anselmian Theism', *Philosophical Quarterly* 58 (2008), 577–96.

Nietzsche, Friedrich, *Beyond Good and Evil; Prelude to a Philosophy of the Future* [*Jenseits von Gut und Böse*, 1886], trans. R.J. Hollingdale (London: Penguin, 1973).

Nota, J., Max Scheler: Een worstelen om het wezen van den mens (Utrecht/ Brussels: Het Spectrum, 1947).

Nussbaum, Martha, 'Commentary on Edmunds', in J.J. Cleary (ed.), *Proceedings of the Boston Area Colloquium in Ancient Philosophy*, vol. 1 (University Press of America, 1985), pp. 231–40.

Nussbaum, Martha, 'Madness, Reason, and Recantation in the *Phaedrus*', in Martha Nussbaum, *The Fragility of Goodness* (Cambridge: Cambridge University Press, 1986), pp. 200–233.

Nygren, Anders, *Agapé and Eros* (London: SPCK, 1953).

O'Brien, Dan, *A Critique of Naturalistic Philosophies of Mind* (with a foreword by Professor C. Hookway), (New York: Mellen Press, 2007).

Osuský, Samuel Štefan, *Prvé slovenské dejiny filozofie* (Liptovský Svätý Mikuláš: Transocius, 1939).

Ott, Ludwig, *The Fundamentals of Catholic Dogma*, trans. P. Lynch (Rockford, IL: TAN Books and Publishers, 1974).

Otto, Eckhart, *Theologische Ethik des Alten Testaments* (Theologische Wissenschaft 3/2. Stuttgart: Kohlhammer, 1994).

Parkinson, G.H.R. (ed.), *Leibniz, Philosophical Writings* (London: J.M. Dent & Sons, 1973).

Partridge, Ernest, 'Why Care about the Future?', in Ernest Partridge (ed.), *Responsibilities to Future Generations: Environmental Ethics* (Buffalo, NY: Prometheus, 1981), pp. 195–202.

Pascal, Blaise, *Pensées et opuscules,* ed. L. Brunschvicg (Paris: Classiques Hachette, 1961).

Perrin, R., *Max Scheler's Concept of the Person* (London: Macmillan, 1991).

Pike, Nelson, 'God's Omnipotence and God's Ability to Sin', *American Philosophical Quarterly* 6 (1969), 208–16.

Plantinga, Alvin, *Does God Have a Nature?* (Milwaukee, WI: Marquette University Press, 1980).

Plato, 'Euthyphro', in *Plato: The Last Days of Socrates*, trans. H. Tredennick (New York: Penguin, 1980).

Plato, *Five Dialogues: Euthyphro, Apology, Crito, Meno, Phaedo*, trans. G.M.A. Grube (Indianapolis, IN: Hackett Publishing Company, 1981).

Posner, Richard, *Sex and Reason* (Cambridge, MA: Harvard University Press, 1992).

Potter, Nancy, 'Gender', in Jennifer Radden (ed.), *The Philosophy of Psychiatry: A Companion* (Oxford: Oxford University Press, 2004), p. 240.

Preuss, Horst-Dietrich, *Theology of the Old Testament*, vol. 2 (Stuttgart: Kohlhammer, 1992).

Primoratz, Igor, *Ethics and Sex* (London: Routledge, 1999).

Prinz, Jesse J., *The Emotional Construction of Morals* (Oxford: Oxford University Press, 2007).

Quine, Willard van Orman, *Mathematical Logic* (Cambridge, MA: Harvard University Press, 1951).

Quine, Willard van Orman, *Word and Object* (Cambridge, MA: MIT Press, 1960).

Quine, Willard van Orman, *Set Theory and its Logic* (Cambridge, MA: Belknap, 1963).

Quine, Willard van Orman, *Pursuit of Truth*, revised edn (Cambridge, MA: Harvard University Press, 1992).

Quinn, Philip, 'Divine Command Ethics: A Causal Theory', in Janine Idziak (ed.), *Divine Command Morality: Historical and Contemporary Readings* (New York: Edwin Mellen Press, 1979), pp. 305–25.

Raine, Adrian, Todd Lencz, Susan Bihrle et al., 'Reduced Prefrontal Gray Matter Volume and Reduced Autonomic Activity in Antisocial Personality Disorder', *Archives of General Psychiatry* 57 (2000), 119–27.

Rawls, John, 'Outline of a Decision Procedure for Ethics', *Philosophical Review* 60 (1951), 177–97.

Rawls, John, *A Theory of Justice* (Cambridge, MA: Harvard University Press, 1971).

Rawls, John, *Justice as Fairness. A Restatement*, ed. Erin Kelly (Cambridge, MA: Harvard University Press, 2001).

Reid, Thomas, *Inquiry and Essays*, eds Ronald E. Beanblossom and Keith Lehrer (Indianapolis: IN: Hackett Publishing Co, 1983).

Rice, Hugh, *God and Goodness* (Oxford: Oxford University Press, 2003).

Ruse, Michael, 'Evolutionary Ethics: A Phoenix Arisen', *Zygon* 21 (1986), 95–112.

Sandberg, Joakim and Niklas Juth, 'Ethics and Intuitions: A Reply to Singer', *Journal of Ethics*, published online, 29 July 2010.

Scanlon, T., *What We Owe to Each Other* (Cambridge, MA: Belknap, 1998).

Scheler, M., 'Der Mensch im Weltalter des Ausgleichs' (1927), in Max Scheler, *Späte Schriften* (Bern: Francke AG Verlag, 1976), pp. 145–70.

Scheler, M., 'Die Stellung des Menschen im Kosmos' (1928), in Max Scheler, *Späte Schriften* (Bern: Francke AG Verlag, 1976), pp. 7–71.

Scheler, Max, *Der Formalismus in der Ethik und die Materiale Wertethik* (Bern/ Munich: Francke Verlag, 1966).

Schellenberg, John L., *Prolegomena to a Philosophy of Religion* (Ithaca, NY: Cornell University Press, 2005).

Schellenberg, John L., 'Imagining the Future: How Scepticism Can Renew Philosophy of Religion', in David Cheetham and Rolfe King (eds), *Contemporary Practice and Method in the Philosophy of Religion: New Essays* (London: Continuum, 2008), pp. 15–31.

Sedley, David, *The Midwife of Platonism* (Oxford: Oxford University Press, 2005).

Shafer-Landau, R., *Moral Realism* (Oxford: Clarendon, 2003).

Sidgwick, Henry, *The Methods of Ethics*, [1874], 7th edn (London: Macmillan, 1907).

Singer, Peter, *Practical Ethics*, 2nd edn (Cambridge: Cambridge University Press, 1993).

Singer, Peter, 'Ethics and Intuitions', *Journal of Ethics* 9 (2005), 331–52.

Šmatlák, Stanislav, *Dejiny slovenskej literatúry: Od stredoveku po súčasnosť* (Bratislava: Tatran, 1988).

Sober, Elliott (ed.), *Conceptual Issues in Evolutionary Biology. An Anthology*, 2nd edn (Cambridge, MA: Bradford/MIT Press, 1993).

Sober, Elliott, *Evidence and Evolution. The Logic Behind the Science* (Cambridge: Cambridge University Press, 2008).

Sober, Elliott and David Sloan Wilson, *Unto Others: The Evolution and Psychology of Unselfish Behavior* (Cambridge, MA: Harvard University Press, 1998).

Soble, Alan, *Sex from Plato to Paglia: a Philosophical Encyclopedia*, 2 volumes (Westport, CT: Greenwood Press, 2005).

Sorley, W.R., *Moral Values and the Idea of God* (Cambridge: Cambridge University Press, 1918).

Spader, H., *Scheler's Ethical Personalism* (New York: Fordham University Press, 2002).

Sterry, Peter, *A Discourse of the Freedom of the Will* [1675]; reprinted in Charles Taliaferro and Alison J. Teply (eds), *Cambridge Platonist Spirituality* (Mahwah, NJ: Paulist Press, 2004).

StrattonLake, P.J., *Ethical Intuitionism* (Oxford: Clarendon, 2002).

Street, Sharon, 'A Darwinian Dilemma for Realist Theories of Value', *Philosophical Studies* 127 (2006), 109–66.

Street, Sharon, 'Reply to Copp: Naturalism, Normativity, and the Varieties of Realism Worth Worrying about', *Philosophical Issues* 18 (2008), 207–28.

Stump, Eleonore, 'Dante's Hell, Aquinas' Moral Theory, and the Love of God', *Canadian Journal of Philosophy* 16(2) (1986), 181–98.

Stump, Eleonore, *Aquinas* (London and New York: Routledge, 2003).

Stump, Eleonore, 'Love, by All Accounts', Proceedings and Addresses of the American Philosophical Association 80(2) (2006), 25–43.

Stump, Eleonore, 'Suffering, Theodicy, and Defense, in Eleanore Stump, *Wandering in Darkness – Narrative and the Problem of Suffering* (Oxford: Oxford University Press, 2010).

Stump, Eleonore and Norman Kretzmann, 'Being and Goodness', in Scott MacDonald (ed.), *Being and Goodness* (Ithaca, NY: Cornell University Press, 1991), pp. 98–128

Surin, Kenneth, *Theology and the Problem of Evil* (Oxford: Blackwell, 1986).

Swinburne, Richard, *Responsibility and Atonement* (Oxford: Clarendon, 1989).

Swinburne, Richard, *Revelation: From Metaphor to Analogy* (Oxford: Clarendon, 1991, 2007).

Swinburne, Richard, *The Coherence of Theism*, revised edn (Oxford: Clarendon, 1993).

Swinburne, Richard, *The Christian God* (Oxford: Oxford University Press, 1994).

Swinburne, Richard, *The Resurrection of God Incarnate* (Oxford: Oxford University Press, 2003).

Swinburne, Richard, *The Existence of God*, revised edn (Oxford: Clarendon, 2004).

Swinburne, Richard, *Was Jesus God?* (Oxford: Oxford University Press, 2008).

Taliaferro, Charles, *Contemporary Philosophy of Religion* (Oxford: Blackwell, 1998).

Taliaferro, Charles, *Evidence and Faith: Philosophy and Religion since the Seventeenth Century* (Cambridge: Cambridge University Press, 2005).

Taliaferro, Charles, *Philosophy of Religion: A Beginner's Guide* (Oxford: Oneworld, 2009).

Taliaferro, Charles and Chad Meister (eds), *The Cambridge Companion to Christian Philosophical Theology,* (Cambridge: Cambridge University Press, 2010).

Taliaferro, Charles and Alison Teply (eds), *Cambridge Platonist Spirituality* (New York: Paulist Press, 2004).

Thomas, A. (ed.), *Bernard Williams* (Cambridge: Cambridge University Press, 2007).

Thomson, Judith Jarvis, 'Killing, Letting Die, and the Trolley Problem', *The Monist* 59 (1976), 204–17.

Trakakis, Nick, *The End of Philosophy of Religion* (London and New York: Continuum, 2008).

Trivers, R., 'The Evolution of Reciprocal Altruism', *Quarterly Review of Biology* 46 (1971), 35–57.

Vlastos, Gregory, 'Socratic Piety', in Gail Fine (ed.), *Plato 2: Ethics, Politics, Religion, and the Soul* (Oxford: Oxford University Press, 1999), pp. 56–77 (reprinted from Gregory Vlastos, *Socrates: Ironist and Moral Philosopher* (Ithaca, NY: Cornell University Press 1991)).

Vlček, Jaroslav, *Dějiny české literatury*, vol. 2 (Prague: SNKLHU, 1960).

Wainwright, William J., *Religion and Morality* (Burlington, VT: Ashgate, 2005).

Ward, Keith, *God, Chance and Necessity* (Oxford: Oneworld, 1996).

Weiss, Roslyn, *Socrates Dissatisfied* (New York: Oxford University Press 1997/8).

Wielenberg, E.J., *Value and Virtue in a Godless Universe* (Cambridge: Cambridge University Press, 2005).

Wierenga, Eric, 'A Defensible Divine Command Theory', *Nous* 17 (2003), 387–407.

Wiles, Maurice, 'The Reasonableness of Christianity', in William J. Abraham and Steven W. Holtzer (eds), *The Rationality of Religious Belief: Essays in Honour of Basil Mitchell* (Oxford: Clarendon, 1987), pp. 39–51.

Williams, Bernard, *Ethics and the Limits of Philosophy* (London: Fontana, 1985, 1993).

Williams, Bernard, *Truth and Truthfulness* (Princeton, NJ: Princeton University Press, 2002).

Williams, George C., 'Huxley's Evolution and Ethics in Sociobiological Perspective', *Zygon* 23(4) (1988), 383–407.

Williams, George C., *Plan and Purpose in Nature* (London: Weidenfeld & Nicolson, 1996).

Williams, Rowan, *On Christian Theology* (Oxford: Blackwell, 2000).

Wilson, David Sloan, 'On the Relationship Between Evolutionary and Psychological Definitions of Altruism and Selfishness', *Biology and Philosophy* 7 (1992), 61–8.

Wilson, David Sloan, *Darwin's Cathedral. Evolution, Religion, and the Nature of Society* (Chicago: University of Chicago Press, 2002).

Wilson, David Sloan and E.O. Wilson, 'Rethinking the Theoretical Foundation of Sociobiology', *Quarterly Review of Biology* 82 (2007), 327–48.

Wilson, Edward Osborne, *Sociobiology: The Abridged Edition* (Cambridge, MA: Harvard University Press, 1980).

Wittgenstein, L., *Philosophical Investigations*, eds G.E.M. Anscombe, R. Rhees and G. von Wright (Oxford: Blackwell, 1953).

Wolterstorff, Nicholas, 'How Philosophical Theology Became Possible within the Analytic Tradition of Philosophy', in Oliver D. Crisp and Michael C. Rea (eds), *Analytical Theology: New Essays in the Philosophy of Theology* (Oxford: Oxford University Press, 2009), pp. 155–70.

Wolterstorff, Nicholas, *Justice: Rights and Wrongs* (Princeton, NJ: Princeton University Press, 2010).

Woolcock, Peter G., 'The Case Against Evolutionary Ethics Today', in Jane Maienschein and Michael Ruse (eds), *Biology and the Foundation of Ethics, Cambridge Studies in Philosophy and Biology* (Cambridge: Cambridge University Press, 1999).

Wringe, William, 'Is Understanding Evil Morally Dangerous: Fiction, Emotion and Moral Contagion', in D. Medicott (ed.), *Their Deeds Were Evil: Understanding Atrocity, Ferocity and Extreme Crimes* (Amsterdam: Rodopi Press, forthcoming).

Wynn, Mark, *God and Goodness: A Natural Theological Perspective* (London: Routledge, 1999).

Xenophon, *Memorabilia*. eds E.C. Marchant and O.J. Todd, Loeb Classical Library, no. 168 (London: Harvard University Press, 1997).

Yandell, Keith, *Philosophy of Religion: A Contemporary Introduction* (London and New York: Routledge, 1999).

Zagzebski, Linda, *Theodicy in the Old Testament* (Philadelphia, PA: Fortress Press, 1983).

Zagzebski, Linda, *A Whirlpool of Torment: Israelite Traditions of God as an Oppressive Presence* (Minneapolis: Fortress Press, 1984).

Zagzebski, Linda, *Divine Commands and Moral Requirements* (Oxford: Clarendon, 1987).

Zagzebski, Linda, *Divine Motivation Theory* (New York: Cambridge University Press, 2004).

Zagzebski, Linda, 'YHWH and the God of Philosophical Theology', *Verbum et Ecclesiae* 27(1) (2006), 677–99.

Zagzebski, Linda, 'The Quest for a Philosophical Yhwh (Part 3) – Towards a Philosophy of Old Testament Religion', *Old Testament Essays* 20(3) (2007), 669–88.

Index